THE MORTGAGE PROFESSIONAL'S HANDBOOK

*Succeeding in the New World of Mortgage Finance:
Operations, Technology, Service and Compliance*

VOLUME II

EDITED BY
JESS LEDERMAN AND TOMASZ LASOTA

The Mortgage Professional's Handbook
© 2016 AzureStar, LLC. All rights reserved.
ISBN-13: 978-1519748300 (CreateSpace-Assigned)
ISBN-10: 1519748302
LCCN: 2016900041
BISAC: Business & Economics / Finance / General

TABLE OF CONTENTS

PREFACE — I

CHAPTER ONE
Designing The Loan Origination Process:
A Call For Evolution — 1
Jennifer Fortier | CMB Senior Associate
Stratmor Group

CHAPTER TWO
Residential Mortgage Underwriting:
Investment Properties, Jumbo Loans,
and Self-Employed Borrowers — 14
Shelley Callaghan | Senior Marketing Program Manager
Vicki Woeckener | Manager, Credit Policy
Deya Araiza | Underwriting Production Manager
MGIC

CHAPTER THREE
Ground Zero: The Impact of Mortgage Fraud — 26
Constance "Connie" Wilson | CMB, AMP, CFE
with contributions by Matt Merlone, CFE

CHAPTER FOUR
Quality Control Audits — 45
Alvin Wali | CEO
Alliance International Corporation

CHAPTER FIVE
Working With Mortgage Insurance Companies — 57
Kyle Benson | Business Technology Operations Director
David Schroeder | Director, Claims Business Systems
MGIC

CHAPTER SIX
Mortgage Cooperatives:
Efficiency and Profits Through Scale — 65
Tom Millon | CEO
Capital Markets Cooperative

CHAPTER SEVEN
Lebowitz: Technology Past, Present, and Future — 73
Jeff Lebowitz
Bend, Or

CHAPTER EIGHT
Automating Toward the Future   **107**
Jonathan Corr | President and CEO
Ellie Mae

CHAPTER NINE
eClosings and eMortgages   **125**
Harry Gardner | Vice President, eStrategies
Ellie Mae

CHAPTER TEN
Reverse Mortgage Loan
Origination Software Technology   **140**
John Button | President & CEO
ReverseVision

CHAPTER ELEVEN
The Pendulum of Regulation   **146**
Chris Appie | Vice President and Counsel
Compliance Systems

CHAPTER TWELVE
Fair Lending   **175**
Stephen M. McGurl | Managing Director
McGurl Risk Advisors LLC

CHAPTER THIRTEEN
Mortgage Servicing   **197**
Marianne Lamkin | Senior Vice President
American Mortgage Consultants

CHAPTER FOURTEEN
Choosing and Working With A Subservicer   **210**
David J. Miller, Jr. | SVP, Business Development
Cenlar FSB

CHAPTER FIFTEEN
Residential Mortgage Special Servicing   **218**
Bill Coppedge | Senior Managing Director
Fay Financial, LLC

PREFACE

I first started publishing books for mortgage professionals in 1987, with *The Secondary Mortgage Market*, the first book on that subject, and only the second on what was rapidly emerging as a mega-industry and one of the largest sectors of the U.S. capital markets: mortgage banking. It was a heady time; mortgage brokers were emerging as a force, feeding product to wholesale mortgage lenders; mortgage-backed securities (MBS) were coming into their own, and private-label MBS were finally providing ample liquidity for jumbos and other non-Agency loans; managing mortgage pipeline risk was becoming a science; and it was starting to become evident that servicing sometimes was worth more (or less!) than one point.

But the 1980's were also a sobering time: the savings and loan industry had just been wiped out, mortgage fraud on low-doc loans had recently run rampant, and toxic mortgages (95 LTV negatively amortizing GPM ARMs, aka "the loans that ate Texas") wreaked havoc.

Think history ever repeats itself?

The Mortgage Meltdown of the late 2000's was even more traumatic and transformative than the upheavals of the 1980's, which is saying a lot. Futurists sometimes speculate about what it would be like if a sudden disastrous event set the world back technologically, overnight. No electricity! No planes or automobiles! How would you manage?

Well, those of us in the mortgage industry faced the financial equivalent of just that scenario in the latter half of 2007. After nearly thirty years of spectacular growth and widespread acceptance in the global markets, the private-label MBS market *entirely shut down*. There was no liquidity for jumbo, Alt-A, and subprime loans (indeed, they were the "loans that ate Iceland"). To find an historical parallel to what happened next, you'd have to go back 60 million years, to the time when an asteroid struck the Yucatan peninsula and wiped out the dinosaurs. Financial mass extinction!

The unthinkable became commonplace: behemoth institutions with massive resources went bankrupt or were merged out of existence; the "quasi," was deleted from "quasi-governmental institutions" when people talked of Fannie Mae and Freddie Mac. Brokers, often unfairly targeted by politicians and the press, and the mom-and-pop shops that had provided such invaluable service for decades, scrambled to merge into larger mortgage bankers, or simply closed up shop. Regulators moved in, reminding some of carpetbaggers heading south in the wake of the Civil War. New regulations settled over the land, driving production costs multiples higher and slowing closings.

To some, the mortgage industry had become about as attractive as the icy gray landscape of a nuclear winter.

It was a magnitude 10.0 earthquake on the financial Richter scale, and we're still feeling the aftershocks.

However, there's simply too much talent, energy, and creative genius in the world of mortgage finance for doom and gloom to prevail for long. If many large institutions went the way of the dinosaurs, all of a sudden there was room for many smaller shops—community banks, credit unions, and some agile mortgage bankers—to emerge and prosper in the mortgage sector, much as what were once merely small furry mammals took over the earth once the dinosaurs went away.

The past is prologue to a future fraught with both peril and possibility, and the three volumes of *The Mortgage Professional's Handbook* look back at the lessons of the past and, yet more important, look forward to what it will take to succeed as the 2010's become the 2020's.

Volume I: Industry Overviews and Loan Production begins with nine chapters which provide a wide-ranging perspective from many of the leaders of this industry: the CEOs of MBA, NAMB, the Independent Community Bankers Association, the National Association of Federal Credit Unions, MGIC, and Ginnie Mae, and senior executives from Fannie Mae, Freddie Mac, and FHA. Part Two provides ten chapters covering multiple facets of mortgage production: new models for loan origination; tactics and strategies for marketing to real estate agents and direct to consumer; approaches to the creation of joint ventures; and four chapters covering sales techniques, recruiting, training, and coaching.

Volume II: Operations, Technology, Servicing, and Compliance covers those topics in extraordinary detail. The first seven chapters explore how companies can rethink traditional operational practices to meet the radically new demands of the new environment. Reengineering workflow, underwriting, quality control, fraud, and the emergence of mortgage cooperatives are all considered. The next four chapters provide an in-depth look at how technology will continue to transform mortgage finance, including state-of-the-art applications for new approaches and products. Two comprehensive chapters on compliance and three on loan servicing, working with subservicers, and the new world of special servicing for troubled loans conclude this volume.

Volume III: Secondary Marketing and Financial Management focuses on the capital markets, but should also be required reading for any mortgage broker, with chapters dedicated to whether and how to make the broker-to-banker transition, find and work with a warehouse lender, selecting and working with correspondent lenders, and contracting all or part of secondary marketing to a third-party firm. Beginners and veterans alike will find a treasure trove of advanced insights, techniques, and strategies in chapters covering pipeline risk management, pullthrough analytics, best execution, the trading and valuation of servicing and non-Agency product, pricing strategy,

PREFACE

and prospects for restoring global confidence in the U.S. mortgage market. Weighty chapters are also included on financial benchmarking and modeling.

The contributing authors to this work are 59 of the best and brightest — and most successful — in the industry. All of us are working pro bono so that 100% of the proceeds from sales of these volumes can go to four charitable organizations:

ALS Therapy Development Institute (als.net): The Institute and its scientists actively discover and develop treatments for ALS. They are the world's first and largest nonprofit biotech focused 100 percent on ALS research. Led by people living with ALS and their families, they understand the urgent need to slow and stop this disease.

The ALS Association (alsa.org): By leading the way in global research, providing assistance for people with ALS through a nationwide network of chapters, coordinating multidisciplinary care through certified clinical care centers, and fostering government partnerships, the Association builds hope and enhances quality of life while aggressively searching for new treatments and a cure.

MBA Open Doors Foundation (https://www.mba.org/who-we-are/the-mba-foundation): The Mortgage Bankers Association is committed to helping families around the country find comfort in their homes when they are at their most vulnerable. To that end, the MBA Opens Doors Foundation sponsors philanthropic programs focused on home and community support, including helping families with seriously ill children make their mortgage or rent payments.

MyHouse (http://myhousematsuhomelessyouthcenter.com/): MyHouse helps homeless youth to become self-sufficient, productive members of their communities. It offers food, clothing, transitional housing, shower and laundry services, employment services, public health care, mediation services, help with legal issues and support and referral for mental health and substance abuse treatment.

Thank you for supporting these organizations, and best of luck in the years ahead.

Jess Lederman
January 1st, 2016
jess@mortgagebanking2020.com

CHAPTER ONE

DESIGNING THE LOAN ORIGINATION PROCESS: A CALL FOR EVOLUTION

JENNIFER FORTIER | CMB SENIOR ASSOCIATE
STRATMOR GROUP

A look back at the operational challenges that lenders have faced over the last decade of mortgage banking reveals some enduring themes. Lenders struggle with how to transform their operations to be better, faster, cheaper, how to become more nimble and responsive to ever-changing demands of the industry and the competitive environment, and how to maintain a certain standard of service and corporate profitability. These are the typical challenges in any industry, but mortgage industry veterans would argue that these challenges in our industry have been especially intense.

Many of the answers to the challenges lenders face lie, at least in part, in a developing a strategic commitment to developing process-oriented disciplines. While this campaign is not a new one, few lenders have truly embraced the effort. This chapter examines the role of *process orientation* in the future of the mortgage industry, and takes a close look at concepts and constructs that are integral to building and sustaining manageable, scalable, and productive operations, and thereby gaining a true competitive advantage.

LOOKING BACK

In the early 2000's, easy lending policies and high demand for mortgage assets spurred new products and expanded markets. It was a welcome opportunity that, nevertheless, came with a unique set of challenges. Lenders had to be able to quickly reassess risk and corporate objectives, find outlets for new products, and update systems and policies to accommodate those new channels and products. Speed and nimbleness was the name of the game.

The 2008 financial crisis brought tighter standards and expanding regulatory controls that caused lenders to re-evaluate past business approaches. These demands, like the earlier boom, also required lenders to respond quickly. But this time, it was under the pressure of serious threats to their business and unprecedented constraints. *Data accuracy* became even more critical and government rules demanded new processes. Regulatory agencies began calling for *proof of compliance* — a subtle but powerful shift from the 'innocent until proven guilty' approach that had historically prevailed. Precision and accuracy became the new theme.

In response, management shifted the organizational focus to figuring out how to comply with regulatory demands, adjust risk policies, and reorganize staffing to accommodate the new roles and tasks. At the transaction level, staff adjusted to dealing with unprecedented levels of detail, new data-validation steps, and stop-gap measures that are designed to create a strong defense rather than advancing the loan process. On top of the process details, systems required complex updates to support new regulatory rules.

Since 2008, lenders have begun to think about process in a new light as lenders struggle with adapting to the new business environment that had come on fast and with a big bang. Spend a little time with a few lenders and a sense of their struggles is readily apparent. They are drowning in detail. They suffer a persistent nagging frustration that things are just harder than they should be. It seems impossible to get on top of the mountain of minutia. All answers seem to point toward technology solutions, but the solutions either don't provide enough depth to truly revolutionize a process, or the implementation of technology becomes a hurdle itself.

Rising Expenses and Plunging Productivity

The implications of the new state of the mortgage industry were manifested in the creation of new departments and functions, increasingly complex processes, and a deepening reliance on technology to enable the loan manufacturing process and manage data. The impacts of this are seen clearly in loan production expenses and fulfillment productivity.

Since the 2008 financial crises – the primary catalyst for this shift – expenses for fulfillment (processing, underwriting, and closing) have increased an average of approximately $800/loan in the retail, broker, and consumer direct channels. Correspondingly, productivity per fulfillment employee is down more than 37% and 44% in the retail and consumer direct channels, respectively, and down by 50% in broker and correspondent channels.

As bad as that seems, it gets worse. These numbers do not reflect new expenses related to pre-funding quality control and costs for creating and staffing a compliance management process, areas that are not simple or cheap to maintain. Nor do they reflect expanded training requirements and the cost of third party reviews and audits.

THE CALL FOR EVOLUTION

The concept of focusing on business processes has had its ups and down since its inception in the 1980's. At first, it was a revolutionary idea, seen as a panacea for all problems that were, until then, hidden in the complexities of processes and organizational structure. The concept got very popular very quickly, as companies attempted to reengineer their problems away. The term became an overused cliché and the concepts were commonly misapplied; results were difficult to achieve. In the mid 1990's, the business process engineering idea fell to the fate of fads.

From reengineering processes, the world turned to technology to solve problems. The promise of the future was in 'e' solutions that automated work, eliminated the need for tedious processes to be performed by humans, and ensured that errors would be easily detected and minimal. But, while technology brought the potential for real change, it too did not offer easy solutions or meet the lofty expectations for return on investment.

In the 2000's and in the fallout of the dot-com bust, businesses began to reconsider the focus on technology and business processes, this time with more balance and rationalism. New process-management techniques, including Six Sigma and Lean, appeared on the scene as interest and attention to developing a business-process orientation were renewed. Companies began to take a closer look at how their processes were designed and how they could help them achieve competitive advantage.

The mortgage industry has been slow to wholeheartedly embrace the concept of business-process orientation. Traditionally, success in the mortgage industry meant having strong acumen for sales and marketing, customer service, risk evaluation, and transactional management. A process focused perspective was not a prerequisite and is simply not a driving instinct of most seasoned mortgage executives. Good mortgage bankers have largely never been trained to think about or rely on process design as key success factors.

Embracing The Process-Oriented Approach

Few would argue that a little process work would be beneficial, but there is generally a limit to lenders' appetites to invest in developing disciplines around process design and continuous improvement. Considering that most mortgage lenders are primarily sales organizations, management tends to turn to volume to answer many problems under the assumption that market share can overcome the impacts of process problems. Historically, management simply did not *need* to invest too much effort in improving processes in order to be profitable and compliant. More recently, with the rise of fulfillment costs becoming a bigger concern, adding one more expense, especially one that cannot be immediately tied to corresponding revenue, is not particularly attractive. Management may also be hesitant to invest because they feel the payoff is questionable or because they are suspicious of seemingly faddish approaches. Or, worse yet, they are gun-shy after having tried and failed or produced only disappointing results.

But now, lenders face a conflict that may force them to reconsider process design. In the current environment, a strictly sales or transaction-level focus is counter to the demands on the industry. Regulators, the agencies, and even consumers expect predictable, repeatable, well-documented processes that can be monitored and controlled.

A Philosophical Shift for Management

The demand for process-minded business practices has undeniably imposed itself on the industry. While some lenders may simply have never thought to develop a process approach to business, others may actually recoil from the idea. Larger lenders, whose scale demands structure and controls, or lenders whose specific differentiation is an engineered process, are usually comfortable with process-design concepts – it is a key element of their success strategy. But, lenders who thrive on and take pride in their entrepreneurial 'make it work' attitude, and in focusing on the transaction level, will need to make a philosophical shift in how they view their business.

Executive teams will have to develop a leadership commitment to process-oriented management and be willing to dedicate resources whose sole focus is process excellence. Companies who have relied on assigning process design to functional-area managers, expecting them to focus on it in their spare time, will have to abandon that practice and, instead, invest in dedicated, skilled teams. Companies who want to excel at process design will have to build enterprise-level skills and capabilities for evaluating the interrelationships among processes and functional areas, planning processes and system capabilities, executing system changes, and building policies that support the process as intended.

The success of process-focused efforts will be determined by the commitment management makes toward truly embracing the concepts. Management must understand that process design goes far beyond moving job tasks around and implementing or configuring software solutions. A full-scale process approach considers job descriptions and organizational structure, policy and rules that govern how work is performed, decision-making approaches, and approaches to measurements and rewards.

DATA AND THE ROLE OF PROCESS DESIGN

The concept of process-oriented approaches or process design typically draws notions of manipulating workflow and job tasks, adding automation, and adding efficiency and speed. But for the mortgage industry, it is also about collecting good data and being able to use it. Data is at the core of the mortgage process and the industry itself – collecting it, calculating and manipulating it for evaluation, creating it to execute loan transactions and secondary marketing transactions, and storing it for archival, regulatory reporting, servicing, and marketing purposes. Data and data management is the tool for achieving strategic objectives for growth and productivity, driving revenue, staying competitive, and staying compliant.

The Data Management Association (DAMA) defines data management as "the development, execution, and supervision of plans, policies, programs, and practices that control, protect, deliver, and enhance the value of data and information assets." Any process-design efforts must focus on how data is created and managed in the loan manufacturing process, and how that data will be mined and manipulated in the future. Expertise in creating accurate data and managing it is no longer just a cost of business, it is a vital tool to drive revenue and stay compliant.

The Demand for Data
Despite the capabilities of loan origination systems and data compilation and reporting tools, many lenders do not have speedy access to information that is organized in a

useful way. Or, the data may be available, but managers are unsure how to use it to draw meaningful conclusions and make decisions. Lenders must master the ability to collect, compile, and analyze data with speed, accuracy, and efficiency. Management must have mechanisms to manipulate and use data to serve multiple purposes:

Data for the Consumer: Consumers are increasingly expecting a stream of timely communications and a convenient menu of options to deliver and receive information about their transaction. Consumers want self-service and fast, meaningful information with a high-touch feel.

Data for Agencies and Regulators: The agencies are collecting massive amounts of data designed to track trends and control risk in the secondary market. Regulators require precise data to prove compliance, often organized in ways that are not inherent to the origination process. And, as regulators' perspectives and interests change over time, lenders must be able to anticipate the need to respond to changing expectations for burden of proof.

Data for Sales and Operations Management: Managers need data to control costs, manage and motivate employees, set competitive pricing, and control loan-level risk. All of these activities rely on the compilation and presentation of loan data and details of the flow and timing of work.

Data for Risk Management: The ability to detect and control risk is rooted in data analysis. Analysts need highly detailed data that can be sliced, diced, and 'tortured until it confesses.'

Data for Marketing: As consumers change their approach to shopping for and selecting a lender, lenders will need to be better at making an impression on potential borrowers before the loan transaction actually starts. As marketing and consumer outreach becomes faster and more sophisticated, lenders will need to be experts at analyzing consumer data and responding to consumer interests and actions.

TECHNOLOGY AND THE ROLE OF PROCESS DESIGN

In the 1990's, the mortgage industry was looking toward the promise of technology and automation to solve the puzzle of optimizing processes and data management. In 1993, early in the conversation about technology and the mortgage fulfillment process, Jeffrey F. Butler framed the COO's dilemma – how do you get the most out of technology to justify the expense? As an industry, we have yet to satisfactorily answer that question. The implementation of technology, while requisite and critical, has become a source of pain itself – how do we implement technology and execute change effectively and quickly with the intended results?

Lenders spend time and resources searching for and evaluating systems to craft a 'complete solution,' with an expectation that the collection of systems will add up to an optimized process. They expect the systems they invest in to enable them to produce clean, reliable data, in a simple and manageable way. And, the systems should introduce new capabilities and process improvements.

All too often, the outcome is far from expectations. Assuming that a system is functional and performs as intended (even if not what was *hoped* for,) the root cause of disappointing results is likely to be that the system was configured or designed without process-focused planning, a clear understanding of business needs, and consideration of how (or if) the technology could meet them. Often, without the benefit of process-oriented planning and requirements development, the implementation team ends up essentially recreating the old system, achieving few of the intended benefits. The features or capabilities of the new system are not realized and the result is just a really expensive version of the old processes and systems that prompted a change in the first place.

A fundamental concept behind that the application of technology is that it is an enabler of, not a replacement for, business processes – it allows businesses to get work done and to produce an outcome. When technology is deployed without the benefit of a strong business process approach, the results are almost guaranteed to disappoint.

The Loan Origination System
There's no better representation of the need for a strong process approach than the implementation of a loan origination system (LOS). The LOS is a primary enabler of the mortgage process and therefore the implementation of the LOS is the most critical technology challenge a lender will face. Sadly, while no lender can live without an LOS, few are entirely satisfied with their implementation.

While most lenders have at least intellectually accepted that there is no silver bullet, they still have a certain set of expectations for the LOS that are often not realized. Lenders assume that the software vendor has figured out a good, or even 'good-enough,' approach that fully leverages the system's capabilities. They expect that if they follow the intentions of the software developers and use the system as the vendor prescribes, the system will automatically optimize processes. Lenders hope the LOS will resolve certain process defects and produce a simpler, more streamlined pathway to a high-quality closed loan. And, along the way, maybe it will solve their key operational problems without requiring too much hard work from the lender or the vendor.

Sidney Harris' cartoon, published in the *New Yorker* magazine sums it up nicely. The cartoon depicts two scientists studying a complex equation. There is a detailed explanation of the problem and equally detailed illustration of the expected results. What happens in between? "Then a miracle occurs." When there is a weak process-management discipline, it is hard (or impossible) to determine the requirements for system capabilities and how to apply them. From this weak position, the lender looks to the system (and, by default, the vendor) to answer these questions, to define a process, and to solve operational problems that may be poorly understood or not even rooted in technology.

Results of a 2015 STRATMOR Technology Insights survey suggested that lenders who built their own LOS were more satisfied than those who purchased a commercial-off-the-shelf solution. Perhaps the distinction is that those who built their own system *had* to take a business process approach and apply process management disciplines – there was no one else to do it for them, no vendor to solve their problems. Without a strong process-oriented discipline, lenders, like Harris' scientists, cannot work out the problem in the middle of the equation.

BUILDING THE PROCESS-ORIENTED DISCIPLINE

Process-oriented disciplines require enterprise capabilities – leadership, culture, and structure – and capabilities to execute process-design projects. Building the process-oriented discipline does not happen accidentally, the company must make a strategic commitment.

Change Starts with Leadership Commitment

Companies that are able to achieve success with process-focused practices have commitment from leadership. Senior executives believe in the value of building capabilities in the organization, focusing on customer services, building a culture of accountability, and investing in people who can redesign processes. The leadership team must take responsibility for building a process-focused improvement plan, but empowering employees to contribute.

Build A Process-Design Team

Once leadership understands the organization's current process-engineering capabilities and where they need to be in the future, they must create a dedicated design team charged with process redesign, communications, project development, and change management.

The initial team should be a small one, made up of people who understand and believe in the concept of process design as a strategic advantage. The team must be willing and able to learn methodologies to examine all aspects of processes and formulate solutions. They must develop standard procedures for process improvement and serve as a model for developing an enterprise-wide appreciation for process disciplines. This team acts a consultant to the organization, performing analysis and providing recommendations to the business, and as problem solvers who formulate solutions to business issues.

Effective process-focused teams must be staffed with people who have an analyst's perspective. They must be talented all-rounders with a natural skill for seeing the interrelationships of activities and outcomes, sorting out the distractions from the *real* issues, and anticipating unforeseen problems. At the same time, they must have a good understanding of the mortgage process and its complexity; and, they must be familiar with the terms, actors, and constraints of the industry.

A key challenge for mortgage lenders is finding and developing the talent to make this shift. One approach is to look for it outside of the industry and groom a process-design task force. But the mortgage process is incredibly complex, requiring years to master the breadth of knowledge required to add meaningful value. Companies who must limit investment in these types of resources simply may not have the time to invest before seeing a good return – they need competent, productive people quickly. The alternative is to seek from within to identify individuals with the propensity to fill this role and develop their skills.

Focus on The Enablers
Workflow and technology are the most obvious process enablers and the ones that seem to get the most attention. It is tempting to focus only on workflow and systems; but process design is not as simple as automating a task, tweaking system configuration, and shuffling process tasks around. There are other factors that need to be considered and built into process design, which if ignored, potentially will drive the failure of change efforts.

These factors are referred to as *enablers* – capabilities that contribute to the success of a process or project.

Policies and Rules
Policies and rules govern how and why people perform the tasks they perform. If people do not have assessable, clear, and consistent guidance, they cannot carry out even the most carefully designed process. Policies may exist formally, evidenced by corporate-provided job aids (the checklists that are so prevalent in the mortgage industry), training materials, manuals, and system configuration. Or, perhaps they don't exist at all and exist only informally, created by the people who perform the job and often in many variations that may or may not meet management's objectives.

When mortgage lenders hear the term "policies" or "procedures" they typically think in terms of product guidelines. But policies and rules as a process enabler is not specific to product eligibility or investor requirements. Policies and rules are about who is responsible for achieving certain outcomes, what to do when the policies do not address a particular situation, and about establishing standard approaches or "norms". A glaring example of the effect of the lack of clear policies is evident in very typical complaints from processors regarding underwriting conditions. Underwriters draw from their own past experiences or personal opinions about what is appropriate regarding conditions. While most report that they go by agency guidelines, the guidance often leaves much room for interpretation. Each has his own philosophy on how to apply conditions. As a consequence, processors cannot predict what an underwriter wants, causing poorly submitted files, rework, and overall frustration. Developing a corporate philosophy that governs how agency guidelines are interpreted and applied would enable a more streamlined and coordinated effort.

Metrics and Rewards
Metrics, or measurements, and rewards are key drivers of behavior and must be in line with the process design. It is relatively simple to create a fairly long list of metrics and

'key performance indicators,' but it is more difficult to align with management objectives and process design. And it is surprisingly easy to undermine process objectives with numbers that focus on the wrong things.

A typical example of metrics undermining process objectives is underwriting-file submission deadlines. Imagine this scenario: The lender has implemented a process change aimed at improving file quality and resolving problems associated with incomplete, poorly organized, or haphazardly reviewed files submitted to underwriting. However, in the past, management placed prominent focus how quickly a loan moves through the process. Performance indicators measure how fast the processor submits to underwriting. The indicators are widely distributed within the company and the processors' incentive bonuses are reduced if they fall below a certain threshold. In this example, the processor has very little incentive to focus on quality; speed trumps quality. This process initiative is very likely to fail.

Rewards tied to metrics will most certainly drive behavior; but informal rewards can have a dramatic impact on process execution. Praise and encouragement and social norms are powerful motivators. Imagine a process-design project aimed at standardizing procedures to eliminate variation in how work is performed. If management continues to praise the processor for going out of the way, and outside the standard procedures for that special originator or demanding borrower, any interest in standardization will fizzle out quickly.

Recently, there has been progress in technology that helps lenders track and monitor key performance indicators. Real-time data is available on simple interfaces. People in different positions in the company have access to see information related to their goals. However, because the technology exists and is fairly simple to deploy, lenders must be cautious that the data actually supports management's objectives.

Job Roles and Capabilities
Job roles and capabilities define who does what work and what skills they must possess. Roles and capabilities must be aligned with the process objectives. An effective process redesign may call for redefining job roles, granting new authority, and empowering employees with new latitude to make decisions. It may require a shift from functional organization to team organization, or some hybrid of the two.

Management may need to invest in building the capabilities of employees if their skills and knowledge are not sufficient. Process design should not be limited to crafting jobs that fit individuals' current skill set; training or job reassignment may be appropriate. If the new process calls for different skills and capabilities, management must ensure that the people in the role are up to the job. This can be a difficult fact for management to accept and takes care and sensitivity to implement *and* maintain positive morale.

Job design or roles must also be well suited to the types of people who perform them well. Jobs that call for people who thrive on challenge and critical thinking must be broad and interesting enough to keep them fulfilled. Those that call for people who enjoy simple, structured routines must be simple, structured jobs.

OPPORTUNITIES AND CHALLENGES

The most obvious motivations for mortgage lenders to adopt a business-process approach are fairly straightforward – controlling skyrocketing fulfillment costs, controlling risk and loan quality, and providing responsive customer service. Along the way, some unexpected benefits are likely, and some of the same old challenges will continue to hang on.

Opportunity: Align Processes And Strategy

There's often a considerable disconnect between a company's strategic intentions and the execution of the loan production process. Consider the potential range of strategic positioning: perhaps it is high-touch service, low cost provider, or specializing in niche products. Now consider the loan manufacturing process and attempt to identify specific things that support (or counter) that strategic objective. For example, a lender may state that they are a high-touch provider, but the process has no mechanisms to invoke communications with the customer at certain milestones, customer communications are cryptic and difficult to understand, or the consumer carries more of the processing burden than they would like.

As processes are designed, they should be tested against the strategic objectives. Does the process support the objectives or work against them? Are the planned changes contributing to the strategy, or are they only 'nice to haves' that distract from achieving more meaningful goals? Too often, lenders embark on process projects without a clear intent or objective, hoping that a random collection of incremental changes will amount to a recognizable benefit that shows up on the bottom line.

A business process approach is a tool for executing strategy. Lenders that invest in building a process-oriented approach to executing strategy will be able to clearly tie efforts to goals and test the validity of projects. Too often, companies design a strategy, but process happens accidentally. Management turns over process development to production people who are not trained or are not singularly assigned to *designing* a process that aligns with strategy.

Change Strategy or Identify New Ones
Process-management disciplines can illuminate new opportunities to gain market share that were previously unapparent. For example, a retail lender whose key strategy is attracting a retail sales force with high compensations plans may focus on building a robust consumer portal to reduce overall costs. Along the way, the lender may realize that they have a unique competitive differentiator that sets the stage for expansion into the consumer direct channel.

Opportunity: Fully Engage A New Workforce

The aging of the mortgage industry population is a prominent theme at the moment. Few lenders are attracting young employees. In fact few are trying. Lenders typically have a 'hire only experienced people' approach. Consequently, as a whole, the industry is self-inflicting the aging workforce problem by imposing the experience conundrum on young workers. Companies that are process-oriented and engage in thoughtful process engineering can create a platform that provides the structure and support on which less experienced workers can quickly and successfully provide value.

Companies that make the investment in developing less experienced employees would find themselves in a happy 'chicken or the egg' dilemma. The exercise of creating processes and systems that allow a less-seasoned worker to accurately execute tasks while building a base of knowledge also result in a process and system does not necessarily require seasoned employees.

Challenge: Focusing on All of The Enablers
Many companies embark on process improvement with the idea that it is a one-time event. Or, management sets the bar for improvement quite low – 'quick wins' and 'low hanging fruit' - and hopes it is enough to collectively result in significant recognizable benefits.

In the effort to gain momentum and build excitement, it is tempting to skip the hard work of establishing the true strategic objectives and prioritizing focus. Sure, the processors would love to automate the USPS validation and it would certainly be a quick win, but does that really support management's primary objective of improving customer communications? While there is merit to quick wins and easy fixes, unrelated incremental changes do not add up to enough benefit for the effort to feel worthwhile.

One tendency is to dive right in, identify and solve small problems and hope that this somehow add up to a true process advantage. Another is to avoid the harder enablers - those more emotionally driven, such as rewards and job roles. This haphazard approach is a disservice to the initiative. If the changes are not deliberately intended to achieve a predetermined outcome, it is too difficult to make an impact that is meaningful and identifiable. Employees need to see a clear connection between the intention, the change, and the result. Otherwise, they will not become convinced that process-focused projects are worthwhile and will eventually lose faith in the concept altogether.

Challenge: The Powerful Stronghold that People Have on Process
An individual's process is also not always aimed at the same objectives that management would place first. While management is concerned about risk, efficiency, costs, and service, a processor may be concerned about avoiding the wrath of an impatient originator, ensuring that his decisions will not later come under scrutiny, or simply avoiding the effort and discomfort of overcoming inertia to learn or adapt to new processes.

Most fulfillment processes, despite automation tools, data validation techniques, and system services, are still highly manual in most lender shops. Management often operates on the assumption that a seasoned employee's past experience is a sound and trustworthy way to produce satisfactory results. Policy and rule development that drives employee decision-making and action is not typically well-developed, perhaps on the assumption that seasoned employees do not need detailed direction.

Regardless of why, the combination of the two dynamics means that the employee has a very high degree of control over how they execute processes. The problem that is difficult to solve is how to drive employees' behavior and approaches to produce a reliable, predictable process that is aligned with the company's strategic objectives. Management typically has little visibility into the nuance of each individual's techniques and approach; yet these techniques and approaches are the very heart of the business.

There are plenty of examples that probably feel familiar to a lot of lenders:

- Deciding to take five steps to complete a task, when two would do, in order to feel confident that they have not missed any details.
- Taking it upon oneself to perform more work than is required due to distrust of the upstream process or because of sense of personal satisfaction for being very thorough.
- In an attempt to maintain a sense of control, putting up artificial obstacles in response to feelings of being overwhelmed or frustrated.
- Over-executing because of fear of accepting responsibility for decisions.

Challenge: Practicing Patience

The management team must understand that meaningful changes will not be quick or easy. It will take time and effort to build capabilities and transform the culture of the organization. There will be the usual bumps and perhaps temporary inefficiencies in the course of introducing changes. Management must be patient and recognize that building skills and seeing results is not an immediate gain, it is an investment for the long term. And, finally they must have the resolve to remain committed and to ease nerves and provide encouragement and leadership as the organization deals with the natural fear of change.

Process design is one of the few opportunities to get better at manufacturing mortgages, become more profitable, successfully grow, and gain a real, sustainable competitive advantage. The good news is that companies that invest in developing a business-process orientation and disciplines to design and improve processes have access to new opportunities to achieve real competitive advantages. For lenders which have traditionally relied on sales acumen and the ability to capture markets as the primary (or perhaps, the only) true competitive advantage, recognizing the opportunities in process design can be invigorating and transformative.

ABOUT THE AUTHOR

Jennifer Fortier, CMB, has 15 years of comprehensive experience in mortgage banking. Prior to joining STRATMOR, Jennifer was Senior Vice President and shareholder for an independent mortgage bank, where she was closely involved with corporate planning, strategy, and execution. Jennifer provided oversight and guidance in numerous areas, including regulatory compliance, quality control initiatives, and operational procedures.

Her primary functional responsibility was running the secondary marketing department and overseeing the lock-desk and shipping and post-closing functions. In addition to her formal role in secondary marketing, she managed many corporate-wide technology projects and established enterprise-wide communication and documentation protocols.

Jennifer participated in the MBA School of Mortgage Banking and the Future Leaders program in 2004. She was awarded the Certified Mortgage Banker designation in 2005. She participated in numerous committees, including the MBA Secondary and Capital Markets Committee, the Louisiana Mortgage Lenders Association Board of Directors, and the Louisiana Residential Mortgage Lending Board.

Prior to entering the mortgage banking industry, Jennifer worked with a start-up broker/dealer, a product manager for an industrial manufacturing company, and filled a systems analyst role on a team focused on an HR system for the U.S. Department of Defense. Jennifer held an appointment as an adjunct professor at Tulane University teaching business management and marketing. She holds a Bachelor of Science in Industrial technology from the University of Southwestern Louisiana and a Master of Business Administration from the A.B. Freeman School of Business, Tulane University. Jennifer currently resides in New Orleans, LA.

CHAPTER TWO

RESIDENTIAL MORTGAGE UNDERWRITING: INVESTMENT PROPERTIES, JUMBO LOANS, AND SELF-EMPLOYED BORROWERS

SHELLEY CALLAGHAN | SENIOR MARKETING PROGRAM MANAGER
VICKI WOECKENER | MANAGER, CREDIT POLICY
DEYA ARAIZA | UNDERWRITING PRODUCTION MANAGER
MGIC

When underwriting loans, especially low-down payment loans, it is important to think in terms of the tried and true four C's of underwriting. Additionally, as down payments decrease, the importance of paying close attention to the layers of risk in a transaction increases. Evaluating all of the factors together helps an underwriter evaluate the overall risk of a loan as we all work toward a common goal — successful property ownership.

THE FOUR C'S OF UNDERWRITING: CREDIT, COLLATERAL, CAPACITY, AND CAPITAL

Credit refers to the borrower's willingness to repay. A borrower's credit history (and representative score) generally reflects the borrower's willingness to repay their debt. Past credit management is the best indicator of future credit performance.

Capacity is the borrower's ability to repay. Several components are used to determine a borrower's capacity. Some of the key factors that are considered are Debt-to-Income Ratio (DTI), income stability, employment history, and reserves.

Capital zeros in on the borrower's investment in the property ("a.k.a. "skin in the game"). The amount and source of funds are reviewed when determining the borrower's investment (aka down payment or funds to close).

Collateral is the property's value and marketability. A residential appraisal is the primary document used to assist in determining if a property's value is supported by like properties in the subject properties location. Another consideration is the future marketability of the property in the unlikely event that it must be sold to satisfy the debt.

Some of the key risk factors to consider when underwriting a loan for mortgage insurance include loan-to-value (LTV), DTI, loan type, occupancy, employment type, and reserves. Borrowers with higher credit scores, stable employment/income, and more reserves are less risky than borrowers with lower credit scores, unstable income,

CHAPTER TWO: *RESIDENTIAL MORTGAGE UNDERWRITING* 15

and low reserves. The more high-risk factors (lower credit scores, less reserves, etc.) on an individual loan, the riskier still that transaction becomes. The combining of multiple high risk factors on a single transaction is known as *risk layering*.

UNDERWRITING INVESTMENT PROPERTIES

An investment property is a non-owner occupied property that is acquired for the purpose of making a profit. A borrower may be purchasing an investment property for many reasons including: generation of monthly income from rents; profit from renovating and reselling the property (known as property flipping); or potential future value appreciation (speculation). When underwriting such transactions, it is important to know the intended purpose, because the underwriting approach will vary due to the different risks involved. Historically investment property loans have required a significantly higher down payment than an owner-occupied residence.

Risk Factors

Investment properties represent a higher risk for many reasons. Among the considerations during your evaluation should be the borrower's history of owning rental properties. A borrower with no experience in owning rental properties may face many of the following challenges:

- *Compliance with laws:* tenants rights, additional building and safety codes
- *Decrease in value:* reduced profit at time of sale, potential impact on monthly rent
- *Property maintenance :* will the tenants take good care of the property when the owner is not present, costs of repairs
- *Renting the property:* advertising, screening potential tenants, rent collection, and eviction
- *Multi-family properties:* unique properties, market support

An investment property can also be a multi-family residential property. Today 1-4 units are considered residential properties, while properties with five or more units are generally considered commercial properties. In general, a borrower who purchases multi-family properties is doing so for positive monthly rental income. While a property's monthly rent may appear to support the operating costs, there are many additional challenges due to the additional maintenance and the work involved in marketing and renting multiple units.

Underwriting an investment property requires a more cautious analysis of all risk factors, because the borrower is not living in the property, the monthly mortgage is dependent on the monthly rents, and unknown maintenance expenses may deplete a borrower's liquid assets or increase their liabilities.

Credit

The credit history of a borrower purchasing an investment property must be documented with a history of traditional credit (installment, mortgage, revolving) and carefully evaluated. In the market following the Great Recession market, a borrower who is purchasing an investment property is typically expected to have a credit score of 700 or higher. Historically, investment property loans become delinquent at a higher rate than loans or primary residences, so it is important that the borrower has a demonstrated history of managing credit. The credit score alone, however, may not tell the entire story. It is also important to look beyond the score and analyze the entire credit report. A borrower with a history of late payments, a bankruptcy, or a foreclosure would require careful scrutiny. If there are any derogatory credit items, it is advisable to look for strengths in the other "C"s such as higher down payment (greater capital) or lower DTI (greater capacity).

For borrowers who have a high DTI, it is very important to review their use of credit. If a borrower has multiple revolving accounts with the unpaid balance at or near the available amount, this may be indicative of a monthly-cash-flow concern.

Income (Capacity)
A history of stable income and employment is very important when underwriting a loan, and for an investment property, an indication of instability is an even higher risk. A borrower's employment income is calculated in the same manner whether they are purchasing a primary residence, second home, or investment property; however the use of rental income from the subject property varies.

The documentation to support rental income will vary based on transaction type (purchase vs. refinance), and when the property was acquired. For example:

- Properties acquired during the current year should require an operating income statement or copies of the current lease agreement.
- Properties acquired prior to the current year should require the most recent two years' signed personal federal tax returns.

The calculation of rental income also varies based on when the property was acquired. For example:

- Property acquired during the current year
  - Monthly Rent (lesser of operating income statement or current lease)
    - Expenses (greater of 25% or operating income statement)
    - Proposed monthly housing payment (Principal, Interest, Taxes, & Insurance)
    = Net monthly amount
  - Positive income is added to the borrower's qualifying income
  - Negative net monthly amount is added to the borrower's monthly obligations

- Property acquired prior to the current year
  - Monthly Rent (based on a two-year average from Personal Federal Tax Returns Schedule E)
    - Expenses (based on a two-year average from Personal Federal Tax Returns Schedule E)

            - Proposed monthly housing payment (Principal, Interest, Taxes, & Insurance)
            = Net monthly amount
- Positive income is added to borrower's qualifying income
- Negative net monthly amount is added to borrower's monthly obligations

For borrowers who have a history of owning investment properties it is important to review the stability of rental income and expenses, including the cost of maintenance. Schedule E of the borrower's Federal Income Tax Return(s) indicates the amount and number of months a property has been in service. Pay close attention to the average cash flow: does there seem to be a pattern of not having a property rented, or significant maintenance costs that may impact the borrower's ability to repay? If so, it could suggest making adjustments to your assumptions about monthly rental income. Or, it could be indicative of management issues. In any event, it is something that should be explored by the underwriter.

Assets (Capital)

A borrower's minimum investment for an investment property is significantly higher than for a primary residence. In the aftermath of the Great Recession, a 1-Unit Investment property typically requires a 15% down payment, while a 1-Unit Primary Residence may allow as low as a 3% down payment.

In addition to the increased down payment, investment properties should require greater borrower funds (as opposed to gift funds), and the number of months of reserves required is greater than with a Primary Residence as well. All of these are designed to help to mitigate the risk of a borrower defaulting on the loan.

A strong history of savings and liquid reserves is also very important. A borrower with limited liquid (eg.checking, savings) reserves is considered a higher risk due to the potential impact on the borrower's ability to make payments (in case of a vacancy) or to maintain the property in the case of unforeseeable repairs. If a borrower's reserves are not in the form of a liquid asset, attention should be paid to their ability to access the funds if necessary.

Collateral

Investment properties bring a unique challenge, since you are not only trying to determine value and marketability, you are also trying to determine if the monthly rental income is reasonable given the market in which the subject property is located.

Some questions to consider during collateral review include:

- Is monthly rental income being used for qualification?
- Are the comparable sales similar to the subject property (e.g. number of units, size and room counts)
- Does the Comparable Rent Schedules (used to determine fair market rent compared to similar properties in the subject properties location) support the monthly rent?
- Is the property in average or better condition?

While having comparables of similar design and appeal is always important, it is even more important when rental income is being used for qualification. For example, a one-bedroom unit should not be compared to a two-bedroom unit, since the demand for the number of bedrooms and the fair-market rent would be significantly different. Also, while property condition is always important due to repair costs, with a rental property the underwriter must also consider how long the work will take due to the impact on rental income.

Investment Property Summary
A borrower's motivation to own investment properties is generally very different from the motivation of someone who is going to live in a property. Careful analysis is required to identify the layers of risk. When underwriting an investment property, the underwriter needs to recognize these risks and consider any compensating factors. For example, a property with market rent less than comparables may be acceptable if a borrower does not need the rental income to qualify. In the end, the goal is for a borrower to have a successful investment in a residential property.

UNDERWRITING JUMBO LOANS: BIGGER LOAN, BIGGER RISK

Jumbo loans have loan amounts that exceed the conforming loan limits. Conforming loan limits for residential mortgages are set annually by the Federal Housing Finance Agency (FHFA), and prescribe the maximum loan amount purchasable by the government-sponsored enterprises (GSEs), better known as Fannie Mae and Freddie Mac. By definition, jumbo loans are "nonconforming" and are not eligible for purchase by the GSEs. Instead, they are funded entirely by private capital.

Historically, sources of private capital have included proceeds advanced by portfolio lenders, real-estate investment trusts (REITs), hedge funds, as well as funds raised from investors through the issuance of private-label securities (PLS) backed by pools of jumbo loans. With the exception of the PLS boom of the mid-2000s — a period in which the PLS market was dominated by subprime and Alt-A lending — jumbo loans have represented the largest share of PLS. Yet, in stark contrast to the subprime and Alt-A loans, jumbo loans are generally fully documented loans made to borrowers with good-to-excellent credit. They are typically manually underwritten and require a reasonable down payment from the borrower (capital), a substantial amount of reserves (capacity), and other compensating factors. This is not to say that jumbo loans are necessarily low-risk. Rather, the most prominent risk factor is their sheer size — a large loan on an expensive property — and the limited marketability of the property in most markets as compared to most properties with conforming financing. These factors accentuate the importance of collateral review.

Jumbo or Super Jumbo?
As of late 2015, the conforming loan limit for a 1-unit property in most real estate markets was set at $417,000, and as high as $625,500 in higher-cost markets. To help spur home buying through increased access to credit during the Great Recession, FHFA

introduced "conforming high-balance" loan limits, enabling the GSEs to purchase loans exceeding the $417,000 and $625,500 thresholds. Under the conforming high-balance limits, the GSEs today are eligible to buy loans on 1-unit properties up $625,500 nationally, and as high as $938,250 in higher-cost markets.

Some use the term *super jumbo* to describe loans with an original principal balance (OPB) of $1,000,000 or more. As the dollar values increase, so does the challenge (and importance) of the collateral review. To compensate for this increased risk, lenders often lower the loan-to-value (LTV) ratios and increase the credit score threshold at which they are willing to lend.

The cost and availability of jumbo loan financing may fluctuate depending on geography, market conditions, and access to capital. Jumbo loans typically have higher interest rates than conventional conforming financing, typically in a range on 0.125% to 0.500% higher. Additionally, it is routine that lenders obtain private mortgage insurance (MI) on jumbo loans with LTVs exceeding 80% to reduce their exposure to loss.

Risk Factors

Jumbo loans generally represent a higher risk to the lender, more so due to the size of the loan as opposed to the credit quality. The risks associated with larger loan amounts are many when compared with smaller loan amounts. Consider the potential adverse outcomes of originating one $1,000,000 mortgage, versus five $200,000 mortgages. With the $1,000,000 mortgage

- risk is concentrated in one borrower and one property, as opposed to being dispersed across five separate transactions;
- finding comparables can be more difficult, exposing the collateral property to more valuation volatility; and
- there is certain to be a smaller pool of potential buyers, which can increase marketing time and cost when looking to dispose of a property repossessed in a foreclosure.

With larger loan amounts come higher property values, and unique, potentially over-improved custom properties which may appeal to fewer prospective buyers. Borrowers typically have more diverse sources of income and types of assets, requiring additional documentation and analysis. LTV, loan type, and loan purpose may also be contributing factors to the overall risk of jumbo lending.

Underwriting

The borrower's willingness and ability to repay, their investment in the property, and the property's value and marketability should be carefully evaluated. Higher-LTV mortgages expose the lender to additional risk, which is of course a risk routinely mitigated with the purchase of private mortgage insurance. Jumbo loans are often adjustable or variable rate mortgages ("ARMs"), because most are held by portfolio lenders. Portfolio lenders typically offer ARMs as a means of managing interest-rate risk. Though not prevalent, interest-only loans are sometimes offered in the jumbo segment as a means of creating financial flexibility for high-net-worth clients.

With any variable-rate loan instrument, there is an inherent payment risk to the borrower if interest rates rise. To help mitigate this risk, borrowers are qualified at a rate that helps ensure they will be able to afford an increase, typically using the greater of (i) the fully indexed accrual rate, and (ii) the note rate plus 2%. Additionally, annual and lifetime interest-rate caps are used to ensure the payment can't rise beyond a known, reasonable level for the borrower.

Credit

Borrowers must have established a strong credit profile that demonstrates their willingness and ability to manage their financial obligations. Credit must be verified using traditional sources. The amount and type of debt may differ, but must be consistent with the borrower's income. Jumbo-loan investors typically require credit scores of 700 and above. In the super-jumbo segment, it is common to see minimum credit score requirements of 720 or 740. Generally, the larger the loan, the stronger the borrower's credit profile required.

Income (Capacity)

A borrower's income must be stable and sufficient to support the new proposed housing payment and other current obligations. Jumbo-loan borrowers generally have more complex income sources and business structures. Many borrowers are self-employed, often with multiple interdependent businesses. Income and business analysis is required to determine stability and continuance, as well as the strength and viability of the business. Large increases in income must be evaluated and determined to be stable and sustainable if they are to be used for qualifying. Each variable must be taken into consideration. *Residual-income analysis* is often used with high income borrowers as a means for determining capacity. For higher income households, a total debt-to-income ("TDTI") ratio can understate the household's capacity to repay due to their greater residual income. As a result, more and more lenders are incorporating some aspect of the residual-income analysis commonly used with the Veteran's Administration (VA) home-loan program.

Assets (Capital)

Assets, savings history, and liquidity must be strong and sufficient to support qualifying income. A solid financial cushion is important to enable the borrower to weather unforeseen financial challenges, and liquidity helps ensure the funds are readily available. A steady savings pattern demonstrates that the borrower is disciplined with their finances. Large balance-increases or new accounts must be verified to ensure the funds are not borrowed and are from an acceptable source.

It is important to consider assets that may be useable as an income source, if necessary. Retirement distributions and interest and/or dividend income are a few examples. It is essential to verify that the borrower will have sufficient funds in the event of a disruption in income. Lenders typically require a minimum of six months reserves. More reserves – anywhere from nine to 24 months — are routinely required with super-jumbo loans and low-down-payment jumbo loans.

Minimum borrower contribution requirements are also higher than with conventional conforming loans. Typically, the entire down payment must come from the borrower's own verified funds, though some jumbo programs do allow for gifts of cash or equity.

Collateral

Higher-priced properties tend to be unique in design, gross living area, amenities, and site size. Appraisals often lack comparables with similar characteristics. They require higher net and gross adjustments, which increases the risk due to subjectivity of value and marketability. As a result, this type of property may be more vulnerable to market changes, and cost to build may not be equal to market value.

Some questions to consider during the collateral review include:

- Is the subject property so unique that it would not appeal to a broad group of potential buyers?
- Has the appraiser provided adequate support in terms of data and narrative to support the value conclusion?
- Are market conditions changing that may impact the appeal of jumbo properties?

If comparable sales are dated or not in close proximity, you should question the resale market for this type of home. It is not uncommon for investors to require second appraisals or review appraisals for certain higher loan amounts, such as for super-jumbo loans, to further support value and marketability.

Jumbo Loan Summary

The GSEs' conforming high-balance purchase programs notwithstanding, the jumbo and super-jumbo segments have historically been served by private capital. In the wake of the Great Recession, and in the absence of a thriving PLS market, it is portfolio lenders, REITs and hedge funds that are writing the rules for jumbo lending today. While investment in this sector is currently fragmented, consistency has emerged in guidelines, with a few exceptions.

Today's jumbo market is a true "A" market as lenders and investors work to mitigate their exposure to the biggest risk inherent in jumbo lending, collateral risk. The market is evolving prudently, while remaining mindful of the long-held belief that the bigger the loan, the bigger the risk.

UNDERWRITING SELF-EMPLOYED BORROWERS

You've heard the clichés: *Follow the money. Cash is king.* When it comes to underwriting single-family residential mortgage loans for self-employed borrowers, these should be considered truisms. But to be even more precise, perhaps we should specify that *cash flow* is king.

Analytical skills and sound judgment are certainly necessary when evaluating self-employed borrowers. Determining whether they can and will repay a loan is difficult, because obtaining an estimate of their earnings from tax returns can be confusing. The challenge is that accountants for self-employed borrowers are experts at reducing tax liabilities by minimizing current net income, while we as mortgage loan underwriters rely on that same net income as a gauge of the borrower's earnings.

The tax return reveals the borrower's taxable income. But what you are really looking to ascertain is the borrower's cash flow, because that is what the borrower will use to pay back the loan.

Risk Factors

The variable nature of self-employed income represents a greater risk than W-2 income because the borrower's day-to-day living and housing expenses are fixed. Some factors to consider:

- Is the business and industry stable, diversified and competitive? *In other words, how healthy is this business?*
- Does the borrower have a good credit history and credit score? *A poor personal credit history could indicate a cash flow problem in the business and prevent the business from obtaining additional financing if needed.*
- What is the marketability of the property? *If the business fails and the borrower loses his/her income, the property is the only asset collateralizing the loan.*

Typically, the industry considers a borrower self-employed if they have 25% or more ownership interest in a business. Because the income is variable, most investors require a two-year history of self-employment and require two years of signed and dated tax returns to document income that is stable and likely to continue.

Legal Structure of Business

Before you can determine the income documentation you will need, you must first understand the different business structures:

- Sole Proprietorship
- Partnerships
- General Partnership
- Limited Liability Company (LLC)
- S Corporation
- C Corporation

Basic Cash-Flow Analysis Concepts

Why use tax returns? You can get a snapshot of a wage-earners income from a W-2 form, paystub, or Verification of Employment (VOE). But a self-employed borrower is different. There is no "independent third-party" to verify employment and income. The most credible source of documentation is the tax returns that have been submitted to the Internal Revenue Service (IRS). Unfortunately, tax returns are not designed to provide a clear picture of cash flow. But, with an understanding of some basic concepts and careful analysis, from those tax returns you can determine the self-employed borrower's cash flow and whether he or she has sufficient income to qualify for the loan.

Tax returns are a starting point for analyzing cash flow. Income is *increased* by the noncash expenses and *decreased* by any real losses or expenses that were not included in the taxable income. As you can see, before you can dive into analysis, it's important to know what is considered income, expense, or loss. Once you understand these basic concepts, you will have a good foundation for conducting a meaningful analysis of both personal and business tax returns. There are three key income/expense components that appear throughout the cash flow analysis — noncash expenses, recurring versus nonrecurring income or loss, and losses and expenses limited by the IRS.

Noncash Expenses: There are generally three types of noncash expenses: depreciation, depletion, and amortization. They are deducted from the business' earnings just like cash expenses such as rent, supplies, and wages. These write-offs are a way for the business to spread out the cost of a long-term asset over its useful life. Because these items do not involve a payment to anyone, they can be added to the borrower's cash flow.

Recurring Versus Nonrecurring Income or Loss: A recurring income or expense item is one that can be expected to continue over time. Generally, the income should be expected to continue over the next three to five years before it can be considered for cash flow. The more the borrowers have to rely on that income to repay the mortgage, the more important it is for that income to continue long into the future.

Losses and Expenses Limited by the IRS: In certain situations, the IRS has limited the amount of loss or expense that a taxpayer can declare. When this happens, the individual reports a taxable income that is higher than what was actually received. A negative adjustment to income will reflect the lower cash flow.

More on Cash Flow

When analyzing cash flow, generally, two years tax returns are required to document the borrower's history of receiving the income, and to determine that the income is stable and likely to continue into the foreseeable future (typically for at least three years). However, in some cases, when an automated underwriting system is used, only one year's tax returns may be required.

Cash flow from the business drives the borrower's income, which will be used to pay back the loan. The underwriter analyzes the tax returns to determine if the self-employed borrower's monthly income will be sufficient to make the monthly payments on the loan. The cash flow needs to be quantified, and a monthly qualifying income figure needs to be calculated. Cash flow for a self-employed borrower is typically determined by two common methods: the Adjusted Gross Income (AGI) method and the Schedule Analysis Method (SAM). The AGI method begins with the borrower's most recent two years' gross total income before adjustments and is adjusted to account for regular/recurring income and neutralizing the income that will be evaluated from each schedule. SAM looks at the income/loss for each tax schedule allowing the underwriter to focus only on the schedules that will be used for determining cash flow, ignoring non-self-employed income sources such as W-2 earnings from employment or Social Security.

The method you use may depend on investor requirements, company policy, or personal preference. Either method should result in the same cash flow for the borrower.

To determine the borrower's cash flow, you'll typically start by analyzing two years of *personal* tax returns (Form 1040 and applicable schedules) and then two-years of *business* tax returns. When reviewing the 1040 tax form and accompanying schedules, you'll focus on the key income/expense components and add all noncash expenses (such as depreciation, depletion and amortization) that impact the borrower's cash flow.

- *Schedule C: Profit and Loss From Business:* Generally analyze two years of Schedule Cs.

- *Schedule K-1 (Form 1065): Partner's Share of Income, Deductions, Credits, Etc.:* Determine borrower's ownership percentage and therefore their share of the income/loss. Income may be used to qualify, provided that there are positive sales and earnings trends, adequate liquidity in the partnership, and the borrower can document access to their share of the income.

- *Schedule K-1 (Form 1120S): Shareholder's Share of Income, Deductions, Credits, Etc.* Same as above except used for an S Corporation.

- *W-2 Form (Wage and Tax Statements) from Borrower owned Corporation:* W-2 wages paid to the borrower from their corporation can be added to cash flow, provided you can document that the corporation is viable.

After analyzing the 1040s (personal tax returns), you'll move on to looking at two years of business returns for Partnerships, S-Corporations, and C-Corporations. Whether or not you will be using additional income from a partnership, S Corporation, or a regular corporation to qualify your borrower, you should still conduct an analysis of the business tax returns to ensure a consistent pattern of profitability. Generally, most investors allow the income to be used as long as the analysis shows profitability, the business is viable, has sufficient liquidity, and the borrower can document his/her ownership.

- *Form 1065: U.S. Return of Partnership Income, Form 1120S: U.S. Income Tax Return for an S Corporation and Form 1120: U.S. Corporation Income Tax Return:* Remember to add or subtract only the borrower's share of income or losses. The borrower's ownership percentage can be found on Schedule K-1 (Form 1065).

- *Year-to-Date Profit and Loss and Financial Statements:* Depending on the time of year you are analyzing tax returns, it may be helpful to obtain a profit-and-loss statement and financial statement to provide a current snapshot of a business over a given period of time (it may be a calendar year or a fiscal year). These documents are not generally used for qualifying the borrower, but rather to support income history, and the growth and stability of the business. Some investors may allow the income identified on the profit-and-loss statement to be considered only if the income is in line with the previous year's earnings. This income may also be considered if it is reported through audited financial statements.

Summary for Self-Employed Borrowers

Your objective in analyzing the tax returns, regardless of the business structure, is to determine that the borrower's business supports a stable income history and will provide continued cash flow necessary to repay the loan. Remember, when it comes to determining a self-employed borrower's ability and capacity to repay, cash flow is king.

ABOUT THE AUTHORS

Vicki Woeckener is a Manager for Credit Policy for Mortgage Guaranty Insurance Corporation (MGIC). In this capacity, Vicki is responsible for the policy and program review team, with a primary focus on interpreting and operationalizing underwriting and credit policy requirements. Vicki has held a variety of positions at MGIC since 1997, including Risk Analyst, Loss Mitigation Specialist, and QC Underwriting Analyst.

Her career in the mortgage industry spans over 30 years, with a variety of responsibilities including new product development, wholesale operations, retail team leader, affordable housing, and-private banking team coordinator.

Deya Araiza, MGIC Underwriting Production Manager, joined MGIC in 1998 and is currently the Underwriting Production Manager for the Seattle office. She manages a team of underwriters focused on MI-only business and is responsible for their overall productivity and work quality. Her experience extends to Contract Underwriting having managed both Contract and Mortgage Insurance teams during her time with MGIC.

Shelley Callaghan, Senior Marketing Program Manager, joined MGIC in the mid-1980's and currently serves as a Senior Marketing Program Manager. She is primarily responsible for MGIC's online and classroom technical-training programs. Through the years, she's worn many different hats, including managing an MGIC Underwriting Service Center and working on MGIC's national Field Operations team. Her technical savvy is built on her extensive practical experience, and drives the value she places on a strong technical foundation.

CHAPTER THREE

GROUND ZERO: THE IMPACT OF MORTGAGE FRAUD

CONSTANCE "CONNIE" WILSON, CMB, AMP, CFE
WITH CONTRIBUTIONS BY MATT MERLONE, CFE

In any discussion of the 2008 mortgage crisis, the topic of fraud usually comes up. Overwhelming evidence points to a pervasive cycle of speculation, abuse, corruption, and fraud during a time period when competition in the financial markets was skyrocketing, regulations were being rolled back, and credit was expanding, thus creating an unprecedented level of economic opportunism. This was not a natural extension of capitalism, and there was little hope of the market self-correcting in time to avoid a crisis. In this chapter we will look back on this "Perfect Storm," illustrate the conditions that existed during the years 2000 to 2006 leading up to the crisis, and then highlight the efforts of lenders, investors, law enforcement, and mortgage service providers to stem the tide of mortgage fraud. Going further we will look ahead to technologies and techniques to combat emerging fraud trends.

In 1973, sociologist and criminologist Donald Cressey came up with the Fraud Triangle to explain criminally fraudulent behavior. According to Cressey's model, there are three factors that must be present at the same time in order for an ordinary person to commit fraud: Pressure, Rationalization and Opportunity.[1] Most sociologists agree that the critical component for white-collar crime is market opportunity, which was omnipresent in the run-up to the crisis. In fact, sociologists David Wolfe and Dana Hermanson updated Cressey's model in 2004, adding a fourth component: Capability.[2] Wolfe and Hermanson recognized that in a crime-facilitative environment where not everyone can walk off the street and carry out a real estate transaction, it takes some level of aptitude and familiarity with the subject. Due to the complexity and number of participants involved, it has often been estimated that 80% of mortgage fraud can be tied back to a lending insider during this timeframe. Perpetrators of mortgage fraud often found the potential high reward for comparatively low risk irresistible; in fact the perfection of the greed cycle inspired innovation amongst white collar criminals who often concocted, and then repeated, far-reaching schemes affecting numerous properties and resulting in millions of dollars in losses.

There were several key conditions or developments that created this environment. Prior to the era dominated by the GSEs and evolution of the secondary market, where pools of loans were sold as mortgage-backed securities, banks were primarily depository

---

1 Donald R. Cressey, Other People's Money (Montclair: Patterson Smith, 1973) p. 30.
2 Wolf and Hermanson, The Fraud Diamond: Considering the Four Elements of Fraud (CPA Journal December 2004) p.38

institutions. From the available pool of deposits, banks would lend to local consumers who wished to become homeowners, effectively tying the institution to the economic fortunes of the local marketplace. In 1938 the government created Fannie Mae out of a need to insulate banks from elevated default rates in these local markets. Fannie Mae and later Freddie Mac created a secondary market for mortgages, and along with Ginnie Mae funded or guaranteed half of all mortgages by 2000. Without an exhaustive look at the predominant market conditions during this time, it would be difficult to name all of the various attributes that made the residential finance system susceptible to collapse, so for our purposes here we will highlight a few key developments:

- The 1998 repeal of Glass-Steagall legislation prohibiting the combination of investment banks and regular FDIC-insured banking institutions.

- Low interest rates made homeownership attractive for consumers, and the higher-yielding MBS pools offered asset managers better investment opportunities than Treasury or traditional bonds.

- Fueled by innovation in the financial markets, the private-label MBS and the "originate to distribute" business model had arrived. This facilitated the segmentation or dissemination of the lending process into components such as origination, funding, servicing, and securitization. This resulted in a new breed of lender, non-bank mortgagee lenders operating under the radar of federal regulation.

- Institutions chasing short-term profits sought to expand credit to underserved and nontraditional borrowers as a way to increase home-ownership rates. This led to exponential growth in Sub-prime and Alt-A programs, which were particularly susceptible to abuse.

- Extreme competition, aggressive financing, and relaxed underwriting standards at the loan level by non-bank private-label lenders led to controversial adjustable-rate, interest-only, low-down-payment, stated-income and stated-asset loan products designed to fast-track originations. In the "originate-to-distribute" model, loans were not held in portfolio, and credit risk was quickly transferred downstream to servicers and investors.

- By 2006 non-bank private lenders were originating more than 80% of Sub-prime loans, without adequate oversight by regulators.

- Compensation structures from the Wall Street level down to the loan-level operations in lending shops incentivized volume over quality of workmanship in order to satisfy the voracious appetites of investors.

- The credit-rating agencies and fund managers treated MBS pools similar to Treasury bonds without applying appropriate due diligence, particularly when it came to high-yielding Sub-Prime pools.

- Creative and mostly unregulated investments utilizing over-the-counter derivatives and credit default swaps gave rise to the term "toxic asset," as pools begin to fail without adequate reserves to serve as a safety net. The speculative environment created at the market level was tantamount to wagering.

- Finally, the home-price appreciation which had been masking many of the warning signs ceased. Home prices began to *depreciate*, accelerating the collapse and leading many underwater borrowers who had little skin in the game to walk away from their obligations. These so-called strategic defaults joined deed-in-lieu proceedings and foreclosures as an ever increasing phenomenon on Main Street.

Given all of the factors contributing to the risk of the residential lending environment, it would be difficult to imagine a scenario where the crash could have been avoided. Although there were some voices cautioning against the unsustainability of the market, they were drowned out and marginalized in the rush for profits and market share. Eventually, Fannie Mae and Freddie Mac also joined the fray as they were losing too much market share to the non-bank entities. The Mortgage Crisis of 2008 was more than a financial meltdown. It eventually had global societal impact as many of the investors in the market were foreign entities, including governments. The unfortunate default of Iceland, which was invested heavily in the U.S. MBS market, is often pointed to as an outflow of the crisis. Overall, the wide-ranging impact has been the subject of movies, books, and academic and government studies. Obviously, to consider the topic in-depth would require a far deeper and broader recounting, but our purpose is simply to set the stage for the next few sections.

In the next section we will focus on what was actually occurring at origination in some mortgage shops, and some common themes around the risks presented with fraudulent behavior, and attempts to mitigate those risks by various participants.

A PERFECT STORM

Causation and Identification of Mortgage Fraud

Across the country, mortgage lenders were springing up everywhere. The non-bank entities sourced their volumes from newly established, but extensive, networks of brokers and correspondents. Large mortgage aggregators purchased the newly minted loans to reap the servicing income streams, and sold the assets onto the secondary market. Generating volume to fill pipelines was the number one priority for a lender. "Feeding the beast" to maintain a pipeline required an endless supply of applicants and a legion of loan officers, processors and underwriters to handle the everyday lending tasks. This led to a significant number of borrowers being shoe-horned into products that they didn't understand, or in some cases were entirely unqualified for, and in some cases were being originated by a cadre of young or unseasoned lending staff. Not surprisingly, this left the door of opportunity wide open for abuse, corruption, and fraud.

Common Elements of Mortgage Fraud

Each type of financial fraud or white-collar crime has its own attributes, but they bear similarities to a general model. The hallmarks of mortgage fraud common to most schemes in one form or another are as follows:

- Intent to Defraud
  - Knowingly commit wrongful act(s)

- Disguise of Purpose
  - Falsification and Misrepresentations

- Reliance on the Ignorance of the Victim

- Voluntary Victim Actions
  - Assisting the offender – may be unintentional

- Concealment

- Conversion
  - Money Laundering / Consumer Goods

Fraud for Profit versus Fraud for Housing

No discussion of mortgage fraud is complete without making a distinction between "Fraud for Housing" and "Fraud for Profit." There are common elements of course; the intent to defraud, and disguising the malfeasance through manipulation and falsification. The FBI defines mortgage fraud as the "intentional misstatement, misrepresentation, or omission by an applicant or other interested party, relied upon by a lender or underwriter to provide funding for, to purchase, or to insure a mortgage loan."[3] Along with the two accepted classifications above, a third and more destructive brand of mortgage fraud may be classified as Fraud for Criminal Enterprise.

- *Fraud for housing* usually entailed misrepresentations by the borrower of their ability to qualify for a loan or to occupy a home. The borrower generally intends to pay the loan back, but would not normally qualify. Because of the magnitude of fraud for profit, and the tendency of fraud-for-housing loans to perform, this was rarely aggressively pursued by lenders.[4]

- *Fraud for profit* involves the collusion of multiple insider participants to defraud a lender of as much money as possible through repeated schemes covering numerous properties.[5] Repayment of the loan is never the intent, although in later schemes the fraudsters would start making payments for up to 12 months to avoid the scrutiny

---

[3] https://www.fbi.gov/stats-services/publications/mortgage-fraud-2010
[4] Association of Certified Fraud Examiners, Understanding the Basics of Mortgage Fraud, 2010 p. 53
[5] Association of Certified Fraud Examiners, Understanding the Basics of Mortgage Fraud, 2010 p. 54

of an Early Payment Default review by investigators and auditors at the investor or servicer level. The FBI estimated that 80% of all mortgage fraud involves fraud for profit. Many are detected only after the property goes delinquent and into foreclosure.

- *Fraud for criminal enterprise* takes mortgage fraud to the next level through money laundering, drug trafficking, and even terrorist financing. Criminals consider fraud in the mortgage industry highly-profitable without the usual risks attending other types of crime. There are numerous examples of high-profile mortgage fraud cases linking directly to domestic and international organized criminal enterprises. Often, proceeds are converted into more property, consumer goods, assets used to further criminal activity, or simply laundered and moved offshore. This type of fraud is not limited to the origination space.[6]

Potential for Abuse

The potential for abuse or opportunities to commit fraud may happen anywhere within a real-estate transaction timeline or lifecycle. Understanding the general timeline of the origination process is a basic requirement of residential lending. Throughout this process, the borrower may come into contact with a number of participants whose responsibility is to shepherd the transaction to the next stage, facilitating the tasks and events necessary to secure a loan against a parcel of property. Disregarding the specifics of distribution channel, retail versus wholesale, or whether the transaction is a purchase or refinance, the general process, participants, and key areas that harbor a potential for abuse during origination are outlined below:

- **Locate Property** – Real Estate Agent, Buyer, and Seller
  On a purchase, the borrower may or may not work with a real estate agent to locate a suitable piece of property for purchase.
  - The agent may be in collusion with the loan officer, seller, and/or buyer
  - The agent may provide fraudulent information or conceal malfeasance
  - The agent may influence the appraiser or otherwise falsify valuation or listing
  - The agent may influence the settlement agent
  - The buyer may not be qualified for the transaction
  - The buyer may be a straw or nominee
  - The seller may unduly influence the transaction
  - The seller or agent may be the orchestrator of the fraud
  - The seller may not actually be the rightful owner of the property

- **Select Lending Product** – Loan Officer
  The loan officer counsels the borrower about lending products, helping them to select the right loan type and amount to serve the borrower's needs. In some cases there may be a pre-qualification and a pre-approval of the borrower.
  - The loan officer may lack adequate training in fraud prevention and detection
  - The loan officer may steer the deal to a lender with lax controls

---

6 Association of Certified Fraud Examiners, Understanding the Basics of Mortgage Fraud, 2010 p. 55

CHAPTER THREE: *GROUND ZERO*

- The loan officer may be in collusion with agent, processor, appraiser, underwriter, or closer
- The loan officer may include excessive yield spread premiums
- The loan officer may be an orchestrator of the fraud
- The loan officer may misrepresent the details of the transaction or the loan product
- The loan officer may intimidate or influence other participants
- The loan officer may exploit inexperienced co-workers

- **Application** – Loan Officer and Processor
  The borrower supplies the information to fill out the 1003 Residential Lending Application or fills out the form themselves detailing information about their intended transaction, property, occupancy, and qualifications such as income, employment, and liabilities.
  - The borrower may be coached into filling out erroneous or false information to qualify
  - The processor may lack adequate training in fraud prevention and detection
  - The processor may be in collusion with loan officer and falsify documentation
  - The processor may erroneously clear conditions for loan approval
  - The processor may manipulate LOS, AVM, AUS, or automated fraud-screening tools

- **Collateral Evaluation** – Appraiser and Processor
  Once the property is identified, a licensed appraiser will ascertain the value of the collateral utilizing an accepted process which is most often derived from comparing the subject property to recent similar sales of property.
  - The appraiser may lack adequate training in fraud prevention and detection
  - The appraiser may falsify the value of the subject property or comparable properties
  - The appraiser may be in collusion with other participants to falsify value
  - The appraiser may routinely falsify appraisals to create a "false market"
  - The appraiser may intentionally disregard USPAP guidance
  - The appraiser may approve appraisals conducted by unqualified trainees
  - The appraiser may falsify values in order to maintain relationship with lenders

- **Underwriting** – Processor and Underwriter
  After collecting the documentation to establish the borrower's qualifications, the processor would provide the loan package to the underwriting department. The underwriter would analyze the transaction looking primarily at the capacity, collateral, and character of the borrower, the so-called 3C's of underwriting.
  - The underwriter may lack adequate training in fraud prevention and detection
  - The underwriter may be in collusion with other participants to grant approvals
  - The underwriter may manipulate LOS, AVM, AUS systems
  - The underwriter may waive conditions without justification
  - The underwriter may be susceptible to influence due to inexperience

- **Closing, Funding and Settlement – Closer and Settlement Agent**
  Once the transaction has been approved by the underwriter, it is passed over to a

closer or funder who prepares the loan documents and assists the borrower in satisfying any remaining loan conditions, then schedules a closing. The closing may be held at a real estate attorney's office or at a title company that handles loan settlements, or, as became commonplace, a mobile notary may be utilized. It is important to note that the Settlement Agent does not work on behalf of the lender, but rather on behalf of the buyer and seller of the subject property.
- The settlement agent may facilitate unauthorized payouts on HUD-1 Settlement Statement
- The settlement agent may be in collusion with the real estate agent and/or loan officer
- The settlement agent may turn a blind eye to identity of buyer, seller or notary
- The settlement agent may skim fees off of the HUD-1 Settlement Statement
- The settlement agent may ignore signs of property flipping

Motivation to Defraud
Obviously, the motivation to engage in illicit behavior is traced back to money; however it may be helpful to understand that the "production culture" also instilled a propensity for participants to regularly overlook borrower and property inconsistencies in favor of funding the loan as quickly as possible and moving it off of the books. Many interviews with perpetrators indicate that they started down the path of fraud out of a desire to move deals through the system quickly, effectively cutting corners and cutting costs. Simply making deals work despite risk concerns quickly escalated to outright fraudulent behavior. There are a number of reasons for this outside of directly profiting from the malfeasance; being seen as a go-getter, or not being the squeaky wheel, and avoiding the intimidation from peers perceived to be senior mortgage personnel, for instance. Even in shops that did not openly encourage illicit practices, risk-mitigation efforts carried out by the quality control departments were met with formidable resistance from the business operations ("Operations") and sales team ("Sales"). Typically, at the end of each calendar month, quality control would report findings to a production committee. Loans that were cited were then subjected to an onerous dispute process pitting Sales and Operations against quality control staffs, and often even legitimate concerns were rolled back if they threatened to impact a commission or bonus. Eventually, the dispute process was reincarnated as the repurchase requests began to come back to the lenders who were still around after 2007.

There were abundant examples of insider fraud committed specifically to obtain commissions, bonuses, and regular fee income. The "production culture" incentivized volume without regard to loan performance at almost every level. For example, if manipulating the automated underwriting system with multiple submissions over and over again, changing only minor details until the approval was granted, qualified a participant for a larger bonus, then that was just business as usual in some shops. Similarly, an appraiser might be influenced to push a value to ensure that the normal deals would keep coming their way. Serial refinances along with creative lending products were actively pursued for borrowers by loan officers whether they made sense or provided a tangible benefit to the client or not. Along the way, insiders were becoming landlords at unprecedented levels as the process proved so lucrative, and with the involvement of fellow insiders approvals were nearly guaranteed. Often times, when investigating a serial fraud case where the borrower was an insider, you could see that over a short span of time, qualifying income and assets seem to increase with each new loan application, as more real-estate owned was being acquired by an insider. Occupancy was also routinely falsified to receive preferred interest rates for primary residences. Proof of rental income was enhanced to ensure the debt-burden guidelines were being met. Examples go on and on, and this is where that fourth component of capability was really starting to surface.

Risk Layering
The snowballing of risk was also enabled further by lax underwriting standards with an over-reliance on credit scoring as a predictor of loan performance. Clearly, identity theft and straw buyer scams were providing evidence that credit history alone was not sufficient to establish the borrower's intent to repay. Along the way, where fraud was detected by the lender and proved too blatant to ignore, the insiders might lose their jobs, but they were rarely prosecuted. Subprime lenders were loath to admit fraud within their ranks, as it would negatively impact their standing with investors and servicers, so the insider usually resurfaced at any number of competing institutions and picked up where they left off. The mounting pressures of maintaining an excessive lifestyle ensured recidivism among many of the participants who were identified. A contributing factor to bear in mind was federal law enforcement in the post 9-11 world was singularly focused on counter-terrorism efforts, while local law enforcement did not have the manpower or acumen in most cases to pursue complex white-collar crimes. All of these factors resulted in the rise of the professional mortgage fraudster.

Once home prices began to depreciate and the delinquencies were mounting, investors and mortgage insurers began actively pushing loans back to originators by the thousands, starting in 2006 and continuing through 2011. A major shift in resources within the surviving larger institutions saw origination staff re-tasked as collections and loss-mitigation personnel. With the collapse that occurred in 2007 and 2008, most of the egregious offender institutions were closing due to bankruptcy and insolvency. In subsequent years, fraudsters re-branded themselves as loan workout specialists, foreclosure rescue scammers, and short sale flippers.

Schemes, Mechanisms, and Red Flag Indicators
When we talk about mortgage fraud in the larger sense, there is a lexicon or vocabulary that goes along with the discussion. It is imperative to break that down from the perspective of someone whose main goal is to detect and prevent fraud. We encourage those in the fight to be cautious about fraud-scheme naming conventions. The name of a particular scheme does not necessarily tell an underwriter what to be wary of, or give any clue as to how an investigator can proceed to document the fraud. It may be derived from what a victimized lender's experience was or how it was perceived by media. It is far more instructive to be cognizant of the individual mechanisms of fraud; also because so many terms are used interchangeably, it is beneficial to speak the same language.

The nomenclature around fraud schemes refers to the general process of the fraud that was perpetrated. There is quite a bit of variability in what schemes are called depending upon who is reviewing it, and what the perspective may have been at that time. For the purposes of fraud prevention, the term used to describe a scheme is far less important than fraud mechanisms and red flag indicators that are present. Listed below are some typical scheme names used in the years leading up to the mortgage crisis and beyond, along with a brief description:

- **Straw Borrower or Nominee Loans** – A technique to misrepresent the credit and identity of a borrower to the lender by using a stand-in "straw" borrower, who may be paid or unpaid by the scheme orchestrator. Almost always entails falsified income, employment, assets, and occupancy.[7]

- **Builder Bailout / Air Loans** – If a builder is plagued with unsold inventory, they may concoct a scheme to unload properties to free up cash. Usually involve hidden seller financing or incentives, down-payment assistance, gifts, and unauthorized payouts on the HUD-1 Settlement statement. If no willing borrowers can be found, they may fabricate a borrower from synthetic identity, employ a straw borrower or create one from whole cloth. An "Air Loan" works the same way except that the borrower is real, but the property does not exist.[8]

- **Chunking** – A scheme that preys upon unsophisticated borrowers (in some cases paid straws) who are dealing with an orchestrator like a loan officer. Multiple applications are submitted to numerous lenders on a single property with the orchestrator acting as power of attorney (POA) for the borrower. Perhaps the loan officer is also the seller, making the transaction non-arm's length as well. Often entails identity theft and elder abuse.

- **Shotgunning** – This is a variation on chunking, but with HELOC loans. Numerous applications are submitted to multiple lenders on a single property in rapid succession. Generally "rate shopping" is the rationale used to explain away the large number of credit inquiries. May be conducted as a bust-out scam by foreign nationals that exit the country immediately upon consummation of the fraud. This is a favorite technique of international criminal enterprises and offshore money launderers.[9]

- **Churning** – In this scam, the loan officer advises borrowers to refinance within a short time-frame several times. Each time the loan officer would split the yield spread premium with the borrower, and the borrower would avoid paying the mortgage during the interim periods. Typically the loan officer would do this with multiple borrowers, hitting multiple lenders to avoid detection.[10]

---

[7] Association of Certified Fraud Examiners, Understanding the Basics of Mortgage Fraud, 2010 p. 81
[8] Freddie Mac, Fraud Mitigation Best Practices, Jan 2015, p 15
[9] Association of Certified Fraud Examiners, Understanding the Basics of Mortgage Fraud, 2010 p. 67
[10] Association of Certified Fraud Examiners, Understanding the Basics of Mortgage Fraud, 2010 p. 70

CHAPTER THREE: *GROUND ZERO*

- **Identity Fraud and Theft** – Simply put, it is the misrepresentation of identity, either your own or someone else's. Given the number of borrower profiles and loans that can cross an insider's desk, there is nearly a limitless number of identities that may be compromised. Ultimately, identity theft is itself a mechanism that shows up in a great number of other schemes. A further perfection of this scheme is professional identity theft, where the credentials of a licensed or certified person are stolen and then used to create falsified documentation. An example of this would be stealing the license and signature of an appraiser and then create a falsified appraisal.

- **Market Creation** – Through multiple falsified appraisals in a particular area, a false market can be created that is then used to support other falsified values. Works in both an appreciating and depreciating market depending upon the goal of the scheme. May be a mechanism in a larger short sale or flipping scheme.

- **Property Flipping** – Buying low and selling high, and in certain cases it is not illegal. However, illegal flipping involves unsubstantiated changes in value due to phantom renovations and rapid changes in ownership in a compressed timeframe. Often times this was used as part of investment-club schemes. There are numerous examples where properties appreciated many thousands of dollars in the same day. Because real estate is a "relationship" business, the participants needed to carry this out would be the loan officer or real estate agent, appraiser, and settlement agent.[11]

- **Foreclosure Rescue** – As the foreclosures and delinquencies mounted, unscrupulous loan officers and real estate agents would re-brand themselves as a foreclosure rescue company assisting home owners in avoiding foreclosure on their properties. This entailed misdirected mortgage payments, high fees, equity stripping, and leasebacks. Often times this scam was committed by the very same loan officers who placed borrowers in properties that they could not afford in the first place.[12]

- **Short Sale** – Lenders have the option of taking a property back through the foreclosure process and then having to dispose of the property. Since most lenders do not want to be landlords, they are amenable to approving a sale by the delinquent borrower for less than the total payoff amount of the loan.[13] As the collapse gained momentum and origination staff were re-tasked to collections and loss mitigation, obvious instances of collusion were created where the staff responsible for negotiating a short sale on behalf of the lender may be acquainted with the borrower or with a real estate professional who is arranging the sale. In some cases the sale was to a relative allowing the borrower to stay in the home, or it may be that the real estate professional arranged a short sale at one particular price, but then has an undisclosed cash offer pending for the property of which the lender is unaware. Appraisal fraud may be used to deflate the value initially, using a falsified BPO along with an unmotivated listing in the

---

[11] Association of Certified Fraud Examiners, Understanding the Basics of Mortgage Fraud, 2010 p. 56
[12] Freddie Mac, Fraud Mitigation Best Practices, Jan 2015, p 21
[13] Freddie Mac, Fraud Mitigation Best Practices, Jan 2015, p 23

MLS. Another way to artificially devalue property was using one of the 3Ms (Mold, Murder, or Meth) as a way to falsify the value. Lab reports showing the presence of mold or methamphetamines lowering the market value are easily falsified. Violent crime may also be used to influence value unduly.

Mechanisms are those individual techniques which enable the fraud. They may be found to exist across multiple scheme types. These are the things underwriters need to be aware of and investigators must be able to identify quickly. Consequently, as we will discuss later, mechanisms are what automated fraud prevention software and prefunding reviews are designed to catch. Listed below are some of the common mechanisms that were encountered in the years leading up to the mortgage crisis:

- Identity theft or abuse
- Altered identity
- Fabrication of identity using falsified documents
- Falsified power of attorney
- Falsified gift documentation
- Falsified letters of explanation
- Falsified appraisals inflating or deflating the value to perfect the scheme
- Falsified qualification documents such as W2, tax return, bank statements or VOE
- Falsified BPO
- Falsified payoffs and re-conveyance
- Misdirected payments
- Collusion
- Non-arms-length transaction
- Account takeover
- Altered credit reports
- Reverse staging
- Piggyback credit using authorized user trades
- Gaming the system: multiple resubmissions to AUS, AVM, or fraud screening tools

Red-flag indicators are variances or inconsistencies that may be evident prior to funding, but are not proof of malfeasance without validation. These indicators of risk need to be reviewed by qualified personnel. If a lender is diligent, these may be caught in processing, underwriting, appraisal, or during closing just prior to the loan funding. These red flags may be in plain sight, or they may be highlighted through the use of fraud-prevention software, validation of income, employment, or assets, and so on. Generally, red flags are things that just don't seem to be correct, or do not make sense for a typical transaction. Seasoned mortgage professionals are often quite adept at sensing when a red flag exists and should be questioned. Consequently, insiders conducting fraudulent transactions are similarly adept at knowing what needs to be falsified and how to avoid scrutiny.

In order to adequately detect and prevent fraud, lenders must be able to put people and processes in place to efficiently review loans, looking for the hallmarks of risk and inconsistency. During the years leading up to the mortgage crisis there were not enough seasoned personnel making these assessments. Fraud was almost always discovered

CHAPTER THREE: *GROUND ZERO*

after the fact when loans became delinquent. The financial and systemic innovations which were appearing each year with greater frequency presented opportunities for exploitation that initially were not well understood. Up until this time the mortgage industry was a very manual and labor-intensive process. Advancements in technology allowed lenders to close more loans in a shorter period of time. However, to those insiders who were motivated towards fraud, it also became an enabler. Case in point would be automated underwriting systems, automated valuation models, and automated fraud-screening tools. In each case, this software was able to streamline the review of lending criteria by an order of magnitude. Over time, motivated insiders found that they could "game" these systems by manipulating inputs. Advances with imaging and desktop publishing made document alterations possible without the white-out or cut-and-paste step.

Origination Fraud during the Crisis
To put some quantification around the fraud which was occurring in the origination phase, we can look at it in terms of the 3C's of underwriting, Capacity, Collateral, and Credit. Estimates from the GSEs place capacity at the head of the list for mortgage fraud prior to 2008. Slightly more than half of the instances of fraud fell into that bucket. Falsification of debts and income would allow a borrower to qualify for a larger loan by creating room in the debt burden calculation that did not actually exist. Collateral was next in line, followed by credit. Keep in mind that these estimates are not exact figures, as a loan may exhibit fraud in multiple categories and the classifications of frauds was not standardized at that time.

- Capacity 51%
    - Income 21%
    - Liability 24%
    - Assets 6%

- Collateral 35%
    - Occupancy 24%
    - Property Type 9%
    - Value 2%

- Credit 14%
    - Identity 8%
    - Credit Score 6%[14]

Fighting Back: Prevention and Detection

Response
Law enforcement was not prepared for the exponential growth of mortgage fraud, or for any white-collar crime, for that matter, during this time frame. The sheer magnitude of

---

14 Association of Certified Fraud Examiners, Understanding the Basics of Mortgage Fraud, 2010 p. 72

the number of potential fraud instances was difficult to address for the multiple agencies tasked with combating the problem. We often hear that cases were primarily handled by the FBI, but there were and still are several agencies in the fight. In no particular order, listed below are the federal agencies tasked with mortgage-fraud investigations:

- United States Department of the Treasury
- United States Department of Justice
- United States Secret Service
- Federal Bureau of Investigation
- Internal Revenue Service
- United States Postal Service Office of Inspector General
- Department of Housing and Urban Development Office of Inspector General
- Federal Housing Finance Administration Office of Inspector General

Lenders are required to document information via a Suspicious Activity Report (SAR), which is then submitted to FinCEN.gov, which is organized by the Department of the Treasury. All federal agencies have access to this repository of SAR reports. From the late 1990's to 2005, SAR filings grew over 1000 percent, due in large part to the mortgage fraud prevalent during the crisis.[15] Federal law enforcement, stretched thin due to the September 11, 2001 terrorist attacks on New York City and the Pentagon, were ill-equipped to deal with this burgeoning crisis.

Compounding the lack of available agents and intensive case load was the fact that mortgage fraud did not fit neatly into a statute for prosecution. Mortgage-fraud schemes are often charged as bank fraud, mail fraud, wire fraud, conspiracy to commit bank fraud, and identity theft. As the crisis continued, individual states in the hardest-hit areas began developing specific statutes around mortgage fraud. The state of Georgia was the first to create such a statute.

In the ensuing years, mortgage-fraud task forces were created to link the efforts of federal and state law enforcement with regulators and lenders at the state and local market levels. The federal government, along with industry regulators and law enforcement, was forced to consider unique methods and tools used to combat mortgage fraud. This included retooling or repurposing existing statutes, writing new legislation and standardizing unregulated industry activities as follows:

- RICO – Racketeer Influenced and Corruption Organizations Act - 1970
- False Claims Act – Law from Civil War era to combat corruption against the government
- Qui Tam Lawsuit – Whistleblower protection
- FERA – Fraud Enforcement and Recovery Act of 2009 Includes language around regulating non-bank entities
- SAFE Act 2008 – Secure and Fair Enforcement for Mortgage Licensing Act
- NMLS 2005 – Mortgage licensing system
- HOEPA 1994 – Home Ownership and Equity Protection Act amending TILA

---

15 FinCEN.gov

CHAPTER THREE: *GROUND ZERO*

- HVCC 2008 – Home Valuation Code of Conduct
- Dodd Frank and Consumer Financial Protection Bureau 2010
- UDAAP – Unfair Deceptive Abusive Acts or Practices
- Fannie Mae Loan Quality Initiative (LQI) 2010
- FinCEN SAR Filing Expansion 2012

Even with the response from law enforcement and industry regulators, the avalanche of cases and lengthy time-lag from investigation to indictment and eventual conviction meant that only a limited number of cases were being adjudicated. Compounding the fact that lenders were not eager to prosecute due to the enormous drain on resources posed by lengthy investigations, the discussion turned to fraud prevention as the only viable option.

Damage Control from the Lending Community
While law enforcement was pursuing the most egregious cases of mortgage fraud, the lenders and investors had turned their efforts to fraud prevention. Developing a robust defense was recognized as the best strategy, because recovery of loss was a time-consuming and ultimately ineffective method to address the problem. A culture of change was gaining ground in the lending community due to the impact of risk and fraud upon lender profitability, leading lenders, investors, and insurers around the country to fund proactive methods of fraud prevention and investigation, including the following:

- Participation in mortgage-fraud task forces

- Engaging with the Mortgage Bankers Association and others around fraud and risk trends

- Creation and maintenance of robust watch lists and ineligible lists – keeping tabs on the growing number of insiders and bad actors that were originating defective and non-performing loans or committing overt acts to defraud

- Investing in quality control and fraud investigation
  - Hiring independent third-party reviewers
  - Implementing changes in loan sampling strategy for better coverage
  - Implementing changes in reporting structure – moving quality control out of Operations and reporting directly to executives
  - Early Payment Default ("EPD") and First Payment Default ("FPD") reviews – oftentimes fraud was detected only after a loan had gone into delinquency; soon EPD and FPD reviews became policy
  - Investigative reviews to purge insider frauds – internal reviews were conducted when fraud was discovered to ultimately remove bad actors
  - Forcing repurchase or rescission in cases of fraud – rise of the repurchase boom. Lenders, investors and mortgage insurers would send non-performing loans originated fraudulently back to the originator if they were still in business
- Education and training of origination staff

- Lenders acknowledged the need for robust training around the identification and mitigation of fraud schemes that included red-flag training, data-integrity screening, fraud-ring analysis, and incorporated these concepts into newly revised quality control programs

Investigator's Toolkit
Just as technology was enabling fraudulent schemes and mechanisms, it also provided a new generation of fraud fighter with tools to validate information quickly and pursue leads efficiently at a time when case-loads were expanding like never before. Subscription-based investigative tools allowed for quick searches to locate persons, property, and associations. Desktop investigations soon supplanted actually having investigators travel to the local market to access county records, interview borrowers, and inspect property. Open-source intelligence providers were also continually evolving in this timeframe, providing a cost savings to investigations as well. Google Earth, for example, made Air Loans with fictitious properties obsolete as a scheme. While the results of these types of investigation were not always sufficient to pursue a legal case in the courts, they were more than adequate to evaluate the extent of fraud rings and to mitigate future losses by tagging the participants involved as ineligible to do business with the institution. The aptitude of the investigative staff also played a role in the repurchase and rescission efforts to push loans back to originators responsible for defective loans.

CHANGING THE GAME: AUTOMATION AND ANALYTICS

Automated Fraud Screening

Automated fraud-screening tools began to appear as early as 1995, but full adoption has only been achieved as a response to the mortgage crisis. Prior to 2005, lenders deemed up-front fraud screening to be too expensive on a per-unit basis. The review costs of high-risk loans necessary to resolve inconsistencies were seen as burdensome. It was assumed that a certain level of fraud was inevitable and just a cost of doing business. Another point of contention for lenders was that false positive rates were too high, or that they did not handle the various loan products equally.

Over time, however, through successive iterations and collaboration between lenders and service providers, screening tools became finely-tuned and in fact increased ROI for lenders by streamlining traditional validation and verification efforts previously handled manually by large processing staffs. Along with the improvements to workflow there was also a commensurate improvement to the workmanship of loan production as the data integrity of loans continued to be refined.

Today, the use of automated fraud screening technology is a major component of pre-funding quality control review efforts. Quality initiatives such as Fannie Mae's LQI suggest pre-funding quality control on 100% of the origination pipeline, and automation has become essential to achieving such a review rate. Lenders often use automation to segregate workflows, focusing human-powered reviews only on the riskiest loans in the pipeline, or they may use it as a way to identify the propensity for fraud or the predictability of default. Through continual evolution, automated tools have become a preferred method to cost-effectively mitigate risk and prevent fraud.

In an environment where automated fraud prevention exists on a pre-funding basis, there is a logical opportunity presented for comparison during the post-closing quality-control audit process. Balancing the efficacy of automation against a human-powered forensic review provides the user with a unique first-hand validation result. The automated quality-assurance efforts need to exhibit findings consistent with those of seasoned quality control auditors. Through the re-validation of loan data on a post-closing basis, we may conclude that the tool is working as intended. We can demonstrate that the areas of risk that have been identified by the tool are in line with the forensic-review findings. The residential mortgage industry is awash in an expanding universe of data. Harnessing the available comparisons of real-time risks against first-hand experiences is crucial to profitable lending.

We also cannot ignore the profound impact that regulatory action has had on fraud risk, which is manifested in a number of ways. The ability-to-repay portion of Dodd-Frank has affected employment and income risk because, post-crisis, lenders have tended to execute on the 4506-T, Request for Transcript of Tax Return, for each loan. With exact figures on income and correspondingly accurate debt-to-income (DTI) ratio figures, it is more difficult to falsify income without filing falsified returns, which has become an additional deterrent to fraud.

We must bear in mind that the lending community has also been forced to divert resources to appropriately account for loan compliance. This may come with a corresponding reallocation of fraud-prevention resources, reinforcing the need for automation to fill in this gap.

The Dawn of Data

As of this writing, we are almost eight years post crisis, and the regulatory environment has changed, as has the credit-risk appetite of lenders. The dialogue has changed from one of fraud prevention to a broader concept of risk mitigation. Accounting for this change is where the advanced analytics come into play. Data scientists are able to apply analytics upon the scoring from fraud, risk, valuation, and underwriting tools to provide lenders and investors valuable holistic insights around loan quality. Making full use of the aggregated data we can create insightful derivative analytics driving down the number of loans that must be manually reviewed by placing the focus clearly on the risk. Predictive modeling and feedback loops of client-contributed data can provide significant lift to the lending community, helping lenders to identify their risks through collaboration and to make changes to credit policy in real time. Technology can greatly enhance loan performance through the following techniques:

- Predictive modeling
- Linking data sets
- Creation of self-learning models

- Risk attribute clustering
- Real time comparison to market data

Emerging Threats

We mentioned earlier in this chapter that the innovation and evolution of fraud risk is enabled by technology, and this is where major concerns around cyber fraud and theft of personally identifiable information are truly being felt. The headlines today are filled with news of breaches and hacks that companies were not prepared for, and in some cases were not even aware of until the consumers were affected. Fueled by domestic and international organized crime along with foreign nationals, cybercrime is the number one growing area of threat to the soundness of the residential mortgage lending industry. There are vast amounts of data provided on borrowers and properties in the lending process that can be misused by criminal elements. Awareness, education, and prevention of cyber threats will dominate the mortgage-fraud discussion in the future. Listed below are descriptions of some of the techniques currently being utilized:

- Personally Identifiable Information (PII) Theft – hacks and breaches target data that can be resold on the dark web to commit identity theft in the future
- Account Takeovers – by leveraging a number of methods to compromise accounts such as social engineering or e-mail compromise, the takeover of accounts by criminals is becoming more prevalent
- Malware – shorthand for malicious software designed to damage, infiltrate, or disable a computer or network system[16]
- Spoofing – falsifying the true identity of an email or phone call to defeat caller ID or network system identification[17]
- Botnet – a network of private computers infected with malicious software and controlled as a group without the owners' knowledge to execute illegitimate commands[18]
- Phishing – the attempt to acquire sensitive information such as usernames, passwords, and credit card details (and sometimes, indirectly, money), often for malicious reasons, by masquerading as a trustworthy entity in an electronic communication[19]
- Spear Phishing – email that appears to be from an individual or business that you know, but is a hack attempt to obtain credit card, bank account numbers, passwords, and the financial information from a computer or network[20]
- Smishing – a security attack in which the user is tricked into downloading a trojan horse, virus, or other malware onto his cellular phone or other mobile device. SMiShing is short for "SMS phishing"[21]

---

16 http://us.norton.com/security_response/malware.jsp
17 http://us.norton.com/security_response/glossary/define.jsp?letter=s&word=spoofing
18 ibid
19 ibid
20 ibid
21 ibid

CHAPTER THREE: *GROUND ZERO*

- Pharming – a form of fraud where a fake website is created specifically to intercept incoming PII[22]
- Trojan – disguised malware that looks benign or remains hidden in order to be installed on an operating system and then be remotely activated executing malicious commands[23]
- Spyware – malicious software that tracks online activities and transmits data to a hacker[24]
- Data Mining – the act of sifting through proprietary data on a computer using malicious software to extract confidential information in furtherance of a scheme

A typical account takeover is detailed in the graphic below:

1. **Targeting** – Targeted through phishing, spear phishing, social engineering
2. **Malware** – Victim installs malware (key logging & screenshots)
3. **Online Banking** – Victim visits their bank website
4. **Collect Stolen Data** – Malware collects and transmits data back to criminal enterprise
5. **Execute Takeover** – Leverage victims' funds through transfer

CONCLUSION

The profile of a fraudulent loan can be typified and visibly demonstrated, but at the end of the day, risk managers on the front line are humans. Human beings require training, education, and experience to hold that line against fraud and risk. With a renewed investment in the education of staff, and in combination with automation, we can change the risk dynamic.

Moving forward, we see that partnering with technologists and incorporating advanced analytics is the optimal way to counter the deepening impacts of cyberfraud upon the residential mortgage lending business. This brave new world demands a sort of training evangelism to overcome the risks of breach, or the looming specter of social engineering. Dialing in the measurement of data, intelligent gathering of information, and collaborative linking across lending verticals are all means to help lenders, servicers, and investors combat risk.

---

22 ibid
23 ibid
24 ibid

Our industry arose to satisfy and safeguard the human need for shelter, and to do so is a noble pursuit that deserves our finest efforts. Because this intrinsic need is so crucial, we must harness all of our faculties to deliver upon this promise. The essential lesson is that our environment is not static. While the techniques we have employed for a long time continue to have merit, there is not only value in modifying our approach to fraud prevention and detection, there is an undeniable need to adapt and evolve. We may be seeing the early signs of a new normal for mortgage fraud, and the conclusion we find is that there is still much work to be done.

ABOUT THE AUTHOR

Constance "Connie" Wilson, CMB, AMP, CFE is widely recognized as one of the nation's leading authorities on mortgage fraud. She has authored and published an extensive fraud-training program nationwide to financial institutions, as well as state and federal law-enforcement agencies. She often serves as an expert witness in legal cases to convict fraudsters, and is a frequent commentator and contributing author on mortgage fraud trends for media and at industry events.

Connie's broad experience in mortgage banking and lending services spans over 30 years in the areas of first and second mortgages and sub-prime products, as well as underwriting, quality assurance, due diligence, claims and fraud management. Career highlights include executive leadership of Interthinx (now First American), where she was instrumental in the initial design of the company's quality control program and fraud-tracking database for all mortgage loan types. Prior to the formation of Interthinx, Connie was executive vice president for AppIntelligence, one of the two entities merged to form the company in 2005. Her early pioneering efforts involved the design of cutting-edge applications to detect fraud that included an automated data-integrity scoring system, automated desktop appraisal-review program and a property-value verifier and automated valuation model.

CHAPTER FOUR

QUALITY CONTROL AUDITS

ALVIN WALI | CEO
ALLIANCE INTERNATIONAL CORPORATION

Missing signatures and disclosures are one of the most common errors found in Quality Control (QC) audits. The QC auditor finds the error and the processing person is surprised! "They're missing? Don't worry, I'll get them." That was then.

Quality is in fashion now. Here's an "easy A" waiting for every company in our industry — build a process that flows correctly in one direction. Yes, it's easier said than done, especially given the fluid nature of the rules and regulations in our industry. There are four fundamental foundations of a solid QC loan process, set forth below.

- Culture: everyone, including senior management, must emphasize quality.
- Policies and Procedures: document, streamline, and automate every possible aspect of the process.
- Train: new hire training, continued training, and corrective training.
- Reports: read them, interpret them, and makes them available to everyone.

That's it — you really don't have to read any further!

The current QC emphasis should not be viewed as penance for the go-go days of our past. Quality should have always been a part of our platform. Take, for example, the auto industry. The auto industry has reached a point where consumers have come to expect a certain level of quality. Car quality has been growing while manufacturers have also added an immense amount of technology and sophistication. Cars can now do amazing things like drive themselves and order pizza. If you compare the car production process to our loan process, missing documents and signatures are like the door falling off your shiny new car! Why then do we not have a fantastic product? By product, I mean an *error-free loan package*.

Risk mitigation through quality control should be embraced as an integral part of the loan origination process. We owe it to our customers, clients, and community to ensure sound quality in every loan.

BASIC REQUIREMENTS OF QUALITY CONTROL

Timeline

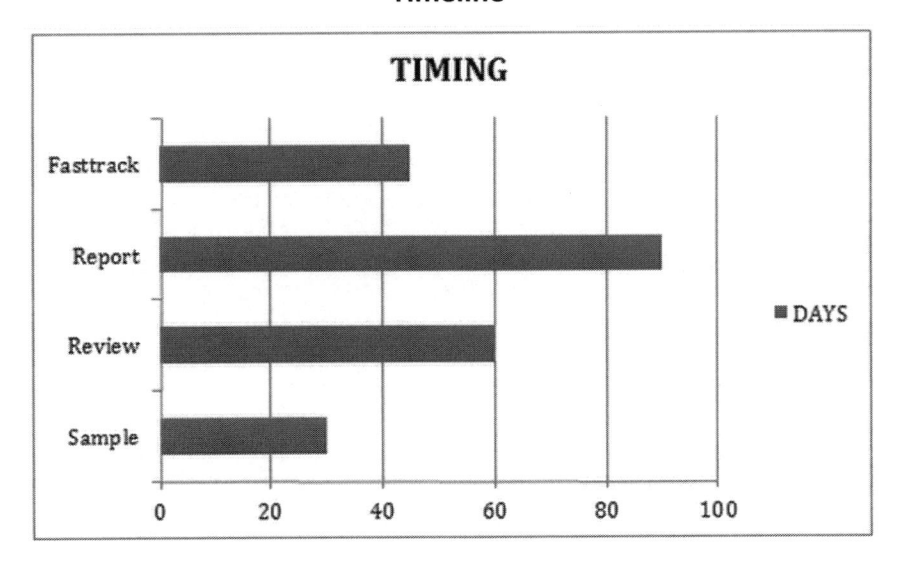

TIMING

Category	Days
Fasttrack	~45
Report	~90
Review	~60
Sample	~30

GSE guidelines allow for a QC cycle of 120 days from the month of closing. The guidance calls for loan sampling within 30 days, review and rebuttal within another 60 days, and final reports to senior management within the next 30 days. However, both Fannie Mae and Freddie Mac recommend a 90-day QC cycle.

That timeline is too protracted to be effective. The broader implication of even a 90-day cycle is that senior management is learning about issues three months after the fact. Any subsequent action will be diluted by the aging of the data. Time is of the essence in our industry. Optimizing processes and leveraging technology can make it possible to reduce the timeline significantly. A "fast-track" process can reduce the timeline by 50 percent while still maintaining quality. *The entire QC cycle from sampling at closing to management-report delivery can and should be achieved in 45 days.*

This will require a commitment of existing resources. A strategic approach to the entire QC process with planned timelines and strong commitments will ensure that each action is executed precisely at a set time, allowing subsequent dependencies to flow smoothly. For example, samples drawn on the day after monthly closing, review completed within 30 days, rebuttals within seven days, and management reports completed within the final seven days. This equates to a 45 day QC cycle, allowing management twice the time to make important decisions.

Sample Size

For post-close audit purposes, the general guidance is to sample 10 percent of the funded loans. Guidance around pre-funding audit samples are a little more relaxed, but an organization would do well to have at least a 10 percent sample size. Smaller organizations should consider a much larger pre-funding audit sample size. A robust

QC process can accommodate pre-funding audits well within 24-hours, which does not significantly impact the overall processing time. These audits normally occur after clear-to-close and are a great tool to rectify errors prior to funding. The payoff from a proactive QC process is far greater than the slight additional time it takes to accommodate them in the general process.

The 10% sample size is to ensure that a statistically significant pool of loans have been chosen for audit purposes. The pool must be a good representation of the book of business channels, geography and products. There are some subtleties of ensuring a truly random audit. Let us assume that a company has two channels such as Retail and Wholesale, is located in two states such as Texas and California, and has conventional and government products. We are also assuming that all segments are equal. In order to ensure that an appropriate number of loans are selected from each population, the sample would need to include 10 percent from each product, then each channel, and then each state. In essence it is a waterfall. The main objective is to have a sample size that represents as much of the business as possible, so that the QC audit reflects the overall business results appropriately.

Depending on the size of the organization and sophistication of the QC process, the mechanics of random sampling can be fully automated or can be a manual process. While there isn't any restriction around a manual process, it is not recommended. Sampling should be automated. An automated process can remove any potential bias, ensure accuracy of set guidelines, and speed up the cycle time. This can range from a self-sustained application-based process to something as simple as a macro-driven Excel spreadsheet. Documentation is very important in order to ensure that these processes are consistent with the latest regulations. Not only does documentation provide a consistent approach, it promotes transparency, which must be an integral part of QC process. The goal of the process is still to ensure that the rules are consistently followed.

Additional discretionary samples can supplement the initial random sample by focusing on potential problem areas. In addition to the random samples it is a good practice to create a *targeted sample*. For example, a company should target new branch locations or product to ensure the required controls are effective. Areas that consistently show up in the random sampled audit deserve additional focus with targeted samples. If, for example, a particular team has received severe ratings over a period of time, the loans generated through that team should be targeted for additional scrutiny.

Reporting
FNMA provides four reports as guidelines. These are the bare minimums that an organization should use. Management needs to have a view into all aspects of the QC findings, action steps, and subsequent impact. Initially there may be a large effort to have meaningful reports. But, over time those reports may not be meaningful with the dynamic changes in the industry. Also, one set of reports may be very useful to one organization while it may serve another very poorly. *The most useful report is the one that gets used.* All stakeholders need to have input and ownership of QC reports. Initial

input will help capture the types of reports an organization most needs. Continued dialogue and input ensures that those reports are used in the timely execution of the overall corporate strategy.

Defect rate vs. Goal is a good start at establishing a key company metric. Management has to be realistic in establishing the target rate. For example, a target rate of 0 is great, but most probably not realistic. Neither is 20 percent. The actual defect-rate trend should paint a picture of a controlled path towards the goal. If the goal is three percent and over the course of a few months the trend is heading towards that, the impact of the reporting and subsequent action plans are taking hold. Otherwise, management needs to determine the root cause of failure. The following graph is an example of a three percent defect-rate goal and the actual defect rate over the course of seven months. It shows an initial trend down from January (seven percent) to June (one percent), but something happened in July. The report should be used to find these behaviors and then investigate further.

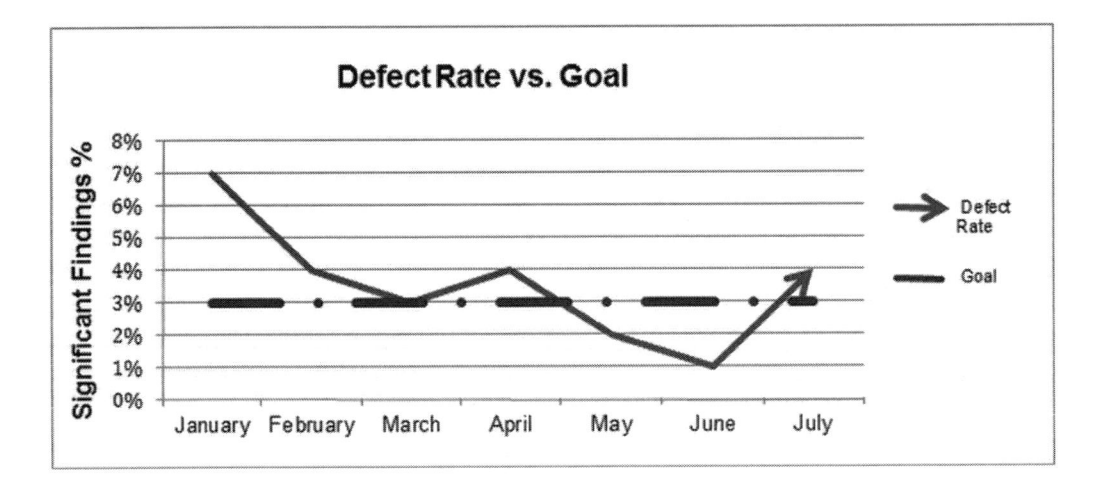

Defect Rate vs. Goal

Discretionary Selection Trend is a good tool to dissect specific areas of potential concern. The following example illustrates the three percent goal against the actual defect rates of "product A" and the "LA branch." The report can be used to better understand the spike in May for the LA branch and July results for product A. This report is one of many that can be used to mitigate product and/or geographical risk.

CHAPTER FOUR: *QUALITY CONTROL AUDITS*

Discretionary Selection Trend

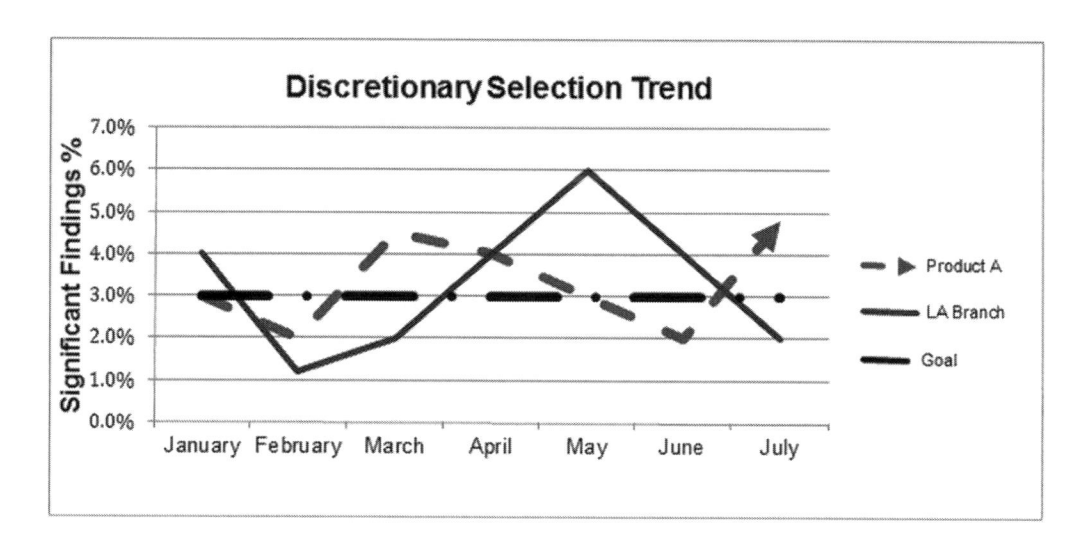

- Product A
- LA Branch
- Goal

Defect Rate by Channel provides a top level look at various channels and the defect trends. This allows senior management to measure channel performance against overall expectations and results. The following graph illustrates three major channels: Retail, Correspondent and Wholesale and their corresponding performance. The Retail channel appears to be trending up while the Wholesale channel is doing well, trending down against a one percent goal.

DEFECT RATE BY CHANNEL

CHANNEL	DEFECT RATE JAN. 2015	TREND FROM LAST MONTH	GOAL
Retail	3.20%	Up	3.00%
Correspondent	2.40%	Flat	2.00%
Wholesale	1.30%	Down	1.00%
Overall	**2.10%**	**Flat**	**1.80%**

Prefunding QC Top Defects is one of the most important reports an organization should have. It can provide near real-time insight into potential issues during the process, compared to the post-close audit. Pre-funding audits are normally done between 24 to 48 hours of the clear-to-close (CTC) trigger. There are process and system enhancement opportunities that can help save more time. For example, pre-funding audits consistently completed within 24 hours of CTC would help improve loan quality significantly. The following graph depicts five of the top defects, allowing the team to zero in on problem areas as they occur.

Prefunding QC Top 5 Defects

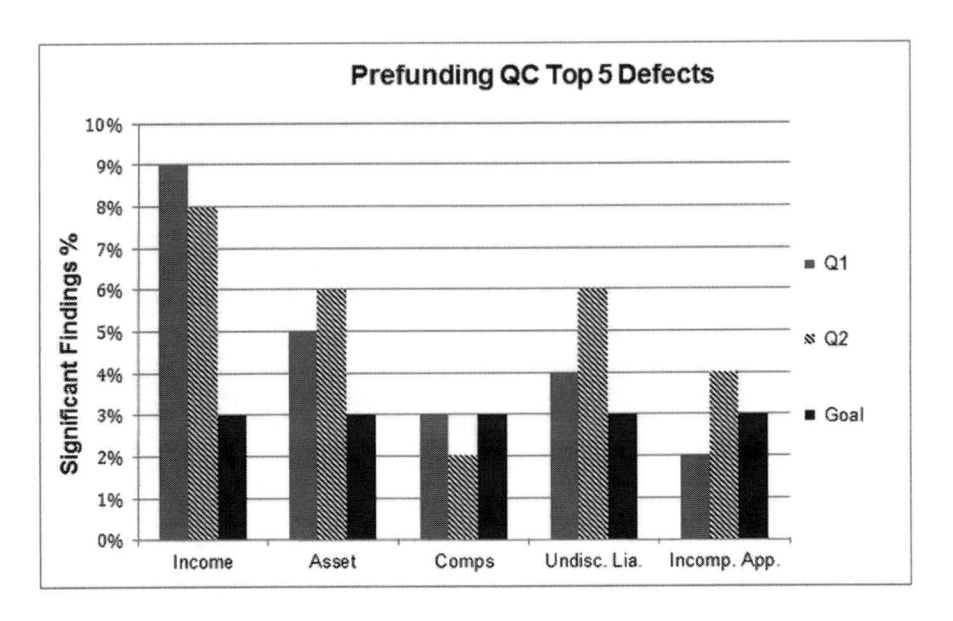

Defect	Q1	Q2	Goal
Income	9%	8%	3%
Asset	5%	6%	3%
Comps	3%	2%	3%
Undisc. Lia.	4%	6%	3%
Incomp. App.	2%	4%	3%

These reports are a minimum standard. A robust reporting mechanism should be at the core of an effective QC strategy. Senior management needs dashboard reports in order to have a consistent view of loan quality and to effectively manage potential problems. Mid-level managers need further detail so that they can help isolate issues, create action plans, and monitor progress. Frontline team members need reporting at a very granular level. This helps them pinpoint how individuals are performing and which specific loans need focus. There are a plethora of reporting tools on the market. Some mortgage applications have in-built report-generating functions. Some organizations choose to create their own reporting database. In short, the reporting system should exist at a very granular level, allowing for the flexibility to generate reports that are useful to all stakeholders.

Grading

Understanding and fully leveraging the grading process is key to an organization's QC strategy. Many companies make the mistake of simply looking at the overall grading and calling it a day. Paying close attention to grading can mitigate risk that, for example, can result in proactively avoiding a repurchase. Strong reporting can help pinpoint areas of concern that can then be studied at the loan-level. Grading can also shed light on best practices. For example, if Team A is consistently receiving a grade of "Excellent," while other teams have low grades, a company can study Team A's best practices and share this across organizations.

Each QC file includes a grade. There are generally four grades, starting with the best being "1. Excellent/Low," to the worst being "4. Poor/Material." The grades reflect the culmination of all the defects in that particular file. There are usually about 10 defect categories such as Income/Employment, Assets, Credit, etc. Each time a defect is found, the category receives a "point." The number and severity of "points" result in a final grade. Each of the four grades tell a distinct story.

1. Excellent/Low: This is the category everyone should aim for. It indicates that the file is sound and everything is in order. No problems were identified with the origination of the loan.

2. Good/Acceptable: These are normally issues identified pertaining to processing, documentation, and decisions. Missing signatures contribute significantly to this category and can be resolved by leveraging the pre-funding audit process. These are "easy fixes" that can be a good area for training.

3. Fair/Moderate: This category runs the risk of quickly becoming a "material" grade if not handled with care. Files may contain significant unresolved questions and/or missing documents. Unresolved issues may create moderate risk. We see a lot of missing verbal verifications of employment (VOE) and non-matching signatures. A timely final VOE may reveal important employment information, and non-matching signatures could be an indication of fraud.

4. Poor/Material: This is the most concerning grade. Issues identified with a "material" grade are serious violations of investor or mortgage requirements that represent an unacceptable level of risk. Missing disclosures, credit reports, bank statements, and incorrect calculations are examples of issues that would be considered "Material/Poor."

What do we do with this information? Protocols should be established for communicating the results and the decisions that need to be made. An informal process of simply reviewing the results with management and passing the decision is not the best strategy. For example, all QC audits with a grade of three or four need to be reviewed with senior management, and a list of actions recommended. The process also needs to include an action plan follow-up to ensure that it was appropriately executed.

EVOLVING RULES

In response to the financial crisis, there has been a significant increase in the number of new rules and regulations. The formation of the CFPB (Consumer Financial Protection Bureau) has seen a consumer-centric consolidated approach to the execution of regulations. It is still an evolutionary process and, as such, dynamic and fluid. The current stage of the regulatory aspect of our industry may be frustrating, but the overall goal is to protect the customer. We must respect and strategically embrace the direction toward which the industry is moving.

Quality control was not the most important goal of many financial institutions prior to the financial crisis. We might have averted a significant component of the crisis if quality had had precedence over quality. Now we live in a post-crisis environment that is focused on quality and rules, and regulations are evolving towards more complex and stringent oversight, rather than regressing towards the historical norm.

There is scrutiny of institutions and of the individuals. The 2010 SAFE act created new licensing requirements and oversight for loan officers, processors, and underwriters. The higher level of expertise required to become licensed has led to many unqualified people leaving the field. Higher quality of people helps improve loan quality, among other things.

THE CURRENT LANDSCAPE

Our industry is still adapting to the "new normal." Quality is still a result of regulatory requirements for most companies, rather than being an integral part of the strategy of most firms. We do not view QC as an investment; it is seen more as a regulatory burden.

QC reporting *should* be part of each executive business review, compensation plan, training, and coaching. Yet it is a disjointed part of the overall business. The executive reviews provide an opportunity for top decision-makers to provide direction and ensure accountability. Compensation tied to quality helps to promote greater focus. Quality control tied to training and coaching is not the norm currently. A planned organizational approach to training and coaching should not be confused with the "talk" a manager has with team members whenever there are issues.

Speed in our business is very important. But, most companies are not required to follow anything shorter than the post-close guideline of 90 days, when 45 is entirely possible. Beyond the regulatory requirements, there are many incentives to have a shorter QC cycle. Senior management has more time to react to potential issues. Loans have not aged as much beyond the close date. Process issues can be addressed before a few more close cycles.

When QC evidence points to a specific area, it is not necessarily indicative of employee mistakes. It may very well be a process or system breakdown. Most companies do not utilize the QC data to study the issues and promote a plan of action.

THE FUTURE

The most important QC issue is cultivation and promotion of a culture of quality. There needs to be a seamless relational process where quality is a part of the larger mortgage banking existence rather than something we need to stop and think about every time a company faces a crisis. Imagine a system overlay that ensures the application and document intake step is fully vetted at the beginning — no more missing items. The processing and underwriting steps are then integrated and the team members are fully versed in the latest regulations. During this step, a pre-funding audit is completed through a combination of system checks and a final review. This can be done in-house or by an external QC audit company. The final post-close audit should be a minimal effort and everyone should get an "A."

One critical aspect of QC auditing is a lack of strong standards. The industry needs to require external QC audit firms to have at least the same licensing requirement for an auditor as there is for a loan officer or processor. The 2010 SAFE act requires processors and underwriters to be managed by a licensed LO, unless working for a banking institution. SSAE16 attestations should be required of all external QC audit companies in order to ensure the safety and integrity of the sensitive information. This will greatly improve the quality of service and ensure minimum service standards to be expected by clients.

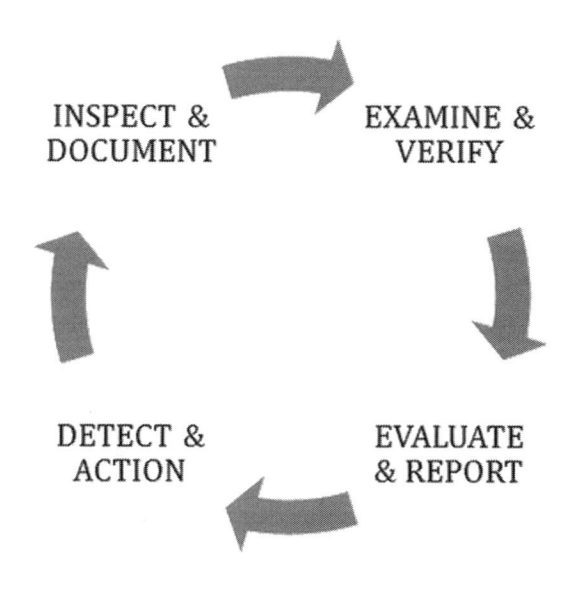

INSPECT & DOCUMENT → EXAMINE & VERIFY → EVALUATE & REPORT → DETECT & ACTION

Quality is not a one-time effort. It is an infinite loop. The first phase is the core function of the QC audit, where loans are tested and the results validated against current regulations, laws, and processes. This should never be a checklist effort. The best method is a combination of an initial system-vetting and a final manual examination. The next step involves taking the observed data, generating reports, and analyzing the results. Do we have major errors? Are they isolated? The third step involves interpreting the results to correctly pinpoint the areas of most importance and create action plans. For example, if results indicate a large number of errors in a particular branch, then the plan of action lists specific steps to improve the error rate. The next step is to document the action plan and sharing the results with the branch and all vested parties. We then go back to the first step and begin the loop. The desired result should be a measurable impact resulting from the actions taken during the last cycle.

As with most aspects of a business, QC is not an isolated effort. A company cannot derive the full potential of a QC effort if it is isolated to only the Compliance department. There are a number of partners that need to have transparency into and engage actively with the quality control program. The principal partners are sales, operations, training, and senior management. With rules and regulations, increasing QC will play a greater role in organizations. In order to successfully navigate towards the future, every organization must create a strategic partnership that preemptively plans a symbiotic execution of responsibilities within their respective areas. The old thinking of QC being a "gotcha" exercise needs to be forgotten. Everyone in every department needs to feel that they are a collective part of a greater effort to improve loan quality. External QC audit firms and internal Compliance departments should take the role of customer service towards the stakeholders, such as sales and operations. Interaction between QC and the Field should be transparent and supportive. The Field should rely on the QC department like a trusted advisor from whom they can seek proactive guidance on any and all issues. QC should embrace a "customer-service-centric" approach where the data is derived to help the Field.

REAL-WORLD CASE STUDIES

Our industry has become much more quality conscious since the financial crisis. It would have been very interesting to compare actual case studies from 10 years ago to the current time. The general findings would have probably pointed to a much more lax environment, disregard for QC, and a greater focus on revenue growth compared to risk mitigation. It is safe to say that many of the companies that did not place an importance on QC are no longer in business. The premise is not that a lack of QC was the only cause of their downfall, but it significantly contributed to their demise. With the disintegration of major financial institutions, we would expect the survivors to have learnt their lessons. But, unfortunately, many institutions still are operating on unstable financial "tectonic plates." What follows are three real-world examples of companies and their QC strategy. Names have been modified to protect the innocent.

Let us start with *Big Bank*. This institution is quite profitable, has good management, and relatively good systems. The QC strategy is good, not great. CFPB would check off most of the QC audit box. But Big Bank has not derived the full potential of its QC strategy. It may be an indication of a larger issue, but the process and systems are disjointed and there is a lack of transparency.

The pre-funding and post-close audit areas are distinctly separate and report to two different senior executives. This unintentionally results in slow or no communications between the two departments, and thus between the stakeholders. Team members do not have a clear vision and do not derive the benefits of easy interaction. This is the perfect storm for an "us versus them" mentality which can further degrade the efficiency and impact of the QC team.

Another major issue with Big Bank is the systems. There are a lot of systems and sub-systems, yet a "black market" of Access databases exists as a patchwork. Anytime a sub-process is created, we have to ask what the original question was. The combination of the systems create a tremendous amount of data, but the underlying code is not clearly documented, and thus not clearly understood. This has the potential for a lot of false-negatives. The most important action for Big Bank is to evaluate the entire QC strategy with a fresh set of eyes. It would be very beneficial to bring in subject-matter-experts (SMEs) from Sales, IT, Operations, and other stakeholders. They need to ask if the reports and underlying data are correct, timely, and useful. They also need to ask if the QC process is the best it can be.

Regional Mortgage Company was a more complex case. While this entity was much smaller than Big Bank, it suffered from a lot more issues. Larger institutions tend to suffer from a bit of bureaucracy and slow adaption to the necessary changes, while smaller entities are expected to be much more nimble and efficient, but this was certainly not the case with Regional Mortgage. The vision and direction of most successful companies is set at the top. In order for QC to be an important aspect of a company strategy, senior management must champion it. Regional Mortgage was focused on revenue growth and cost cutting, and QC was squashed in the middle of those two efforts.

Senior management did not have involvement in most QC matters except for early payment defaults and buy backs. *This is an indication of a reactive approach.* Mid-level managers were reluctant to bring up any issues, and when they did it was too late. The QC audit cycle time was just below 120 days in most months. Reporting was another area that could have been vastly improved through communication and stakeholder involvement.

The high turnover also contributed to a lack of both ownership and of a relational basis for the QC department and the Field to work on. The most concerning issue was the quality of the investor files. QC scores were in the 3-4 range on a lot of audits and the monthly trend was far above the target. If someone could overlook all of the prior issues, it was very concerning to see the way the investor files were compiled.

Yes, Regional Mortgage has issues with its QC strategy. It is indicative of a much larger organizational issue. There must be a larger strategic approach that takes QC into consideration and ties the firm's efforts into one holistic approach.

Thomas Bank is a great example of how a QC program should run. Thomas Bank has a number of locations in a particular state. While it has a long pedigree, it is very receptive to new ideas that balance revenue growth with risk mitigation. Thomas Bank takes very calculated risks. They have clear strategies that are consistently reviewed.

Thomas Bank does not have complicated systems. Most of their systems seamlessly talk to one another. The data is audited and produces strong reports on which good decisions are made. Thomas Bank understands which reports serve them best, and works with an external firm to create, modify, and discuss the reports. They take a proactive approach to all aspects of the QC process. During a CFPB audit-prep consultation engagement it became very clear that Thomas Bank's employees clearly know the QC process and how they fit into the overall strategy. This indicates that all stakeholders are being kept in the loop. All aspects of the QC process are well-documented promoting transparency.

The size of a company should not determine its commitment to its quality control program. Ultimately the key is the importance that *leadership* places on QC.

CONCLUSION

Quality control should be quality enhancement. One of the most competitive advantages a company can foster is to change the view towards quality. Instead of controlling quality, companies should embrace a continuous improvement cycle of quality. The impact and results are more important than automated tools or manual processes. Each company needs to assess what process works best. Loan quality will certainly improve profitability, but the larger goal is to ensure the best product for the investor, portfolio, community, and client.

ABOUT THE AUTHOR

Alvin Wali serves as CEO at Alliance International Corporation, a FinTech company specializing in managed services for the mortgage industry. He has successfully led initiatives leveraging disruptive technology to support one of the most expeditious and accurate processing platforms in the industry. Alvin has 15 years of banking experience with leadership roles at Citibank, Fujitsu, and Bank of America. He successfully oversaw areas in audit, finance, accounting, asset management, wires, PMO, and systems implementation. Alvin led globally dispersed teams in Europe and Asia, working across time zones and cultures.

Alvin also serves on the board of The Nari Project, a nonprofit supported by the Clinton Global Initiative. Nari provides crisis kits to victims of domestic abuse in America, India, Bangladesh, and Vietnam. Alvin is passionate about socially responsible business and has promoted profit commitments from Alliance to Nari, and introduced paid volunteer days-off for all employees to give time to any cause of their choice.

CHAPTER FIVE

WORKING WITH MORTGAGE INSURANCE COMPANIES

KYLE BENSON | BUSINESS TECHNOLOGY OPERATIONS DIRECTOR

DAVID SCHROEDER | DIRECTOR, CLAIMS BUSINESS SYSTEMS

MGIC

Mortgage insurance is a financial guaranty against loss in the event a borrower defaults on a mortgage *and* the property value is less than the amount owed. Generally speaking, if a borrower defaults and title is transferred, the mortgage insurer reduces or eliminates the loss to the insured. Having protection against potential losses from default gives lenders the ability to expand their lending criteria, therefore allowing more people to become homeowners.

There are two types of mortgage insurance: Government — through programs provided primarily by the Federal Housing Administration (FHA) or Department of Veterans Affairs (VA) — and private mortgage insurance (Private MI). While both forms protect against losses, there are some distinguishing characteristics. At a high level, VA and FHA loans are backed by the federal government, and therefore taxpayers are ultimately responsible for any losses. On the other hand, Private MI relies on private capital to cover claims. Another important difference is that Private MI introduces the concept of co-insurance (or aligning of interests with the lender), as FHA covers 100% of losses while Private MI generally covers a portion of the loss. At the individual program level, VA loans are typically made available to United States veterans and current Service members, and is paid with an upfront premium and no ongoing expense. FHA loans offer less stringent and more flexible qualification requirements in comparison to Private MI. However, with FHA insurance, the borrower will pay both an upfront fee and a monthly premium. Also, for a 30-year mortgage, the FHA typically does not allow the monthly MI payment to be cancelled unless there was at least a 10% down payment and the loan is a minimum of eleven years old, whereas Private MI can be cancelled.

A loan that is neither insured by the FHA nor guaranteed by the VA is considered a conventional loan. For this type of loan, Private MI is often used to mitigate risk. Typically it is applied to loans with a loan-to-value ratio (LTV) of greater than 80 percent. Private MI, when compared to FHA insurance, offers a wide variety of premium plans that often allow for faster equity building, a lower cost option for many borrowers, and has the added benefit of having borrower-paid premiums automatically cancelled by the servicer when the loan amount drops to 78 percent of the property value at loan origination. The borrower may request earlier cancellation based on a new appraisal.

REGULATION OF PRIVATE MI

Providers of Private MI are governed by the laws and regulations in each state where they operate. On a state-by-state basis, the regulatory agency, generally the State Insurance Department (SID), monitors activities and reviews the financial condition and standards of conduct to be maintained by the insurer for the protection of policyholders. In addition to setting standards for the financial health of the insurance companies, the SID also examines and approves the insurance company's policy and rates, and oversees the licensing of individuals selling the insurance products. The National Association of Insurance Commissioners maintains the Mortgage Guaranty Insurance Model Act (which has been adopted by many states) which, among other things, addresses solvency regulation of mortgage-guaranty insurers. There are also several federal laws and regulations applicable to mortgage insurers. Federal laws that affect mortgage insurers include, but are not limited to, the Equal Credit Opportunity Act, Fair Credit Reporting Act, Fair Debt Collection Practices Act, Gramm-Leach-Bliley Act, Truth in Lending Act, Real Estate Settlement Procedures Act, Unfair Claims Settlement Act, and the Homeowners Protection Act of 1998.

Since the 1990's, Fannie Mae and Freddie Mac (collectively referred to as the Government Sponsored Enterprises, or GSEs) have purchased the majority of mortgage loans insured by private mortgage insurers, and therefore, have been the largest beneficiaries of mortgage insurance policies. The GSEs set requirements that any mortgage insurer must meet in order to be eligible to insure loans that are sold to them. These Private Mortgage Insurer Eligibility Requirements (PMIERs) set specific standards covering minimum financial and operational requirements.

WORKING WITH A PRIVATE MORTGAGE INSURER

While no two Private MI companies are exactly the same, there are some commonalities among them. For starters, each company has a master policy to which customers must agree. This is a contractual agreement between the insurer and an insured lending institution (the insured) that sets the terms and conditions under which the mortgage insurer provides protection in the event of an insurance claim being asserted. Mortgage insurers work with all types of mortgage originators, including mortgage brokers, mortgage bankers, commercial banks, community banks, non-bank lenders, and credit unions. Mortgage insurers have some variation in how the sales, underwriting, servicing, claims, and loss mitigation departments operate. These functional areas work in conjunction to follow the loan from origination through to when the policy is either cancelled or a claim is paid.

To obtain insurance, a prospective lending institution must apply for and receive a master policy before submitting loans for approval. The insured can then submit applications for insurance on individual loans. Once a loan is approved, the insured is issued a mortgage insurance commitment. When the loan closes, provided that there are no changes to the loan information that would cause the terms of the commitment to no longer be valid, the commitment will become certified. The commitment and certificate are subject to the terms and conditions spelled out in the master policy. The policy stays with the loan even if it is ultimately sold onto the secondary market.

MANAGING RISK

The risk of a mortgage insurer having to pay a claim can be separated into two parts — the risk of borrower default and the risk of foreclosure. To control for these risks, mortgage insurers set underwriting guidelines. When considering a loan for insurance, the insurer evaluates the ability of the borrower to repay a loan, the collateral value of the property, the historical performance of the lender, the risk of the loan program, and the market risks (see Chapter 2 of this volume). Examples of criteria used when evaluating the borrower's ability to repay the loan include the borrower's credit history, debt to income ratio, loan-to-value ratio or down payment, the purpose of the loan, and the intent to occupy the property. When underwriting the property, a mortgage insurer generally considers such factors as the type of property and the property's appraised value, but could also include market location.

Published guidelines can change as market conditions change. These changes can be across the board or tailored to reflect the risks in a particular region, a particular lender's business mix, or segment of the market. Regardless, a mortgage insurer's guidelines provide reference points for the underwriter and minor variances from underwriting guidelines are not unusual.

COST OF PRIVATE MI

As previously mentioned, private mortgage insurers offer a variety of premium plans. These allow lenders to best meet changing market needs. While the specifics of how the various products are priced and executed are determined by the individual insurer, common options include:

Payer
- Borrower-paid mortgage insurance where the borrower pays the MI premium, generally as part of their monthly mortgage payment
- Lender-paid mortgage insurance where the lender charges the borrower a higher interest rate to cover the cost of the premium

Frequency of payments
- Single-premium plans, in which a cash payment in full is required at the time the policy is issued
- Monthly-premium plans
- Annual plans where premiums are paid for a year in advance

Most mortgage insurers use some form of risk-based pricing to determine what they will charge for their products. They set pricing based on factors such as the percentage of coverage, the premium payment plan selected, the LTV ratio of the loan, and the borrower's credit score. That said, methods for evaluating risk can vary widely from one company to another. However, all mortgage insurers are required to receive approval from state insurance departments which require submission of insurance plans, rates and forms prior to use. Due to this approval process, there may be differences in the rates, and programs available for use in certain states even within a single company. The best source for current pricing and program information is to contact a specific company's sales representative or visit the company's web site.

CLAIMS

Even in the best of economic times there is the risk that a borrower will default on a loan and lose the property to foreclosure or an alternative to foreclosure, resulting in the need for the insured to file a claim. A mortgage insurer's claim process is designed to honor its obligation to the insured, but it also works to reduce the incidence and severity of claims. Typically the mortgage insurer becomes aware of a potential loss when it receives a Notice of Delinquency (NOD) from the insured when the loan goes delinquent (typically after two missed payments). From there one of the following will occur:

- The loan is brought current by the borrower and a cure is reported to the mortgage insurance company
- The insured works with the borrower to resolve the delinquency through methods that are acceptable to the insurer, thereby allowing the borrowers to bring the loan current and maintain possession of their homes (e.g. modified loan terms temporarily reducing monthly payments)
- If the delinquency cannot be cured the insured may work with the borrower on an alternative to foreclosure, such as a presale or voluntary conveyance of the property, that is acceptable to the insurer and results in the borrowers losing possession of their home
- The insured takes title through a foreclosure action

Options that are effective for borrowers who wish to keep their properties and who have an ability to pay include temporary indulgence, repayment plans, forbearance plans and loan modifications. These are generally referred to as *loan workouts*. If the borrower cannot repay the delinquent payments or maintain future payments, or no longer wishes to fulfill their contractual obligation, a presale or deed in lieu of foreclosure may be a better option for all parties involved.

Assuming a loan workout plan cannot be accomplished, foreclosure proceedings are initiated by the insured. When a loan becomes delinquent, the insured may be instructed to preserve and/or establish the mortgage insurance company's deficiency rights at the foreclosure sale. A deficiency right is an unsecured money judgment against a borrower

CHAPTER FIVE: WORKING WITH MORTGAGE INSURANCE COMPANIES

whose mortgage foreclosure sale did not produce sufficient funds to pay the underlying promissory note, or loan, in full. The availability of a deficiency judgment depends on whether the lender has a recourse or nonrecourse loan, which is largely a matter of state law. Any pursuit of a deficiency recovery typically occurs after a claim has been paid.

Title transfer is a condition to claim filing, either to the lender or a third party. Once the insured takes title through foreclosure or an alternative to foreclosure, they then have the right to file a claim. An insured's claim for loss can include:

- The unpaid principal balance
- Interest due (calculated at the contract rate from the date through which the interest is paid, up to the date that the claim was filed, although some policies limit the amount of interest that can be claimed)
- Reasonable attorney fees incurred in obtaining title
- Real estate taxes, condominium fees and hazard insurance premiums advanced
- Reasonable and necessary property maintenance expenses
- Court costs necessary to acquire title

Less:
- Escrow account balance
- Funds from a pledged savings account or other funds held by the lender
- Rents or other payments collected or received by the lender
- Funds received under fire and extended coverage policies in excess of the cost of restoring and repairing the property

This total amount is then multiplied by the percentage of coverage stated on the insurance certificate. If the insurer pays this amount it is called the *percentage guarantee option*.

Once a claim has been evaluated and it is determined that a claim payment should be made, the mortgage insurer typically has varying choices when settling the claim.

If the property is no longer owned by the Insured or Investor, the mortgage insurer typically pays the lesser of:

- the percentage guaranty option as described above, or
- the actual loss suffered by the Insured (after adjusting for items that are not claimable).

Conversely, on claims where the property is still owned by the Insured or Investor, the mortgage insurer will either:

- pay the percentage guaranty option as described above, or
- pay the Insured the entire amount of the claim (after adjusting for items that are not claimable) and take title to the property. This option is selected when the mortgage insurer estimates that any loss realized from its sale of the property will be less than the percentage guaranty option payment

INTERACTING WITH MORTGAGE INSURERS

It may be easy to conceptualize the process of executing a master policy with an insurer, ordering and certifying a commitment, servicing an active insured loan, and, if necessary, conducting default management and claims activities on the insured loan. However, when you consider multiple insurer relationships spread across thousands of loans within an origination and/or servicing pipeline, the need for automation and well-controlled MI management procedures becomes extremely important. Inaccurately pricing or ordering MI, or allowing MI premium payments to lapse, resulting in the cancellation of coverage, can have severe consequences to the insured. Fortunately, there are many technology solutions offered by the insurers themselves using secured websites, or through loan origination and servicing platforms, that streamline and automate the most common interactions throughout the life-cycle of an insured loan.

Obtaining Premium Rates

Before the advent of automated rate quotes, loan originators had to use a hard copy "rate card" to accurately price the mortgage insurance based on each borrower's unique scenario. Today, loans can be accurately priced by going to each insurer's website (or mobile app), or by using existing connections from leading product and pricing engines (PPEs) and loan origination systems (LOSs). Using automation to price MI ensures that premium rates are correctly quoted to borrowers, and that these rates are automatically updated in key systems and on origination disclosure documents.

Ordering Commitments

In order to streamline the loan production process, pertinent LOS data fields are kept up to date with accurate MI premium information, allowing for the generation of closing documents with accurate MI information. Additionally, automation in the MI commitment-ordering process allows for the commitment document itself to be returned to the LOS and/or the lender's electronic imaging system. Lenders are able to order delegated, data-only commitments, as well as non-delegated commitments which combine a data submission with an electronically transmitted document package for underwriting.

Certifying Coverage

Automated MI certification ensures that the coverage is activated in a timely manner. Industry-leading servicing systems send electronic transactions to MI companies when loans with MI board the system, signifying that the loan has closed and the coverage is now in force. Failure to effectively activate coverage may lead to commitments expiring inadvertently.

Maintaining Coverage

The MI companies support numerous automated transactions throughout the loan administration life-cycle as long as the coverage is in place. Automated renewal billing helps to ensure that recurring premium payments on monthly and annual policies do not lapse, thereby causing inadvertent cancellation of coverage. MI companies require notification of servicing transfers on loans that they insure, and a record of servicing transfer can be automatically sent to the MI companies. Additionally, whether due to regulatory compliance, loan payoff, or another reason, automated MI cancellation notifications can be sent to the MI companies. The major service bureaus and many MI companies' secure websites support some or all of these servicing transactions.

Reporting Defaults

Mortgage insurance companies require that servicers provide monthly reporting on loans that are in default. This reporting can be accomplished through an automated process provided by many of the loan-serving platforms available in the marketplace. Alternatively, a servicer may be able to meet their default reporting responsibilities by utilizing an MI company's website.

Filing Claims

Dependant upon the requirements of the investor, claim filing may be performed by the investor or it may be the responsibility of the loan servicer. Many loan servicing platforms include an automated claim-filing module along with the ability to obtain an electronically formatted Explanation of Benefit detailing the components of the claim payment. Alternatively, claims can be filed on websites provided by the MI company. While utilizing paper to file a claim is an option, it is generally not as efficient as the electronic methods described above. It is important that mortgage lenders and servicers work with their MI providers, origination system vendors, servicing platform vendors, and internal IT departments to ensure they are taking advantage of all available automated options with their mortgage insurers.

Leveraging Mortgage Insurers' Expertise and Value-Added Services

MI companies interact with many participants in the residential finance industry, given that mortgage insurance is used by all sizes and types of lenders, servicers, and investors. Additionally, the product spans the life-cycle of a mortgage loan from origination and pricing, through underwriting and closing, to servicing and default management. As such, MI companies are often viewed as a valuable resource of industry information and a provider of various educational and training initiatives, ranging from underwriting training, to sales training, to educational forums regarding emerging regulatory requirements.

In general, MI companies also offer value-added and fee-for-service products. Utilization of contract services, including pre-close underwriting services and quality assurance reviews, and post-close quality control reviews, can help lenders meet fluctuating volume demands and provide extra layers of independently reviewed quality control. Some companies offer post-closing services to help identify new leads and retain existing consumers.

Lenders and servicers should work directly with their MI providers to understand additional solutions that can be provided above and beyond the mortgage guaranty insurance product.

SUMMARY

This has been a high-level overview of the important role that mortgage insurance plays in expanding access to credit for qualified borrowers by protecting against potential losses from default, as well as of the differences between government MI and private MI and the mechanics of private MI coverage. Additional information about how mortgage insurance can help lenders expand their customer base is available directly from the FHA, VA, and individual private mortgage insurance companies. The most important takeaway is that mortgage insurance enables broader access to homeownership by protecting the interests of investors in mortgage loans against credit losses.

ABOUT THE AUTHORS

Kyle Bensen, CMB, CMSP, began his career with MGIC in 1998, and currently operates as MGIC's Business Operations Technology Director. Kyle is responsible for system and operational functions supporting MGIC's policy origination and underwriting production processes. Additionally, Kyle is responsible for establishing and maintaining mortgage industry vendor and business partner relationships to advance MGIC's strategic objectives by developing and maintaining partnerships with key origination, servicing and other mortgage industry technology vendors. Kyle represents MGIC's interests on mortgage technology related committees, industry standards bodies and organizations, and is an active member of the MBA and the Wisconsin Mortgage Bankers Association.

Kyle received a Bachelor of Arts degree from the University of Nebraska in 1998, and a Masters of Applied Sciences in Computer Information Systems from Denver University in 2005. Kyle achieved the highest level designation in the mortgage industry by earning MBA's Certified Mortgage Banker designation in 2012, and he currently holds the Certified MISMO Standards Professional designation.

David Schroeder has worked at Mortgage Guaranty Insurance Corporation (MGIC) since 2000 and is currently a Director in the Claims Department. In this role, he is responsible for a number of Claims operational areas including Quality Assurance, Operational Reporting and Operational Analysis.

David's career in the mortgage industry spans over 30 years with a broad range of experience that includes Sales, Underwriting and Operations Management.

CHAPTER SIX

MORTGAGE COOPERATIVES: EFFICIENCY AND PROFITS THROUGH SCALE

TOM MILLON | CEO

CAPITAL MARKETS COOPERATIVE

Mortgage cooperatives consolidate resources and like institutions in a massive residential mortgage industry.

- More than $10 trillion in residential mortgage loans are currently outstanding in the U.S.
- The U.S. residential mortgage industry is expected to create approximately $1.1 trillion in originations in 2016 — more than five million individual loans.
- There are over 7,000 U.S. financial institutions involved in residential mortgage lending, including banks, savings associations, credit unions, and mortgage companies.
- Originators that produce less than $5B of loans annually comprise 17.2% of annual industry volume.

The cooperative business model brings efficiency and scale to help small and mid-sized mortgage lenders remain profitable and competitive.

- Small non-bank originators face continued regulatory and capital constraints, and many will need to be acquired or align with a cooperative to remain competitive.
- Originators at small to medium-sized banks will need the resources of a larger platform to remain competitive. A cooperative can provide these resources by consolidating origination volume, creating revenue opportunities, and lowering costs.
- A cooperative is able to leverage its unique position to centralize the loan manufacturing process and reduce costs for its members. Lenders continue to pursue strategies involving automation and outsourcing to lower costs, improve compliance and quality control functions, maintain profit margins, and restore investor confidence in non-government mortgage loans.
- The cooperative model may represent a key solution to credit enhancement and the emergence of private solutions in the U.S. mortgage industry. Jumbo and non-agency secondary markets are being reshaped and regenerated, and represent a particularly interesting prospect for origination by cooperative members.
- A cooperative can be positioned in the center of a network comprised of many varied players in the mortgage industry, creating benefits for lenders, vendors, and investors.

EXAMPLES OF MORTAGE COOPERATIVES

Several private-sector cooperatives, a government-regulated series of cooperatives in the Federal Home Loan Bank ("FHLB") system, and a number of influential organizations with cooperative characteristics operate in the mortgage industry.

The cooperative space today includes organizations such as the American Bankers Association, the Independent Community Bankers of America, LendersOne, America's Mortgage Cooperative, The Mortgage Collaborative, the Mortgage Bankers Association ("MBA"), and the Capital Markets Cooperative. Each of these organizations serves a particular type of lender, and provides cooperative benefits in varying ways. The cooperative model is difficult to implement, and a number of cooperative models have tried and failed in recent decades.

Capital Markets Cooperative

The Capital Markets Cooperative ("CMC") is a leading private cooperative that has been highly successful since 2003, and provides a good example of the cooperative business model. CMC has over 200 mortgage lenders as members (which it calls "Patrons"). Its mission statement crystallizes the cooperative model: "Strengthen each of us through the power of all of us." The cornerstones of CMC's cooperative model are partnering and negotiating increased incentives and discounts from nationally-known mortgage investors and service providers; developing proprietary hedging and valuation models and managing interest-rate risk and valuations through its full service trading desk; and coordinating networking and information-sharing events. By leveraging its nationwide network of mortgage bankers, the cooperative delivers innovative products and services, lowers costs throughout the mortgage manufacturing process, and provides growth and profit opportunities to its members.

Collectively, CMC's community bank members hold more than $211 billion in assets, and its entire member base originated over $100 billion in residential loans in 2013:

\multicolumn{3}{c}{2013 Residential Origination Volume (HMDA Data)}
Rank	Originator	Annual Volume ($Billion)
1	Wells Fargo	$198
2	*Capital Markets Cooperative Patrons*	**$111**
3	JPMorgan Chase	$100
4	Bank of America	$86
5	Quicken Loans Inc.	$76
6	Citibank	$47
7	U.S. Bank	$37
8	Flagstar Bank	$28
9	PNC Bank	$22
10	SunTrust Mortgage, Inc.	$21

CHAPTER SIX: *MORTGAGE COOPERATIVES*

America's Mortgage Cooperative

As another example of a successful cooperative, America's Mortgage Cooperative ("AMC") is an organization designed to bring marketing clout and economies of scale to small to mid-size mortgage bankers operating throughout the United States. AMC was founded in January 2000, with the fundamental goal of leveraging the quality of individual companies with their aggregate size to improve their competitiveness and performance in the marketplace.

An important byproduct of AMC has been the development of an informal peer-group network in which members have been extremely open in sharing proprietary information about their companies to their benefit as well as others in the membership. AMC has provided individual members with a valuable resource to ask questions/obtain feedback/explore strategies with executives of other AMC members.

The members organized AMC as a Delaware limited liability company operating pursuant to an Operating Agreement that is shared amongst cooperative members. AMC is a member-managed cooperative governed by a Board of Directors comprised of six members to oversee its operations. AMC has organized committees to manage specific areas of interest. The Committees are: 1) Executive; 2) Regulatory Compliance; 3) Quality Control and Underwriting and 4) Technology. Members are welcome to participate on any committees in which they are interested. Members may also have other individuals from their companies be active on these committees. New committees will be added as the need and the interest of members mandates. For example, the Regulatory Compliance Committee met every two weeks to help members prepare for TRID implementation.

A cornerstone of AMC is the individual member's right to determine for themselves whether to participate in any agreement. An important provision of the operating agreement is a member's ability to "opt-in/opt-out" of participation in any agreement. For example, some members decided not to participate in the cooperative's Fannie Mae partnership.

AMC membership is offered by invitation only. AMC is looking for prospective members that have similar ideals, and a commitment to the highest ethical standards. For example, AMC reviews a prospective member's FHA early default and claim performance in FHA's Neighborhood Watch system. Each AMC member and AMC's partners are asked for input on any prospect. AMC is also only interested in new members that want to be actively involved in the cooperative. Accordingly, AMC expects prospective members to make such a commitment about participation. AMC typically meets three times per year. AMC also holds regular conference calls for member executives (approximately twice a month) to keep the membership abreast of Washington and industry issues. The Compliance Committee and Underwriting and Quality Control committee comprised of managers of these areas also have regular conference calls to discuss issues.

Federal Home Loan Bank System

In the government sector, regulated by the Federal Housing Finance Agency (FHFA), the Federal Home Loan Bank (FHLB) system is comprised of cooperatives. The FHLB regional banks are independent cooperatives privately capitalized and owned by thousands of financial institutions, big and small, from all 50 states, U.S. possessions, and territories. The FHLB cooperative structure distributes and shares credit risk amongst cooperative members. It demonstrates the effectiveness of the cooperative model as a risk-sharing platform, which has been suggested in many forums as a method for reform of the Government-Sponsored Enterprises ("GSE's") and restoration of the private securitization markets. Several leading models for GSE reform call for cooperative platforms to take first-loss positions by standing in front of a catastrophic risk backstop provided by the Federal government. Small-to-middle market originators are simply not capitalized, nor do they typically have the expertise to retain and manage a portfolio of credit risk, and the cooperative model provides a solid solution, as evidenced by the FHLB.

As reported in FHLB marketing collateral: *"To become a member of an FHLBank, a financial institution must purchase stock in their FHLBank, which is held at par value and not traded. As cooperatives, FHLBanks do not have the pressure for high rates of return as do publicly traded companies. They pass their borrowing benefits in the global debt markets on to their members in the form of lower borrowing costs, which are subsequently passed on to consumers, businesses, and communities. The nation's banking system relies on them as a cost-efficient, evenly priced source of short- and long-term funding.*

The country benefits by having this access to credit provided to many institutions of all sizes, types, and geographies. Regional and local needs are better served. Consumers and businesses have greater choice. Capital and credit for jobs, housing, and economic growth flows to communities at a fair cost. The orderly expansion and contraction of funding to members are one of the most fundamental values of the FHLBanks. The amount of advances to local lenders rises and falls depending on demand and broader economic activity."

REGULATORY COMPLIANCE

The cooperative model has been particularly effective in the past several years as a networking and best practices forum on regulatory and compliance matters. The mortgage banking industry is heavily regulated, and lenders face challenges complying with an evolving and sometimes uncertain set of regulations. Cooperative members share ideas, discuss challenges, and seek solutions to improve their respective operations and clear compliance hurdles effectively.

Compliance risk was the top focus of lenders in 2014; in fact, it is a main reason why many institutions have reduced mortgage lending. 62% of small-sized and 84% of mid-sized lenders report that regulations have a "significant impact" on their business. As a result of the financial crisis, a multitude of regulatory mandates have added significant uncertainty and costs to the mortgage industry. The new regulations are complex and have been subject to ongoing and extensive amendments. The Consumer Finance Protection Bureau (CFPB), the Department of Justice (DOJ), Fannie Mae, Freddie Mac, FHA/VA, HUD, and a long list of Federal and state regulators combine to greatly complicate matters. Establishment of the CFPB has raised the cost of regulatory compliance for participants in the mortgage industry, with *industry-wide costs to originate having increased by 30% since 2013*. In addition, over $125 billion in fines and settlements have been paid by leading mortgage lenders and capital-markets participants. The CFPB has recently expanded to bring enforcement actions against mortgage servicers for improper practices.

Regulatory complexity and the increasing costs of compliance have led to an increased reliance on outsourcing. A co-op can provide compliance assistance on an outsource basis to its members, thereby reducing risk and cost, and increasing flexibility of cooperative members' business models. The cooperative model provides an effective platform from which members gain regulatory expertise and find solutions to rapidly changing compliance matters.

SERVICING

Servicer oversight, sub-servicer selection and fees, and servicing benchmarking are areas where the cooperative model adds value. The advantages of networking and sharing best practices are particularly evident in the face of new challenges and changes in business methods. To wit, a huge shift towards mortgage servicing rights ("MSR") ownership by middle-market mortgage bankers began in 2012, and today a significant portion of middle-market players retains MSR. The retention of MSR brings about significant new challenges, and the cooperative model is well-suited to assist.

When a lender retains MSR, it must manage and oversee the entity that performs the servicing functions, whether that entity is internal or external. A cooperative may assist in this regard by sharing policies and procedures, market color regarding specific sub-servicers, and regulatory advice pertaining to servicing.

Many middle-market lenders contract with sub-servicers to collect payments and fees and manage defaults and foreclosures for the MSRs they retain. Networking amongst cooperative peers provides invaluable perspective on the performance and general effectiveness of particular sub-servicers. For smaller lenders, a cooperative may gain advantages of scale by owning MSRs and servicing them on a private-label basis on behalf of its cooperative members.

Further creating value through group strength, a cooperative can benchmark individual lender servicing performance relative to a broad cooperative peer group.

COOPERATIVES AS SERVICE PROVIDERS

A cooperative may also be a service provider to its members. The Capital Markets Cooperative has several businesses under one roof, all of which combine to exemplify the effectiveness of the cooperative model. First is CMC's analytics business, where CMC analyzes, hedges, values and/or trades over $40 billion of mortgage pipelines and mortgage servicing rights ("MSR") annually. It performs MSR valuations and manages pipeline and MSR market risks for its members. A second CMC business is the *lender operation,* a storefront for purchasing mortgage servicing rights (MSRs) and other assets from CMC's Patrons. The third business is the over-arching framework, the co-op. The co-op binds the Patrons together by providing greater access and better prices than any one or handful of lenders could otherwise obtain. The co-op exists to serve and service its Patrons, passing along the discounts, bounty, and goodwill that group buying-power creates. It's a Costco or Sam's Club for mortgage bankers.

As for the value proposition for Patrons and would-be patrons, value is derived from the co-op model. It's efficient and drives several benefits. Centralization is the core concept thanks to the economies of scale residing there. Some Patrons use CMC's risk management pipeline software and trading operation. Others want an investor, whether an agency aggregator or a portfolio buyer, with sufficient and consistent purchasing power to acquire their loans and MSRs. Still others want these services along with more standard co-op benefits, like savings on investor charges and business supplies.

To be a CMC Patron, a lender must engage in at least one of CMC's businesses. Such participation opens the door to the co-op, which provides discounts on services from an array of mortgage investors and service providers. Historically, MSR values have been volatile and both difficult and expensive to hedge, and the past few years have seen a huge shift towards MSR ownership by smaller players. CMC's MSR analytics practice performs valuations on the MSR portfolios of many of CMC's Patrons, and advises on many MSR strategies. CMC's pipeline analytics and advisory practice manages Patrons' pipelines: locks loans, secures investor take-outs, and hedges the loans' interest-rate risk through closing and delivery.

The co-op gets special pricing thanks to both the larger volumes aggregation can offer smaller originators and the quality of its Patrons. CMC does business with a very attractive group of lenders, who form a source of solidly performing collateral. Its capital-market structure and nature, combined with CMC's adaptability, enhances Patrons' strong loan-performance metrics. Add in the economies of scale and scope from aggregation alongside carefully monitored lenders, and investors can justify better prices. CMC passes along the savings to its Patrons, deal by deal, several basis points at a time.

The exchange of ideas in a large cooperative network elevates the business of each individual member. This flow of open communication amongst co-op members is designed to foster continued development of solutions, shared tips, and best practices, providing members with a competitive edge. The power of the network matched with a mortgage-services infrastructure produces substantial savings and earnings for cooperative members and helps members solve complex business challenges.

SUMMARY

A cooperative is positioned as a single point of contact to deploy products and services across a large market share, and is able to leverage the collective volume to provide substantial economic benefits. A cooperative network of large size and scale brings a number of opportunities. It provides a platform to develop and quickly launch new products and services. It offers market insight into performance of loans and servicing rights of all shapes and sizes. It serves as a "one-stop shop" for a number of vital services that small- to mid-sized lenders require. A number of ancillary benefits, such as improved vendor pricing and networking opportunities, further knit cooperative members together.

In the highly-regulated and competitive mortgage industry, it is critical for small- to mid-sized lenders to reduce costs. Lenders must increase operational flexibility and loan-sale execution strategies to compete with established national banks and the growing population of large, independent mortgage companies. Cooperative members are typically small- to mid-sized financial institutions, independent mortgage companies, and credit unions that lack the scale and buying power of their larger competitors. A cooperative is a trusted marketplace of vetted business solutions for its members, who rely upon the cooperative and its vast information network to help make buying decisions. Further, cooperatives like AMC provide ongoing support and advocacy on behalf of its lenders.

A cooperative network is a broad information source regarding new investors and products, and serves as a single point of contact for investors and vendors to access a diverse population of small- to mid-sized residential mortgage lenders. Cooperative members rely on the cooperative network for investor and product introductions. Cooperatives drive savings on services ranging from sub-servicing to flood certifications to technology solutions to overnight shipping. The additional revenue a vendor would receive from an agreement with any single small- to mid-sized lender may not compensate for the associated selling and marketing expenses. However, by using a cooperative to access a broad network of lenders, vendors are able to quickly expand and diversify their customer base with minimal additional fixed expenses.

ABOUT THE AUTHOR

Tom Millon, CFA, CMB, is CEO, President, and Founder of Capital Markets Cooperative ("CMC"), and one of the top executives in the U.S. residential mortgage industry. He is an expert in mortgage finance and a frequent public speaker. Mr. Millon founded CMC as a one-man operation in 2003, and has grown the firm to one of the nation's leading mortgage banking operations. CMC's national client base of community banks, credit unions, and independent mortgage bankers originate over $100 billion of residential mortgage loans annually, ranking CMC among the top five mortgage originators. Prior to founding CMC, Mr. Millon built several leading mortgage trading and risk management operations, and was a trader on Wall Street and the Chicago Board of Trade.

Mr. Millon graduated from the Wharton School of Business of the University of Pennsylvania in May 1986. He holds the Chartered Financial Analyst (CFA) and Certified Mortgage Banker (CMB) designations. Mr. Millon is the Chairman of CMC's Board, and he is on the Board of the Wharton School's Institute of Urban Research. He is a member of the National Futures Association, the Association for Investment Management and Research, and the Security Analysts Society of San Francisco. Mr. Millon provides significant time and support to charitable organizations focused on autism research and on mentoring disadvantaged student athletes.

CHAPTER SEVEN

LEBOWITZ: TECHNOLOGY PAST, PRESENT, AND FUTURE

JEFF LEBOWITZ

BEND, OR

If you want to know the theory and methods of revolution, you must take part in revolution. All genuine knowledge originates in direct experience.
Chinese Proverb

Technology change is occurring in faster cycles. Similarly, waves of change in mortgage banking are not quieting, but are increasing in amplitude. What is in store for the industry is "Future Shock'. Shock waves will come from a technology revolution, a new management and organizational paradigm, and the reconstruction of trading relationships.

It is long past time for the industry to lobby for and reduce the amount of capital allocated to regulatory compliance. Overreach of the regulatory agencies has stunted internal business growth. The major technology expense has been in remediating legacy systems. The flow of truly innovative spending has been squeezed down as capital available for technology startups has dwindled.

Technology intensity (technology investment in proportion to business activity) has fallen. Focus on compliance has limited the possibilities in product diversity and in the quality of customer experience. The world outside the mortgage market increasingly has gone digital. The value of digital enterprises has soared as the value of technology suppliers to the mortgage market has been constrained. The future requires lender innovations that modernize the command over business processes, that customize cash flow patterns of mortgages to synchronize with individual borrower profiles, and that anticipate changing customer and business partner behavior.

Partly due to changes in capital requirements, and partly due to a lagging shift to a digital business model, banks have lost market share to non-banks. *Inside Mortgage Finance* of Bethesda, MD has estimated non-bank share of origination volume at 37.5% in 2014, a 40% increase from 2013.

Indeed, the industry is undergoing a tectonic shift. Underlying the changing structure of the mortgage industry lies a technological catalyst.

A BRIEF HISTORY OF MORTGAGE TECHNOLOGY

Lenders' relationship with technology has been uneven. Most lenders (perhaps 80%) originate less than $500 million in mortgages in a year. Most lenders do not have the funds or the specialized staff to manage technology. Technology applied to the mortgage industry is traceable to an early ancestor of Back Knight Financial Services. Computing and Statistical Services was founded in 1962 in Jacksonville, Florida. In 1969, Computing and Statistical Services incorporated under its new name: Computer Power Inc. (CPI). Its primary offering was a loan-servicing technology platform called the Mortgage Servicing Package (MSP). (Note: IBM did not announce its mainframe S/360 computers until April 7, 1964.)

For all intent and purpose, automation of mortgage processing began in 1973. Wang Labs brought out its flagship minicomputer, the Wang 2200. The 2200 was an integrated information system running native word processing and data processing on one machine. Over the years, several large technology companies made brief forays into mortgage technology. They included Google, IBM, Intuit, and Microsoft. Generally, the size of technology spend in the industry (±$4 billion) is too small to engage very large technology companies. Most often, marketing to the mortgage industry is combined with bank marketing.

The industry has seen a great number of mergers and acquisitions among its technology suppliers. Mortgage technology largely remains the domain of specialized vertical applications vendors. The fragmented structure of demand and the supply of information technology, the wickedly cyclical nature of mortgage banking, and now suffocating industry regulation, caused the industry to lag technologically behind the whole of the financial sector in the U.S.

THE ERA OF NEW TECHNOLOGIES

The mortgage industry is about to exit its Victorian era of technology use. Regulators have corseted the industry into making small-ball, prudish technology decisions. A quick assessment of the condition of technology use signals the need for a new, antithetical regime of business investment. The current technology use is uninspiring.

The very near-term future is no better than desultory. In a tormented business and regulatory environment, new investments in the mortgage value chain have been made halfheartedly. The major themes enveloping the industry are

- Lenders display a diminished appetite for technology risk
- Investment commitments are remedial and not particularly innovative
- Technology supplier mergers sap energy from leading-edge start-up ventures
- Regulators and not strategy are dictating technology priorities
- Technology-based outsiders are being permitted to attack industry borders

Investment capital generally has been immobilized. Risk-averse lenders are operating with legacy technology. Using traditional management practices, they cannot foresee the impending industry transformation by a new operational paradigm.

Temporarily inaccessible to most mortgage lenders is a revolution in decision-making, in process engineering, and in management techniques. The financial crisis of 2007-2008, and rules promulgated by vigilante regulators, have obscured lenders' vision into and participation in the imperative to change. As the Chinese proverb instructs, "If you want to know the theory and methods of revolution, you must take part in revolution."

The revolution is spear-headed by data scientists. The new paradigm of business is being constructed on a foundation of fact-based decisions that in turn are grounded on bounteous data. Traditional decision-making informed primarily by personal experience will be supplemented with and then replaced by management-by-model algorithms. A very new way of organizing mortgage operations is around the next corner.

In 2012, the highly-regarded French management consultants, Capgemini, released an important study of how businesses are changing. The study found that nine out of ten business leaders "believe data is now the fourth factor of production, as fundamental to business as land, labor, and capital." That report concludes: "Big Data represents a fundamental shift in business decision making." Facile users of data-based decisioning, the "Digirati", have significantly higher financial performance than their less digitally-mature competitors.

While it is unlikely that a mortgage banking company will make the Boston Consulting Group's list of most innovative companies, innovative change has become a management imperative. A good start would be to plan for implementation of digital and data-based technologies. Technology is moving from departmental operations to becoming a foundation for business model renovation.

Using detailed survey data on the business practices and information technology investments of 179 large publicly traded firms, researchers from the Massachusetts Institute of Technology found that firms using data-driven decision making (DDD) have productivity that is five to six percentage points higher than what would be expected given their other investments and information technology usage.[1] Few lenders have integrated DDD into their businesses. Rather, for the past five years, lenders have been focusing on compliance with regulator mandates.

The financial meltdown, and now a pervasive regulatory regime, suggest that the industry operating model was seriously flawed. Assuming that is a true assessment, there is evidence that regulators are tinkering around the edges of revolutionary change that could be needed. Regulators (i.e., CFPB) are preoccupied with an historic problem:

---

[1] Strength in Numbers: How Does Data-Driven Decision-making Affect Firm Performance? Erik Brynjolfsson, MIT and NBER, Lorin Hitt, University of Pennsylvania Heekyung Kim, MIT. April 22, 2011

the financial crisis of 2007–08. Keeping Fannie Mae in conservatorship limbo and investing heavily in MISMO 3.4 data standards show as the French say, *plus ça change, plus c'est la même chose* — the more things change, the more they stay the same.

"At the direction of our (Fannie Mae's) regulator, the Federal Housing Finance Agency (FHFA), Freddie Mac and Fannie Mae (the GSE's) are working together on the Uniform Mortgage Data Program® (UMDP). The UMDP is a multifaceted, ongoing program in which the GSE's develop and implement mortgage data standards for the single-family loans we purchase and/or securitize...."[2]

Fungible, high quality data undoubtedly are important. Without credible scenarios for the technology platform of the future, where in the industry construct does data quality fit? Of all the industry technology requirements, what priority should be assigned to data management? How much of the industry's technology funding should be invested in projects such as UMPD? Ultimately, the industry will be reformed not by enforcement, but by adapting to a new operating paradigm. The new paradigm will be defined by investments in both knowledge systems and integrated transaction flows.

TECHNOLOGY ACCOMPLISHMENTS

What is most important and too little understood is what drives lenders' willingness and ability to absorb technological innovation. The complement of this is: what factors drive lenders' investment decisions? Over the years, some have described mortgage banking as the "industry of slow adopters."[3]

Fundamental change in the mortgage industry occurs slowly and often reluctantly. There are few technology risk-takers in the industry. Research[4] showed that only one in twenty lenders is willing to experiment with new technology or innovative processes. Lenders have managed technology as an operational tool. Technology investment largely has been allocated to production channel integration, electronically linking to trading partners, extending the use of XML (data transport), standardizing interfaces to customers and trading partners, and generally updating infrastructure and back-end systems (updating hardware and software).

The evolution of a technology-based paradigm in mortgage lending began in 1973, when Wang Laboratories, Tewksbury, Massachusetts, founded the mortgage origination technology industry. It was then that Wang Laboratories published instructions for mortgage-rate calculations and loan amortization for its Series 2200 mini-computer. In 1973, Wang made news in financial-services industries. Until then financial institutions relied on printed tables for mortgage amortization schedules. In that year a Wang

---

2 FHFA Announces New Timeline for Fannie Mae and Freddie Mac Mortgage Data Implementation, 12/14/2011
3 The Industry of slow adopters. Mortgage Banking Magazine, April 2001
4 MORTECH: Annual Survey of Mortgage Lenders Use of Technology, Bend Oregon, 2000.

banking customer spot-checked a mortgage table against calculations generated by his Wang 2200. The banker found a computational discrepancy between the two sources.

As it turned out, the Wang calculation was correct. The printed table had the wrong figures. As they say, the rest is technology history.

In the past decade, a number of new technologies and technology applications have been brought into the industry. The most impactful of these have been automated compliance systems, definition of data standards, introduction of mobile computing, networking key components of the mortgage value chain, and installation of smart systems to improve adherence to business policies.

IMPACTFUL TECHNOLOGIES 2001-2014	
Technology	**Industry Impact**
Mobile	Conduct business on multiple platforms
Automated compliance	Manage financial and regulatory risk
Networked value chain	Integrate transactions and management decisions
Smart systems	Rules-based adherence to business policies
Data standards	Improved decisions, loan quality and asset transfer
Social media	Extended business reach
Source: MORTECH, LLC	

Of these, three have a little more significance than others: mobile computing, automated compliance, and operational integration.

Mobile Technology
The development and worldwide use of mobile technology is (and will be) the most impactful of technological innovations. Mobile phone subscriptions in the world come close to universality. The numbers describing mobile technology use simply are staggering. The International Telecommunications Union (ITU), Geneva, Switzerland, estimates that in 2014 there are almost as many mobile-cellular subscriptions as there are people in the world. Mobile cellular subscriptions approximated 7 billion by end 2014. This is a household penetration rate of 96% — staggering!

In the U.S., "The ubiquity of mobile phones is changing the way consumers' access financial services..." In its Consumers and Mobile Financial Services 2014 report, the Federal Reserve Board found:

1. Eighty-seven percent of the U.S. adult population has a mobile phone, not much changed since 2013.
2. Seventy-one percent of mobile phones are smartphones (Internet-enabled), up from sixty-one percent a year earlier.

Mobile has become the locus of application development. Gartner Inc., Stamford, Connecticut, estimated that by 2015, there will 205 billion functional mobile applications downloaded to mobile devices around the world. The utility of phones makes them the future's communications platform. What started out as a convenience and a form of entertainment has become the dominant protocol for how we communicate and transact.

Generally, smartphone, tablet, and Web apps are easier for customers to use and provide more current information than do legacy back-office platforms. This will influence the future design of mortgage marketing and service sales channel. The business problem is how best to design tablet and Web apps for customer use and to provide more current information than do the legacy back-office platforms.

Automated Compliance

Regulators have intensified their scrutiny of lender data, processes, risk management and financial reporting. The development of automated compliance systems has been crucial for lenders to respond to a fluid regulatory regime. Technology has enabled lenders to make compliance part of the operations workflow and to cost-effectively respond to frequently changing regulatory dictates. Every lender has been preoccupied with the demands of untested, but prevalent regulatory interventions.

These systems have brought a plethora of capabilities which lenders require for managing regulatory risk. The most important feature is the automatic identification of operational incidents. Lenders have become armed for risk identification and remediation with integration into risk assessment workflows. Applications that integrate with external event databases help identify risk events that other lenders had experienced. General systems requirements include:

- An external risk event repository
- Incident management workflow
- Root cause analysis
- Risk scorecard/dashboard capabilities.
- Scenario analysis capabilities
- Statistical modeling capabilities
- Predictive analytics

Few lenders had the near-disintegration of the world's financial system written into their operations strategies. Now, automated compliance is regarded as more critical than the likes of workflow integration, business intelligence, and mobile commerce. The downside has been refitting compliance operations, displacing lenders' investment in infrastructure and emerging core operations technology.

Integration of Operations and Systems

Operational integration and networking have been highly impactful for the industry. The *Holy Grail* for operations people is integrating functions into a straight-through processing architecture. Lenders and investors alike aspire to automate transaction-processing fully, from the point of borrower inquiry to final settlement.

Straight-through processing requires industry-wide use of common message standards. Standard data and transaction definitions are necessary in order to exchange transaction data electronically and without interruption. A primary benefit of industry-wide standards is that standards help dissimilar processing systems become compatible (or interoperable). Incompatible data definitions and mismatched networks require that employees and trading partners input the same data manually at various points during the lending process. Manual intervention in transactions creates increased human error, faulty loan descriptions, more loan buybacks, longer turnaround times, and rising processing and transaction costs.

It is not always easy for market participants to agree and use a common standard. The history of MISMO exemplifies the chore of gaining industry-wide adoption of a standard. Discussions of industry data and transactions standards began with the formation of the MBA Mortgage Technology Work Group in 1988. The MBA Technology Committee took up the challenge in 1990. Fourteen years ago, the Mortgage Industry Standards Maintenance Organization (MISMO) evolved to explore the possible uses of XML in the industry.

Depending on how we count, the industry has been looking for universally-adopted trade standards continuously for 25 years. Now, the torrent of regulatory changes has made the work of MISMO (and its subscribers) all the more urgent. The edicts issued by the Consumer Financial Protection Bureau now are driving standards definitions. Rick Hill, MISMO Executive Vice President, has said that "MISMO is focused on helping the industry by updating the standards to assist in complying with the regulations." MISMO Version 3.4 was released for comment in October of 2015. The new release updated support for the TILA/RESPA Integrated Disclosures (TRID) rule, the proposed Home Mortgage Disclosure Act (HMDA) rule, and the GSE's Uniform Mortgage Data Program (UMDP).

Degree of integration is the ultimate standard by which efficient business operations are judged. Data standardization is a facilitator of efficiency; but, physical and logical bridges across technologies, departments, and customers are the wellspring of excellence.

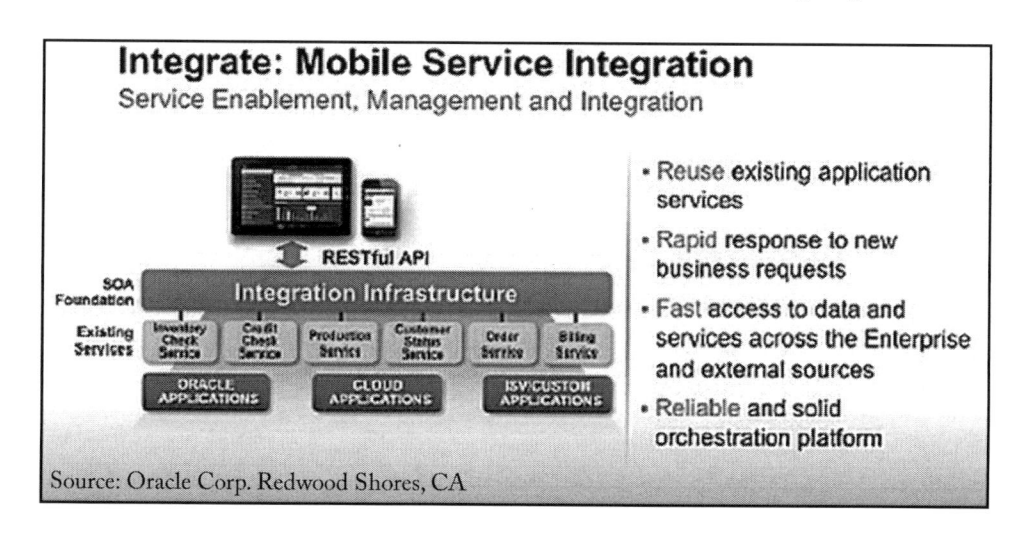

Integrate: Mobile Service Integration
Service Enablement, Management and Integration

- Reuse existing application services
- Rapid response to new business requests
- Fast access to data and services across the Enterprise and external sources
- Reliable and solid orchestration platform

Source: Oracle Corp. Redwood Shores, CA

Online and mobile channels are converging. This convergence places a development priority on a seamless, optimized experience for lenders' customers and business partners. Integrating distribution, operations, and decision analytics into an intelligently functioning network is the most impactful on lenders' business architectures. From integration comes streamlined operations, workflow integrity, immediate access, and fast response times.

MODEL-BASED MANAGEMENT

The 1990's saw the beginning of a new paradigm of risk assessment in the mortgage industry. The marker of fundamental change was the advent of statistical modeling through Automated Underwriting Systems (AUS). AUS was the first instance of mortgage bankers relying on automated statistical tools to manage a core business function. Other model-driven capabilities introduced in the 1990's were automated valuation models, automated fraud detection, and risk management systems.

PMI (Private Mortgage Insurance) Aura was the first automated underwriting application to predict default over the life of a mortgage. Despite having so-called "first mover" advantage, AURA quickly was displaced by Fannie Mae Desktop Underwriter and Freddie Mac Loan Prospector.

After two decades, commercialized AUS models became requisite to managing a mortgage company. In the mid 1990's, lenders made major commitments to using data to better manage the front ends of their businesses. In five short years from the GSE commercializing AUS, lenders relied more on statistical models than on human underwriting. By 2000, more than 80% of lenders had implemented an AUS. An estimated 65% of new production then was being underwritten with an AUS. At the same time (2000), automation of other primary decision functions were not nearly as well accepted as was AUS: 28% of lenders deployed an AVM; 33% of lenders implemented an automated fraud detection system; 35% incorporated credit or rate risk management systems.[5]

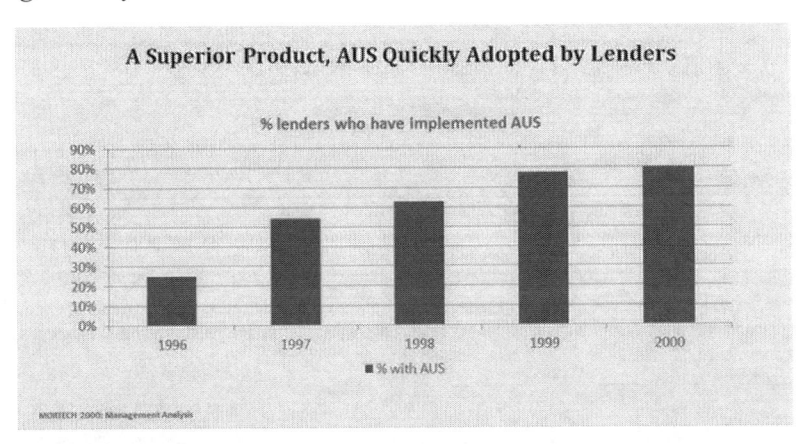

A Superior Product, AUS Quickly Adopted by Lenders
% lenders who have implemented AUS

MORTECH 2000: Management Analysis

---

5 MORTECH2000, MORTECH, LLC; Bend OR.

CHAPTER SEVEN: *TECHNOLOGY PAST, PRESENT, AND FUTURE*

The AUS from Fannie and Freddie were superior to other AUS in one respect. It was not that their design and execution were better than the mortgage insurers or applications providers (i.e., Fair Issac). GSE technology was adequate; but, the GSE's embedded their technology in the business contract between GSE and the loan sellers. The GSE's waived reps and warranties on loans submitted and accepted by their respective AUS. These were solid financial incentives for lenders to adopt Fannie Mae Desktop Underwriter® and Freddie Mac Loan Prospector®.

GOVERNMENT VERSUS PRIVATE SECTOR INVESTMENT

"The greatest advances of civilization, whether in architecture or painting, in science and literature, in industry or agriculture, have never come from centralized government." Milton Friedman, Nobel Laureate, 1962.

Given how lenders and technology vendors have responded to increased regulation, the question arises: "Has government interrupted the natural and necessary allocation of resources to technological innovation?"

It is easy to believe that large government bureaucracies hinder technology innovation. The incentives to succeed in government rarely align with private sector values.

To the contrary, there are many examples of government and private partnerships having been technologically very productive. This happens in very special contexts.

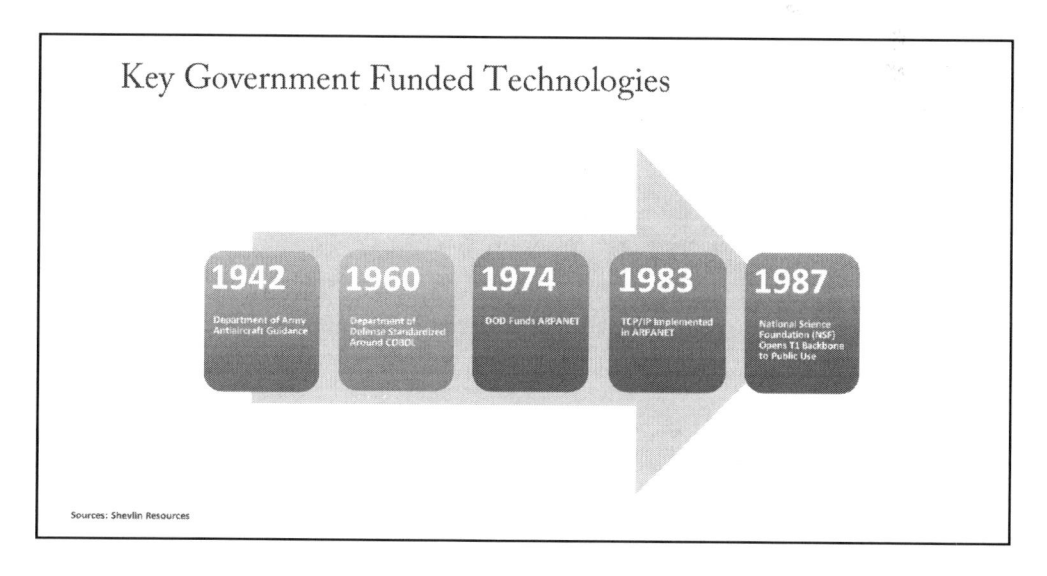

Key Government Funded Technologies

- **1942** – Department of Army Antiaircraft Guidance
- **1960** – Department of Defense Standardized Around COBOL
- **1974** – DOD Funds ARPANET
- **1983** – TCP/IP Implemented in ARPANET
- **1987** – National Science Foundation (NSF) Opens T1 Backbone to Public Use

Sources: Shevlin Resources

For seventy years, the federal government has facilitated or has underwritten foundational information and networking technology. Most often, new technologies grew from Department of Defense national security needs and from defense programs. While designed from government requirements, use of these technologies eventually was transferred to the private sector. Considered "spin-offs", technical algorithms, network infrastructures, and software were made available through licensing, funding agreements, and expert assistance.

In order to maximize benefits to commerce and society, government-supported innovation necessarily would run on open and novel technology platforms. Government technology research and development should be visionary. Government funding must be durable and it should be patient. It is not unusual for the government to underwrite technology projects all the way from the exploratory stage through late commercialization.

Historically, pioneering government technologies were offered to, but not forced on the private sector. Government/private-sector partnerships provided incentives and subsidies to technology transfers.

Technology transferred to private users, however, has not been totally free. Depending on the type of technology, general applicability, the work required to make ready for a secondary application, and effort to launch often are expensive and resource intensive.

DODD-FRANK DAMAGE TO INDUSTRY INFRASTRUCTURE

In general, Dodd-Frank Wall Street Reform and the Consumer Protection Act (the ACT) is legislation with limited vision. The mortgage industry is on the frontier of a new technology paradigm at a time when Dodd-Frank discourages risky technology investments. The ACT in no way contemplates future technology exigencies of the industry. Consider that throughout 2300 pages of the Act, the word technology is mentioned only nine (9) times. At that, the technology referred to is intended for use by employees of federal agencies. The Act is bereft of concern for what technology framework would be needed to reshape (re-form) industry business practices.

As Dodd-Frank issued forth, lenders could see the writing on the wall. A remarkable 92 percent of lenders responding to the "MORTECH 2009" technology survey thought that regulation would force up the cost of doing business with the government-sponsored enterprises (GSE's). By mandating additional processing and greater documentation, the federal government created a de facto mortgage franchise tax on mortgage bankers.

In 2015, after six years of enhanced regulation, legislator and regulator mandates still create excessive cost and regulatory uncertainty. By overburdening the loan process, The Dodd-Frank Act has been a scourge on financial entrepreneurship. Dodd-Frank was estimated to have imposed $21.8 billion in added costs and caused an additional 60.7 million paperwork hours spent in compliance.[6]

Small scale financial institutions have seen that "the cost of regulatory compliance as a share of operating expenses is two-and-a-half times greater for small banks than for

---

6 Andy Winkler, Ben Gitis, and Sam Batkins, Dodd-Frank at 4: More Regulation, More Regulators, and a Sluggish Housing Market (July 15, 2014),

large banks."[7] Keep in mind that 80% of mortgage originators bring in $500 million or less in loans originated per year (MORTECH Surveys). These are small financial companies. For them, the regulatory burden has been unaffordable.

With all the regulatory changes, the mortgage process remains highly paper-intensive. Added processing costs reached as much as $3,500 per loan — a cost which is added to the borrower's customary 20 percent down payment.[8]

As reported in the MBA's "2015 Second Quarterly Mortgage Bankers Performance Report," compliance contributed a great deal to increasing the net cost to originate a mortgage. To make matters worse, regulatory complexity has extended the time it takes to close a loan.

On December 16, 2015, the Origination Insight Report released by Ellie Mae® indicated that loan-closing rates reached their highest point since tracking began in August 2011. The average time to close a loan increased by 3 days to 49 total days in November, the longest time to close since February of 2013.

The average time to close FHA, Conventional, and VA loans all increased to 49, 49, and 50 days, respectively. The Report cited the increases as being caused by lenders adjusting to the new RESPA-TILA ("Know Before You Owe") regulations.

Per Loan Cost of Producing A Mortgage Has Steadily Climbed

YEAR	COST	CHANGE
2013	$4,182	-
2014	$5,038	20%
2015	$6,984	38%

Source: MBA's Quarterly Mortgage Bankers Performance Report; Shevlin Resources, Bend, OR.

In the early years of the 21st century, industry planners looked to the reasonable expectation of a five-day loan production cycle (Portner, Lebowitz, "Taming the Paper Tiger, 2004.") and a cost to originate of less than a thousand dollars per loan.

Costs for a lender to process a mortgage have risen rapidly. A good deal of the problem emanates from the misalignment of the objectives of regulators and the business needs of lenders. As opposed to lenders setting priorities for their investment in operations, regulators have jumped the queue by dictating immediate investment in compliance, data quality, and risk measurement.

"Technology is core to the CFPB accomplishing its mission. This means developing and leveraging technology to enhance the CFPB's reach, impact, and effectiveness.

---

[7] Small, Community Banks Suffering Under Dodd-Frank, SBE Council, 20 February, 2015
[8] Technology in the Mortgage Industry: The Fannie Mae Experience. William Kelvie, June 2002.

We strive to be recognized as an innovative, 21st century agency whose approach to technology serves as a model within government."[9]

CFPB is fixed on its own mission. Dictating technology requirements to lenders primarily serves the priorities of the CFPB (and FHFA). Lenders have to obey. Having finite resources, lenders have had to suspend normal capital allocations.

TECHNOLOGY UNDERINVESTMENT

Lenders seem to be underinvesting in technology. According to the Mortgage Bankers Association, the average technology spend to close a loan is falling. At the same time, lender productivity as measured by loans closing per production employee is falling. This result is an anomaly. One would expect that lenders' operations would become more technology intensive to offset falling productivity.

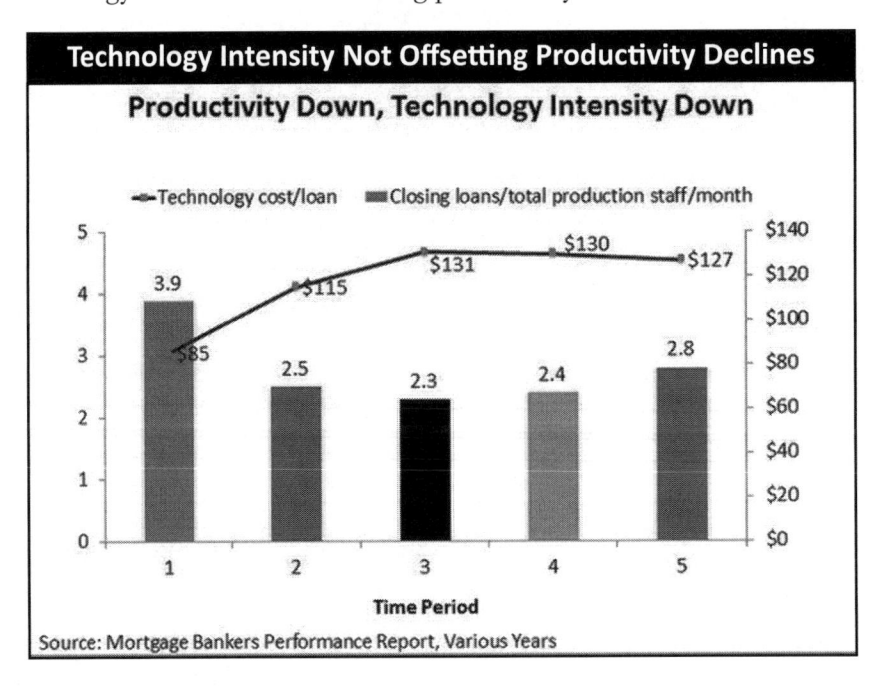

Technology Intensity Not Offsetting Productivity Declines
Productivity Down, Technology Intensity Down

— Technology cost/loan ■ Closing loans/total production staff/month

Time Period	Closing loans/total production staff/month	Technology cost/loan
1	3.9	$85
2	2.5	$115
3	2.3	$131
4	2.4	$130
5	2.8	$127

Source: Mortgage Bankers Performance Report, Various Years

The anomaly implies that centralizing lenders' technology investment decisions with regulators has caused financial and operational distortions. Even representatives of the Obama administration criticize (by inference) the misalignment of the chain of technology decisions. Lawrence "Larry" Summers, the director of the National Economic Council and a top economic advisor to President Barack Obama, states that the most effective paradigm of decision-making requires decentralized thinking. Summers would say that mortgage regulators are out of step: "There is something about this epoch in history that really puts a premium on incentives, on decentralization, on allowing small economic energy to bubble up rather than a more top-down, more directed approach."[10]

---

9 The CFPB strategic plan, 2013.
10 Lawrence Summers PBS Interview, Interview conducted 04/24/01

Current conditions have triggered an irreconcilable conflict between regulators and the lenders they supervise.

THE MORTGAGE TECHNOLOGY INNOVATION CONUNDRUM

As lenders devote extraordinary resources to regulatory compliance, capital is not being allocated to developing competitive tools for the future. Innovation is being limited to developing remedial (not innovative) technology.

Lack of innovation capital means fewer innovative technology startups to lead the mortgage industry. A decade ago, there were more than twenty vendors of loan origination systems (LOS) exhibiting at the MBA Annual Convention & Expo held in Orlando, FL. If there is competition among technology suppliers, lenders get choices of technology architectures. Come the 2015 MBA Annual Convention & Expo meeting in San Diego, the number of LOS companies and vendors of integrated point solutions had dwindled to a handful.[11] The risk of unknowable regulatory liability and uncertainty about the future structure of the mortgage industry has discouraged innovative start-ups.

". . . in the adjacent real estate industry, there have been well over 30 companies being funded by VCs. By contrast, only five mortgage technology firms received funding in the same timeframe; and, they got very small fundings. Since the financial crisis of 2008, technology innovation in the mortgage industry has been crowded out by the persistently harsh realities of the industry."[12]

According to a study by the Santa Clara, CA-based SVB Financial Group; "Innovation Economy Outlook 2015,"[13] the difficult regulatory environment is the top challenge to vendors of financial technology. Forty-three percent of financial technology companies surveyed selected regulations as their chief concern. Bruce Wallace, Chief Digital Officer at SVB Financial Group, pointed out that "many startups begin with just 5-10 employees, making it difficult to navigate or devote resources to compliance."

Further, market reluctance to adopt new technologies also discouraged technology startups. Twenty four percent of tech companies saw lender aversion to taking technology risk as their number one business challenge. The problem has not been lack of money. Only 15% of respondents believed that "access to funding" was their major challenge.

Indeed, there have been a number of factors causing an unprecedented dearth of innovation in the mortgage technology industry:

---

11 The Mortgage Technology Innovation Conundrum,"Jeb Spencer, Co-Founder and Managing Partner of TVC Capital; 2015.
12 Ibíd.
13 SVB Financial, Santa Clara, CA.

1. *The Great Recession Reduced Loan Volumes.* Loan volumes have decreased significantly and remained stagnant since 2003. This partly explains a consolidation of mortgage technology providers and has been a deterrent to new entrants in mortgage technology. Reduced volumes are squeezing out innovation by obstructing the entry of new players.

STAGNANT LOAN VOLUMES INHIBIT INVESTMENT IN INNOVATIVE TECHNOLOGY

1-4 Family Residential Mortgage Origination Volume	
Year	Volume (Trillions)
2003	$3.3
2008	$1.5
2014	$1.1
2018 Projected	$1.3

Sources: FFIEC, HMDA, MBAA

2. *Push towards end-to-end technology solutions.* Historically, the largest banks used a single technology system (and single-source vendor) to manage mortgage processes. Otherwise, most mortgage banks integrated best-of-breed solutions. Smaller and mid-sized lenders selected and spliced together point-of-sale (POS), loan origination (LOS), pricing and product eligibility (PPE), and document management systems. In order to reduce management complexity, and to displace coordination and operations cost, the trend now is toward demanding an end-to-end processing system. This change has resulted in merger and acquisition capital displacing capital from being invested in new and innovative technology.

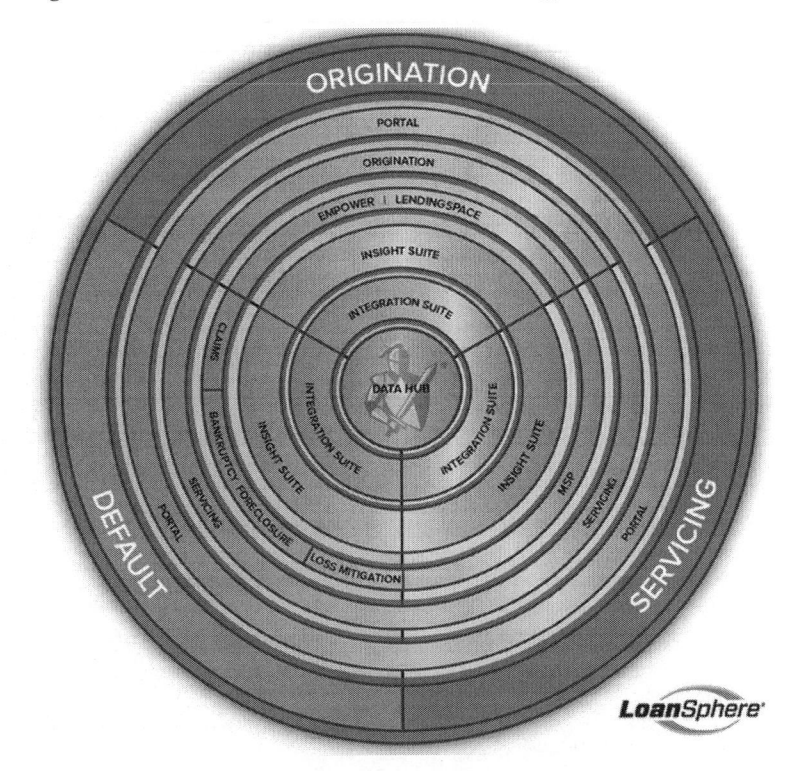

CHAPTER SEVEN: *TECHNOLOGY PAST, PRESENT, AND FUTURE*

BKFS LOANSPHERE TYPIFIES TREND TO END-TO-END MORTGAGE PROCESSING

3. *Industry Regulation and Compliance.* Massively increased industry regulation and increased compliance risk have made it prohibitive for new technology suppliers to enter the mortgage technology space. It is the unpredictable regulatory risk and the fear of predatory civil law suits that have diminished innovative capital investments and have caused the U.S. House of Representative to pass H.R. 3192, the Homebuyers Assistance Act. The implementation of the 1,888-page TILA-RESPA Integrated Disclosure rule (TRID) has prompted congress to shield "any person making a good-faith effort to comply with TRID from being sued for TRID violations."

STARTUP TECH CO'S CHALLENGED BY (CUSTOMERS') REGULATORY BURDEN

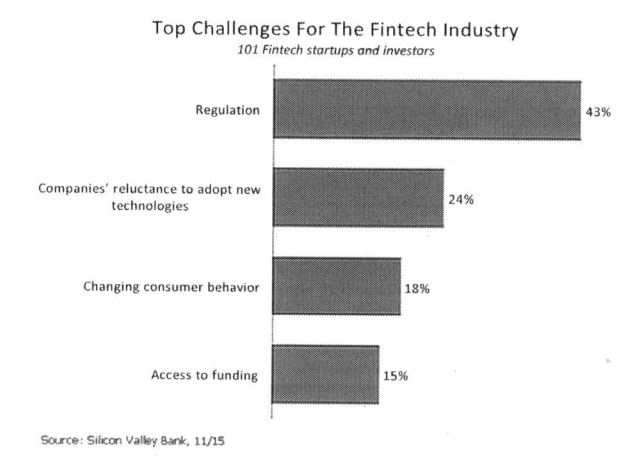

Top Challenges For The Fintech Industry
101 Fintech startups and investors

Challenge	%
Regulation	43%
Companies' reluctance to adopt new technologies	24%
Changing consumer behavior	18%
Access to funding	15%

Source: Silicon Valley Bank, 11/15

4. *Industry Consolidation.* The combination of reduced volumes, financial distress, the prohibitive regulatory environment, and the move toward single-sourced technology have resulted in increased concentration in technology demand and a contraction in the number of mortgage technology vendors. There has been a diminution in cash-on-cash returns to venture capital. Lowered returns have kept the investment community at bay.

Without a profound change in the industry's operating and regulatory environment, the "innovation conundrum" will likely continue into the foreseeable future.[14]

DIGITAL COMPETITORS

Digital-based start-ups use peer-to-peer solutions, social technologies, and advanced data analytics to develop products, manage risk, and improve service. Their technology platforms are more open than those of the conventional technology suppliers.

---

14 "The Mortgage Technology Innovation Conundrum," Jeb Spencer, Co-Founder and Managing Partner of TVC Capital; 2015.

Digital companies are built for continuous innovation and frequent technology upgrades. They maintain a narrow focus on their value-added offerings. They are agile and efficient. Product and processes are updated speedily and frequently. Technology releases update monthly or sooner.

Securities markets tend to value digital-based businesses much higher than they do companies operating with conventional, legacy platforms. This differential attracts venture and late-stage capital. It is only natural that investment is directed to opportunities promising higher valuations. This very fact has reinforced the shortage of innovation capital in the mortgage industry.

MORTGAGE TECHNOLOGY COMPANIES RECEIVE MODEST VALUATIONS

Company	Year Founded	Market Value as Of Nov 30, 2015
Internet Born		
Alphabet (Google)	1998	$264 B
Amazon	1994	$367 B
Facebook	2004	$298 B
Priceline	1997	$62 B
Saleforce.com	1999	$53 B
Internet Adapted		
Apple Computer	1976	$657 B
Oracle	1977	$167 B
SAS Institute	1976	$3 B[1]
Mortgage Vendors Consolidating Traditional Products		
Black Knight FS	2007 (LPS) spin-off	$5.3 B
D+H Financial Technologies	2005[2]	US $2.6 B
Ellie Mae	1997	$1.1 B

[1] Private company – showing year end 2014 revenues.
[2] Public company with Restructured Businesses; Originally founded in 1875.
Source: Shevlin Resources, Bend, OR

Rather than spend money on innovation, investment capital is going toward technology vendor mergers and acquisitions. The uncertainty of return to research and development is pushing vendors to acquire rather than develop. The M&A market for mortgage technology has been extraordinarily active since 2009.

There have been an estimated thirty five mergers or acquisitions of mortgage technology companies since 2009. The greatest number involved services companies. Since these targeted companies often focus on regulatory compliance, the industry has been investing in yesterday's problems. As regulators have expanded the market for compliance services, more often than not, M&A capital has been invested in the old industry paradigm.

MERGERS AND ACQUISITION SCOREBOARD[1]

Acquisition Target	New Product	Extend Product Line	Enter New Market	Total
CRM/Prospects	2	1		3
LOS	3	1	3	7
Compliance	3			3
Servicing		1	1	2
Outsourcing	1			1
Services[2]	7	7	1	15
Private Equity Investor	3	1		4
Total	19	11	5	35

[1] Source: Berkery Noyes Investment Bankers, New York, NY; Shevlin Resources, Bend, OR.
[2] Activities included: Closing, Doc Prep, Appraisal, Default Management, Pricing, GIS, Quality Control, Due Diligence, Public Records

Intense regulatory demands and constraints have led capital to be allocated to suboptimal uses.

DIFFUSION OF TECHNOLOGY

Lenders have adopted financially critical technologies such as risk management, automated collateral valuation, and fraud detection much more slowly than they employed the GSE's automated underwriting systems. What explains the differences in rates of adoption? Ultimately what determines the pace at which an industry transforms itself is the rate at which companies adopt new technology.

- The benefits attributed to the innovation.
- Compatibility with and ease of inserting into work processes
- How easily a new technology can be learned
- Can the technology be tried and tested before a full commitment is required
- After a test run, how easy is it to measure potential advantages from new technology.[15]

---

15 Based on Rogers, Everett; Diffusion of Innovation, 3d. Free Press.

GSE'S CONTROL COMMUNICATIONS CHANNELS

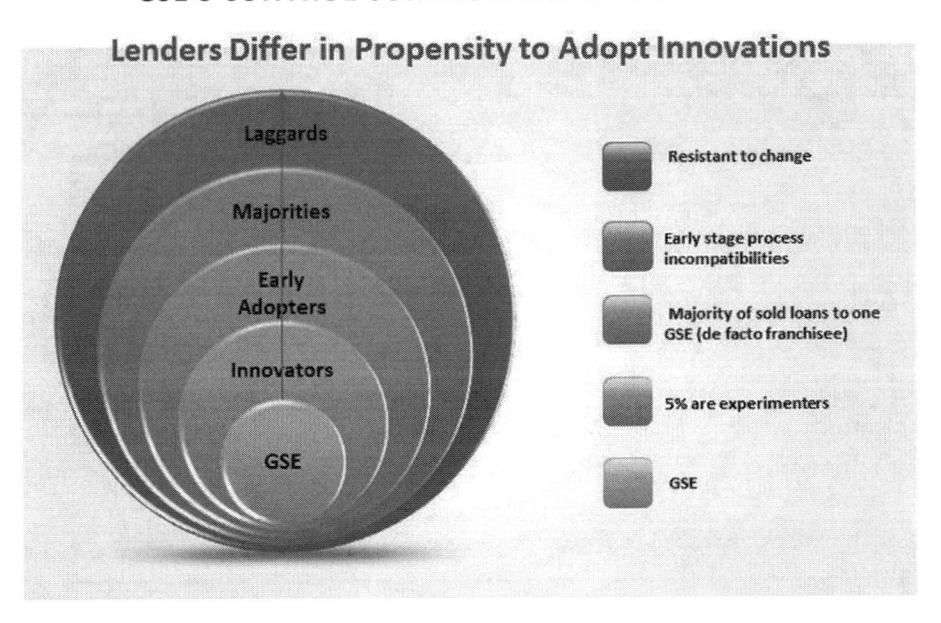

Lenders Differ in Propensity to Adopt Innovations

- Laggards — Resistant to change
- Majorities — Early stage process incompatibilities
- Early Adopters — Majority of sold loans to one GSE (de facto franchisee)
- Innovators — 5% are experimenters
- GSE — GSE

Detractors of the GSE's have ignored how they used their scale to build and distribute useful new technologies. Occupying the industry's central communication node, the GSE's have been in a position to speed up lenders adopting new processing or decision technologies. Short communication channels facilitate rapid adoption of an innovation. Other than the GSE's, no entity in the mortgage industry has universal communication with lenders. There are five agencies of change in mortgage – GSE's, large wholesalers, regulators, mortgage securities issuers, and mortgage banks collectively. But, the GSE's have greater exposure to potential adopters and more influence in mortgage distribution channels. None commands more attention from the news media. If the GSE's are innovative, the industry is elevated. Since the mid 1990's, the mortgage GSE's had made substantial technology contributions to the mortgage industry. They often used their financial and operating scale to invent new approaches to producing and servicing mortgages. In this respect, the GSE's would be hard to replace.

Looking at seven years of technology projects at Fannie Mae, the nature of GSE technology investment changed considerably. Major projects have become remedial updates to legacy systems. These were intended to make doing business with the GSE easier, make it less likely to have data or documents errors, and to reduce transactional overhead.

CHAPTER SEVEN: *TECHNOLOGY PAST, PRESENT, AND FUTURE*

Seven Years of Fannie Mae Technology Initiatives Focus on Transactions with Lenders	
Technology Initiatives	**Purpose**
Servicer and Investor Reporting	Replace 20-year old legacy system
DU RefiPlus	Speed up refinancing
eMortgage Electronic Signing, eDelivery	Support loss mitigation
Centralized Systems Architecture	Operational simplification
Collateral Underwriter (CU)	Validate appraisals
EarlyCheck	Filters for case problems
Servicing Management Default Underwriter (SMDU)	Elicit loss-mitigation options
Vega Analytics	Tools for collateral valuation/ risk management
Common Securitization Platform	Issue single GSE mortgage-backed security
Source: Fannie Mae, Federal Reserve Bank of Chicago/ DePaul U. Risk Conference	

When introducing the PATH act intended to phase out Fannie Mae and Freddie Mac, House of Representatives Financial Services Committee Chairman Jeb Hensarling (R-TX) characterized the mortgage GSE's as follows: "The current system is a government monopoly run by the same types of Washington bureaucrats who run the IRS." Even if accurate, it was not always this way.

There was a time before the financial crises of 2007-2008, that Fannie Mae and Freddie Mac were fierce competitors. There was no collusion between the two. Competitive development of AUS platforms gave lenders a choice of differing logical and technological designs.

Starting with Dodd-Frank, it is the government that has created a true duopoly by repealing inter-GSE competition. Now, with the government underwriting the development of the Common Securitization Platform, the federal government is building a transactional monopoly.

COMMON SECURITIZATION PLATFORM, A PUBLIC GOOD?

CSP has been mandated by the Federal Housing Finance agency. CSP ownership, scope, project management, and development cost set a new pattern for GSE technology projects.

The FHFA began work on the Common Securitization Platform in 2012. FHFA envisioned centralizing all issuing, payment, and reporting functions across the markets for agency and non-agency mortgage bonds. The platform would be used for all non-

Ginnie Mae government-guaranteed securities, but open to nonguaranteed securities (private). CSP also will trade forward mortgage-backed securities (TBA). It is assumed that TBA trades still would settle according to the SIFMA monthly schedule.[16]

The goals of CSP embrace data and security standardization, development of economies of scale, and improved market liquidity for mortgage-backed securities.

Common Securitiization Platform - May 2015

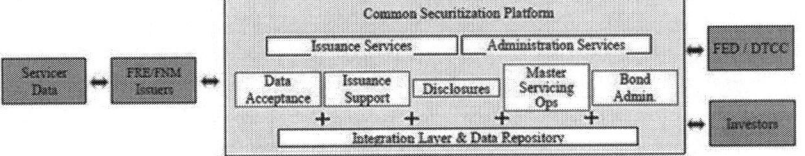

Loans on the securitization platform should be covered by a uniform servicing standard. That standardization is meant to foster prudent underwriting. It also aligns investor and borrower interests. Finally, CSP is expected to add flexibility if securitized loans need to be modified. .

Although a joint Fannie Mae and Freddie Mac project, CSP is owned by Common Securitization Solutions, LLC (CSS). CSS may determine the future structure of the secondary market.

This LLC can be sold, traded or given to private sector competitors. In "A Strategic Plan for Enterprise Conservatorship: The Next Chapter in a Story that Needs an Ending" (2012), FHFA states that a principal tenet of the development of CSP is its "... open architecture that will permit multiple future issuers of mortgage-backed securities to access the platform and it should be flexible enough to permit a wide array of securities and mortgage structures." By government fiat, CSP will inherit a dominant economic position in trading guaranteed securities. Imbued with economies of scale, CSP will be able to compete for non-guaranteed securities trading. CSP would be very attractive to potential buyers who have a stake in the trading business.

In the section above titled *Government versus Private Sector Investment*, it was stated that government technology research and development should be visionary. Further, to benefit commerce and society, government-supported innovation needs to be based on open and novel technology platforms. The plan for CSP subscribes to these principles. CSP plans a fundamental innovation in processing GSE securities. The CSP open platform is intended to benefit broadly private and government guaranteed mortgage-backed securities.

The CSP development team is being watched and guided by politicians as well

---

16 According to the New York Federal Reserve Bank, as of this writing 90% of MBS trading is in TBA's.

as FHFA's Division of Conservatorship. In a letter to FHFA Director Mel Watt, dated March 17, 2015, Senator Bob Corker (R-TN) and a bipartisan group of the Senate Banking Committee raised concerns about the development of the Common Securitization Platform (CSP). The explicit message to FHFA was to move beyond "the duopolistic tendencies of the past." The CSP central feature was to be accessible not only to government-sponsored enterprises (GSE's) Fannie Mae and Freddie Mac, but also to private sector participants.

The intent is clear. CSP is meant to benefit the entire industry. The situation is well defined. Congress fully supports and approves of funding the development of CSP. More so than a private startup, this emerging government operation will be given a chance to reengineer the inner workings of the residential mortgage business.

CSP Oversight, Progress and implications for Technology Applied to the Mortgage Market

Under FHFA, the Division of Conservatorship (DOC) has responsibility for the management of the CSP project. DOC created a Scorecard to evaluate the management, progress, and quality of the CSP program.

For all Scorecard items, Fannie Mae and Freddie Mac (the Enterprises) and Common Securitization Solutions will be assessed based on the following criteria:

- The extent to which each Enterprise conducts initiatives in a safe and sound manner consistent with FHFA's expectations for all activities;
- The extent to which the outcomes of their activities support a competitive, resilient, and liquid secondary mortgage market to the benefit of homeowners and renters;
- The extent to which each Enterprise conducts initiatives with the appropriate consideration for diversity and inclusion consistent with FHFA's expectations for all activities;
- Cooperation and collaboration with FHFA, each other, the industry, and other stakeholders as appropriate; and
- The quality, thoroughness, creativity, effectiveness, and timeliness of their work products.

CSP is a large and difficult undertaking. In January 2015, FHFA Office of the Inspector General issued its CSP "Scorecard". OIG graded the program's state at 30% out of a possible 100%. While, it is rumored that CSP will cost $300 million or more, a successful outcome is not assured.

CSP is a large, government-sponsored development project. Given the provenance of the CSP, it should be declared a "public good." Senators Elizabeth Warren and Bob Corker, members of the Senate Banking, Housing and Urban Affairs Committee, declared that CSP's open platform would "enhance the ability for small and mid-sized lenders to access the secondary mortgage market and help facilitate greater competition in the market going forward."

Access to CSP should be free and open to anyone. Funded by taxpayers, CSP and its services should be provided to all comers at cost. This idea holds whether CSS ends up being owned by the government or by a private organization. Being profitless by charter, CSP likely will remain a public good. As such, lender adoption of CSP should be nearly universal and public utility maximized.

TECHNOLOGIES FOR 2020

Industrial-age thinking has allowed the technology infrastructure of the mortgage industry to stagnate and age. Workflow reengineering has been based on a "factory" linear processing model. The primary objective of reengineering has been to reorganize and cut operating costs.

In the future, organization will be more free form; teams and tasks will be organized extemporaneously.

In the "digital age," operational networks will be built around rapid point-to-point communications. Rigid organizational structures will give way to networks of small groups formed and disbanded according to problem and project requirements. The "ad-hoc" groups will be tied-in for coordinated problem solving. Advanced computation and communication nets will underpin improvements in work accuracy, institutional memory, and better and more-timely decisions. The new organization model will bring together specialists and practitioners for coordinated fact-based problem solving.

In the digital age model, autonomous actors cohere and integrate their various skills and resources. New and advanced computing will guide ad hoc work flows through data sharing and skills integration. Hierarchal work will be replaced by rapidly added and dissolved system nodes within boundary-less virtual organizations. The new organization model will flourish through the use of advanced decision-support systems and massive data stores. The mortgage industry is sitting on the threshold of a management revolution. Whoever crosses that threshold determines the future state of competition. Data analysis and business intelligence are becoming the lingua franca of well-run companies in any industry. Rapidly maturing analytical technology is now available in form and function designed to help teams make real-time decisions.

It is technology that will release the mortgage industry from its ancient business processes and primordial regulatory constructs.

Three dominant technologies for the future

M
- Mobile becomes strategic distribution channel
- Large majority of consumers own smartphone
- Customer-facing processes retooled for mobile
- Mobile employee apps improve productivity
- Employee-facing processes redesigned for mobile
- Frameworks customized for lifecycle management of mobile applications
- mPayments becomes leading application

C
- Proliferation of sources of IT services
- Most core services have cloud-delivered option
- Migration to cloud-based services to conserve capital
- Cloud and mobile applications developed in sync
- Cloud infrastructure allows for appropriate scale
- Used-based pricing conserves cash

A
- Data and fact-based management displaces experiential decision-making
- Large data stores and algorithms become corporate assets
- Leverage on data standardization (regulatory or proprietary)
- Data extend to social media, mobile devices
- Insights from advanced analytics migrate to high-performance desktop computers
- Risk management shifts to life-of-loan analysis (servicers)

Mobile — *Cloud* — *Analytics*

The scope of the technology change to come is so large as almost to defy description.

In 1955, three logicians at Carnegie Mellon University in Pittsburgh, PA, (Allen Newell, Herbert A. Simon and Cliff Shaw) wrote a computer program named the Logic Theorist (LT). LT simulated the problem-solving skills of a human being. Legend has it that in the first class held after Christmas 1955, Simon told his class: "Over Christmas, Al Newell and I invented a thinking machine." Almost sixty years later to the day, this singular event in computing continues to change decision-making — and it will for all time.

For purposes of this essay, we have narrowed all possible technologies with impact on the future of mortgage banking to the central mover (analytics), and two pathways to invoke and to access the prime mover (cloud computing and mobile technologies).

Technology for Analytics

"In ... post-industrial society, the central problem is ... how to organize to make decisions — that is to process information" [17]

Originators are realizing that the primary byproduct they create when originating a loan is risk. Once transferred to the GSE's, virtually all of the prepayment risk and more than half of the credit risk of newly guaranteed conventional mortgages are now

---

17 Simon, H., Administrative Behavior. 3rd. ed. 1976, New York: Free Press.

borne outside of the GSE's.[18] More than in any time in history, mortgage lenders are driven to characterize and quantify risk. To get there, they are seeking technology to help them understand the type and level of risk they face.

Analytics in the mortgage industry date back to the early 1980's. At that time, options theoretic modeling[19] was applied effectively to portfolio valuations and pricing. These models changed the nature of prepayment analysis, securities pricing, and issuance. At the time, there was an uneven distribution of analytical talent. Wall Street "rocket scientists" outdistanced lenders' secondary marketing teams.

Good analytics professionals are rare. They must have both analytical training and business domain knowledge. The work requires data-mining skills and the ability to develop a data perspective on practical business problems. A shortage of highly skilled staff has made it difficult to close competitive gaps between financial institutions and securities underwriters.

To fill the skills gap, specialized analytics consultants formed to support the mortgage industry. Most lenders use these consultants to manage pipelines, analyze portfolios, and to project capital requirements. The consulting pioneers are still serving mortgage lenders and investors. The founders of their trade are Andrew Davidson & Co. Inc. (AD&Co), New York (1992), Applied Financial Technology, San Francisco (1996), and, Quantitative Risk Management (QRM), Chicago (1987). They all are in business today with greatly expanded scope of analytical modeling and services.

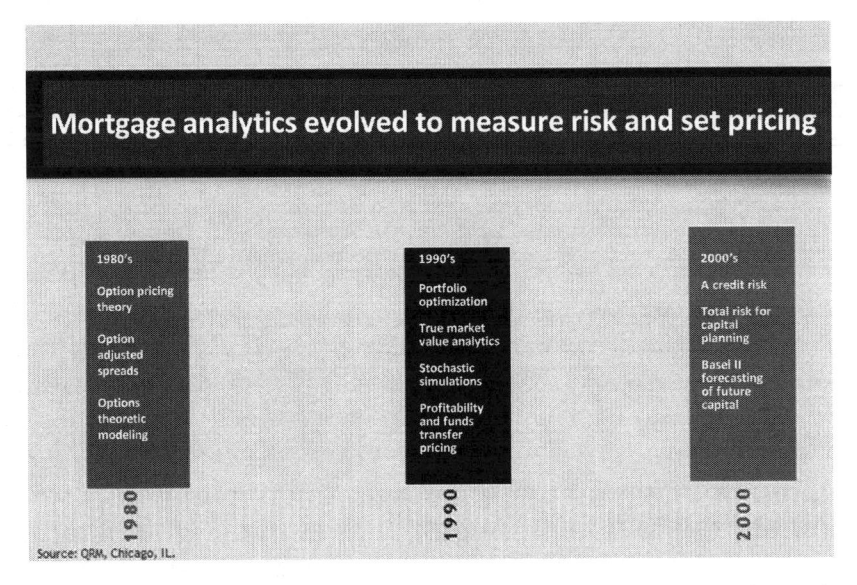

Mortgage analytics evolved to measure risk and set pricing

1980's	1990's	2000's
Option pricing theory	Portfolio optimization	A credit risk
Option adjusted spreads	True market value analytics	Total risk for capital planning
Options theoretic modeling	Stochastic simulations	Basel II forecasting of future capital
	Profitability and funds transfer pricing	

Source: QRM, Chicago, IL.

Since the 1980's, risk and pricing analytics have become increasingly sophisticated. Now, these analytics are being expanded to loan level decisions, capital forecasting, and enterprise management. Fortunately, new tools are becoming available and made affordable for lenders.

---

18 Andy Davidson, **The Quiet Revolution**, letter dated December 11, 2015.
19 Valuation of mortgage loans and mortgage securities using implied puts and calls.

Big-Data Analytics

Digital-based companies are reinventing business analysis. For instance, Google studies search-engine queries to predict unemployment before the Bureau of Labor statistics releases its monthly employment report. To detect and predict consumer buying patterns, credit-card companies sift through 1,024 terabytes of data. The use of big data and high powered analytics has led to improved methods of predicting prepayments, defaults, and fraud. In addition to conventional approaches, big-data techniques will use behavioral, financial, social, and transactions data to individualize decisions.

The use of large stores of data and analytical software will increasingly drive decision-making in the mortgage bank. To leverage analytical capability, lenders will integrate information from multiple data sources. Analytic software will function to change the discipline of decision-making. The gains will be noticeable.

Big-data analytics can create measurable value. Big data analytics brings with it:

- More informed and up-to-the-minute management control
- Streams of information applicable to adjusting business tactics with reduced lag time
- More accurate, detailed performance monitoring
- Continuous forecasting to improve sensitivity to changed business conditions
- Precise and smaller group customer segmentation
- Tailored loan features and pricing
- More relevant add-on marketing
- Improve products and services

In the future scheme of making decisions, real-time is preferred over the traditional batch processing often found in legacy servicing systems.

There are important changes necessary before a lender can convert to a big-data analytics model. Some of these changes are:

- Build a formal data organization that can be synthesized in real time.
- Develop standard definitions for numerical and textual data.
- Implement high-velocity processors to accommodate new data sources such as social media and mobile devices.
- Implement a platform for lenders converting to big-data analytics.

In the (recent) past, big-data decisioning required networks of servers or clusters of high-performance computers. Intel Corporation's HPC Platform Group has bridged the technology gap to bring supercomputing to lenders' desktops. Taking this level of computing out of the data center and giving it to business and operations staff truly is revolutionary.

INTEL 72 CORE CHIP BRINGS SUPER COMPUTING TO THE DESKTOP

Intel Corporation made great strides with its Intel® Scalable System Framework (Intel® SSF). The enhancements promise to bring high-performance computing (HPC) to mid-sized companies. Intel offers the Intel® Omni-Path Architecture (Intel® OPA); thus, they have optimized fabric technology[20], making high performance technology accessible to a broad variety of users.

High-performance computing (HPC) historically was reserved to solve the most complex computational problems (e.g., genome sequencing, weather forecasting, etc.). HPC now is transforming more industries with new tools such as big data analytics. Traditional sectors, such as financial services, are using supercomputer-like capabilities to gain real-time insights from large and complex data sets. As Intel innovations lower the barriers to accessing high performance computing, high performance computing is closer to being mainstream technology.

"We're entering a new era in which supercomputing is being transformed from a tool for a specific problem to a general tool for many," said Charlie Wuischpard, vice president and general manager of HPC Platform Group at Intel. "System-level innovations in processing, memory, software and fabric technologies are enabling system capabilities to be designed and optimized for different usages, from traditional HPC to the emerging world of big data analytics and everything in between. We believe the Intel Scalable System Framework is the path forward for designing and delivering the next generation of systems for the 'HPC everywhere' era."

In order to stay competitive, lenders will learn to use HPC and to quickly and easily extract real-time data. The data will come from desktop and laptop computers as well as smart phones and tablets. Analytical software will reside in memory rather than on disk drives. In-memory applications will run as much as 1,000 times faster than do disk drives.

The coming transformation begins with "the data-creation explosion. Data useful to lenders is coming from Web and mobile engagement, behavior and interactions on a

---

20 Fabric refers to a technology deployment that maximizes information transfer.

global scale and the growing set of tools and talent ability to analyze that data."[21] This trend creates the foundation for the making of modern remarkable companies. The secret to successful transformations lies in turning operationally generated data into performance information.

The bottom line is that technology is evolving in a way that enables smaller companies to access to large sets of data. They will have the ability to mimic large companies and work with self-stylized analyses and reporting.

Motivity Solutions' Mortgage Business Intelligence

There is a good example of sophisticated data management and advanced analytics for Main Street companies. Motivity Solutions, Aurora, Colorado, pioneered a mortgage banker's business-intelligence system for operations.

Their technology, Movation Business Intelligence (MBI), is a suite of analytics optimized for mortgage. Embedded in a lender's operations, MBI produces real-time performance management analytics. Users have access to key performance indicators, to scorecards, to dashboards, and to on-demand dynamic reporting. Interfaces bring in data from sources selected by mortgage banking operations staff.

MOTIVATION: FORECASTING AND PERFORMANCE MONITORING OPTIMIZED FOR MORTGAGE

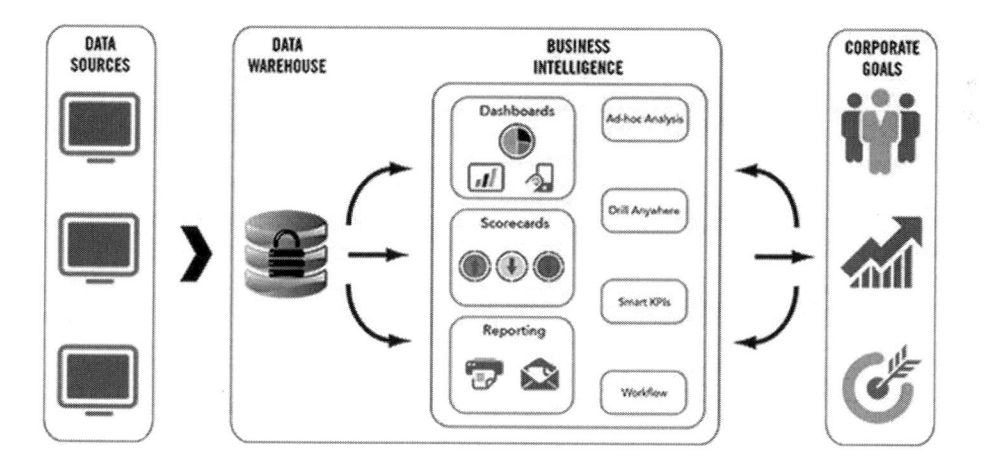

MBI delivers streaming, actionable information for visual reporting and display. Analysis is delivered through three media: dashboards, scorecards, and reports. Output from MBI is easy to read, readily understood, and effortless to retain and share. And, MBI is uniquely mortgage business intelligence.

Big data and business intelligence are coming from small innovators (i.e., Motivity). These pioneers make Pilgrim's Progress in disseminating new approaches to lender

---

21 Dan Feshbach. Founder LoanPerformance Corp. (Acquired by First American Financial in 2005.) Private Conversation.

managers. For them it is a long journey from the "City of Destruction" to the "Celestial City"!

Cloud Computing and the New Paradigm of Collaborative Processing

"Simple to get, easy to own, and a joy to use. These are the three goals and objectives we set for every one of our cloud applications." Oracle Corporation.

The Cloud has been hyped as "the next big thing," "a disruptive force," and even "a shot in the arm for our economy." In simple terms, cloud enables users to purchase software and IT resources as a service. This transforms the burden of capital expenses to a flexible, pay-as-you-go model. Cloud computing resembles a utility that supplies water or electrical power—users are able to access their business applications at any time and from multiple locations, track their usage levels, and scale capacity as needed without large up-front costs.

Lenders use cloud-computing to accelerate conversion of their business processes to digital form. Digital processes ease engagement with customers and with employees. The goal is to improve customer experience and to increase productivity. In the short term, Cloud is looked to for lower fixed capital investment and less working capital expended.

Collaborative Computing

What is new to the industry is the concept that business relationships may be defined within technological or trading *networks*. Wholesale lenders are managing a complex network of relationships. The value of a network is determined in large measure by its overall size (the number of network members).

The value of any network is governed by what technologists refer to as Metcalfe's law (Bob Metcalfe was the designer of the Ethernet method of connecting computer nodes). The two major corollaries of Metcalfe's law are:

1. The value of small networks will be much smaller than those of large networks — that is, it is difficult for small networks to compete with large networks.
2. Once a network grows beyond some critical mass, it has the potential to grow very fast, meaning that it gains general adoption by the user community. The successful network, then, operates as a many-to-many transaction and informational platform.

Metcalf envisioned a company and its trading partners being networked together. But, old habits die hard. Most of the management structures and processes in mortgage banking derive from the model of the vertically integrated lender, whereby the lender controls all of the functions of producing a loan. That clearly should not the case in the future.

The mortgage business, as in the automobile industry, is evolving to shared systems that permit many suppliers to work with a small number of assemblers (wholesale aggregators) on a common platform. In other words, a network is formed to allow suppliers (originators) to use the same platform to work with any of several assemblers or wholesalers.

The potential to redefine the operating profile of the industry depends on several important elements:

- implementation of a collaborative, shared processing platform;
- development of an information and transaction platform open to every entity and person that takes a part in producing a closed loan; and
- equitable distribution of cost savings to all users of the networked processing platform.

Ellie Mae Network (originally ePass Network) is a well-known example of a vertical industry transaction network. The Network is an electronic platform that allows Encompass users to conduct electronic business transactions with investors and service providers. Service providers offer their services electronically to users of Ellie Mae Encompass, their integrated origination platform. To increase use of the Network, Ellie Mae built API's[22] to integrate with leading loan origination systems.

For Ellie Mae's users of the Encompass production system, orders and services delivery are made without having to leave their origination screens. Correspondent investors connect to Encompass Product and Pricing, receive secure tamper-proof data and documents directly from lenders via Ellie Mae Data & Document Delivery Services, and have loans checked against federal and state laws with Ellie Mae's Mavent Compliance Service. Title and appraisal companies invoke "Appraisal and Title Centers" from which to deliver final report and fees directly into originators' loan file. Encompass simulates a networked business model.

For Ellie Mae's users of the Encompass production system, orders and services delivery are made without having to leave their origination screens. Correspondent investors connect to Encompass Product and Pricing, receive secure tamper-proof data and documents directly from lenders via Ellie Mae Data & Document Delivery Services, and have loans checked against federal and state laws with Ellie Mae's Mavent Compliance Service. Title and appraisal companies invoke Appraisal and Title Centers 'from which to deliver final report and fees directly into originators' loan file. Encompass is a networked business model.

Mortgage originators pay for SaaS Encompass[23] either through recurring monthly subscription fees or through monthly fees, based on the number of licensed users and mortgages funded. The Company's additional services are paid on a subscription or transaction basis. Lenders and service providers participating in the Ellie Mae Network also pay fees, generally on a per-transaction basis, for transactions processed through the Ellie Mae Network from Encompass users.

---

22 The acronym API stands for "Application Programming Interface."
23 SaaS. Software as a Service. A form of computing services distributed through the "Cloud".

New Pricing Model

"Success-Based Pricing" models offer lenders a zero-cost per loan technology option when fees are passed to borrowers as part of lenders' origination, document preparation, and processing fees. In 2010, Ellie Mae instituted its revolutionary (to the industry) "Success-Based Pricing" structure. With Encompass360™ Mortgage Management Solution Banker Edition, firms no longer had to purchase the technology. Instead, customers were to pay a fee for each loan closed through Encompass360™. The success fee included the lender's origination, document preparation, and processing fees.

Because cash resources were scarce coming out of the "Great Recession," lenders welcomed a pricing scheme that required additional fees only if an agreed upon minimum level of closed loans was not met.

SaaS solutions such as that operated by Ellie Mae do bring cost-savings, operations efficiency, system scalability, and financial flexibility. It is the SaaS computing vendor that takes on the capital risks and the management of the underlying computing infrastructure – a big advantage to small and mid-sized lenders.

Early Mortgage Processing Cloud

Dorado Corporation, San Mateo, CA (acquired by CoreLogic on March 15, 2011) has been a pioneer in providing cloud computing applications for mortgage companies. In 1999, Dorado Corp. was the first mortgage technology vendor with a Cloud processing platform. That year, Dorado introduced its Loan Center Software as a Service (SaaS) origination product to mortgage bankers. Early on, Loan Center was more SaaS than Cloud (as Cloud it is now defined.) With SaaS, there is no software to distribute or install for lenders.

Knowing that mortgage lenders operated in highly cyclical and volatile markets, Dorado designed technology to give lenders the ability to operate flexibly. Dorado approached SaaS as a new paradigm to deliver both economic and operational benefits to lenders.

Dorado's platform was built according to e-commerce systems requirements. Dorado built around specific core characteristics:

- Openness
- Scalability
- Flexibility
- Integration
- Personalization
- Collaboration

Loan Center was built in collaboration with specialty service providers (i.e., compliance, credit, documents, fraud detection).

What is more, Dorado may be the first of mortgage technology vendors to build software using Service Oriented Architecture (SOA). Service Oriented Architecture is a business-centric IT architectural approach. SOA eases the integration of business functionality as a chain of linked and repeatable business tasks.

Dorado also innovated with embedded customer portals. What started as features for broker and correspondent lenders became important to the retail channel. To this day, Dorado considers self-service as the best way to deliver transparency and satisfaction to borrowers.

Other Forms of Cloud Computing

Platform as a Service (PaaS)
PaaS provides the infrastructure needed to develop and run applications over the Internet. Users can access custom applications built in the cloud, just as they do in their SaaS applications. The lender's IT departments and industry Independent Software Vendors (ISV) focus on innovation instead of complex infrastructure. By leveraging PaaS, organizations can redirect a significant portion of their budgets from "keeping the lights on" to creating applications that provide real business value.

PaaS is driving a new era of mass innovation and business agility. For the first time, developers can focus on application expertise for their business, not managing complex hardware and software infrastructure.

Infrastructure as a Service (IaaS)
IaaS is a cloud service for flexible and scalable computing. Generally, IaaS includes block storage and networking services. Through IaaS cloud and through a self-service portal, lenders are able to set up and manage computing and storage workloads on demand and as needed.

IaaS serves lenders as they move business-critical applications and other workloads into the cloud. Service is provided with a high level of security, high-availability, flexibility, and control. Using predefined deployment plans and scenarios, set-up is relatively easy.

One of the key aspects of IaaS is the provision of "block storage."[24] Depending on planned use, there are two types of storage that can attach to the IaaS server:

1. A standard speed option for customers who just need additional storage on their Cloud server
2. A high performance option for databases and high performance applications, leveraging solid state drives for speed

Both types are priced per gigabyte (GB) of storage, by input/output operations per second (IOPS), which can be difficult to predict or control. The key selling point of IaaS is that lenders only pay for what is used.

From this computing channel, capital expenditures and personnel costs go down and flexible levels of scale are obtained.

---

24 Block storage is networked storage that is attached to cloud servers.

Mobile Computing

Analytics, big data, cloud computing, mobile communications, and social networking are converging as the future business infrastructure. Cloud and mobile together and separately have become the foundation on which innovative technology is created.

Demand for connectedness and interactivity are driving adoption of mobile technologies. Mobile has become a life style for many, particularly the so-called millennial generation (born between 1982 and 2004). Dedication to mobile devices will endure at least until the year 2020.

Mobile devices run similar software applications to those found on traditional desktop computers. Mobile devices are capable of operating, executing, and providing services like desktops. Future applications are being developed specifically for use on a mobile "platform." The fast-changing world of technology and applications makes a case to have mobile applications to be device-agnostic (will work with various systems without requiring any special adaptations.) The best way to accomplish this is through the Cloud.

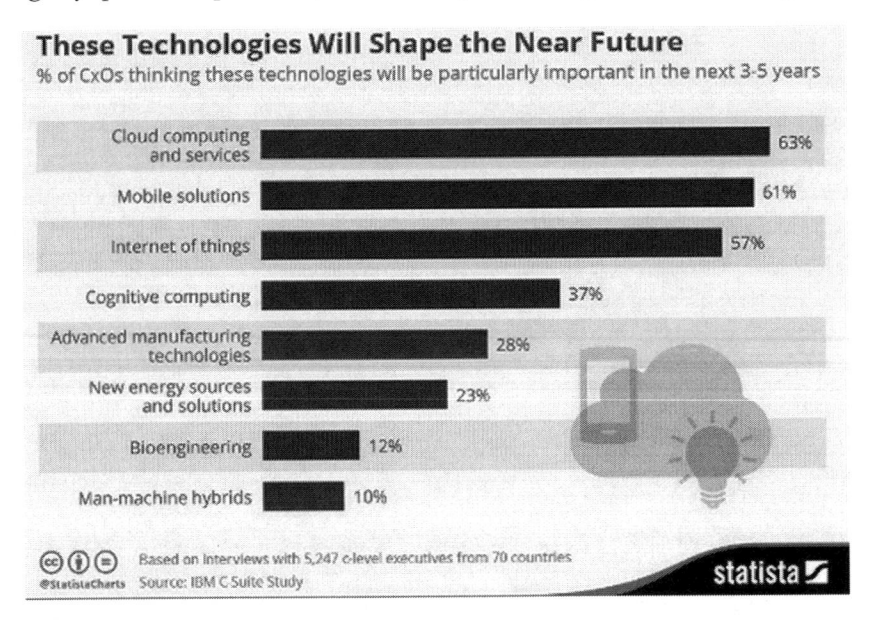

These Technologies Will Shape the Near Future
% of CxOs thinking these technologies will be particularly important in the next 3-5 years

Technology	%
Cloud computing and services	63%
Mobile solutions	61%
Internet of things	57%
Cognitive computing	37%
Advanced manufacturing technologies	28%
New energy sources and solutions	23%
Bioengineering	12%
Man-machine hybrids	10%

Based on interviews with 5,247 c-level executives from 70 countries
Source: IBM C Suite Study
statista

The 2015 IBM C Suite Survey of 5,247 executives from around the world point to Cloud computing and mobile solutions as having the most importance to their businesses over the next 3-5 years. Investing in mobile is a logical imperative to compete in the mortgage industry.

Wireless devices have become omnipresent when consumers shop (including shopping for a mortgage), make payments, and stay in touch through instant messaging (think customer service). Cloud and mobile have revolutionized communications. And, they are early in transforming commercial banking and mortgage banking.

These transformative uses of cloud and mobile devices also enable a flexible and mobile workforce. Employees are able to access systems through the cloud from wherever they are. There are virtually unlimited capabilities with the processing power of a mobile device. With a mobile workforce, lenders will devise new work strategies. Indeed, the design of mobile applications is a crucial product variable. Consumers and workers expect mobile applications to come with a rich and intuitive experience. Users expect an immersive and connected experience. They will compare mobile mortgage commerce applications to the entertaining and meaningful experience had with mobile applications used every day. The universality of mobile devices points to a time when lenders may be operating exclusively through mobile devices

Required: Rapid Mobile Development

Contemporary processing formats are real-time and most suitable for mobile customers and staff. Mobile cloud solutions are being built from the ground up with the most up-to-date operating requirements. Demand for mobile applications is so strong that lenders are having difficulty keeping up. The main focus of mobile app developers has become shorter development cycles. Developers also are expected to shorten the time between functional design and applications launch. Mobile development solutions are being offered to deliver continuous technical and functional enhancements.

Cloud technology is important to mobile app development. Proliferating devices and uses forces the integration and synchronization of mobile applications on multiple devices. Application developed for the cloud enables user on multiple devices to work with the same features, functions, and data. Device agnosticism is prerequisite to making users see value in applications. Lenders (or their vendors) are in the midst of building a platform for rapid application development and universal access for customers, employees, and business partners.

There is a constant flow of new mobile services. Financial applications such as Apple Pay and Google Wallet confirm the durability of the mobile communications and distribution channels. The most profound challenge in mobile commerce is ensuring security and privacy to users. The other challenge is embedding faster speeds and stable telecommunications connections. These features improve every day. The only rational conclusion is that migration to mobile-first is a sure bet for lenders.

Final words: The twentieth century billionaire industrialist, J. Paul Getty, was quoted as saying, "In times of rapid change, experience could be your worst enemy." Mortgage bankers are facing exactly the times described by Getty. An entirely new approach to the business of mortgage banking would be most appropriate.

ABOUT THE AUTHOR

Jeff Lebowitz is widely recognized as a thought leader in mortgage banking. He has spent a career integrating strategic business planning and technology impact analysis. For twenty years, Lebowitz managed scientific surveys of lenders' adoption and use of technology. His twenty-year time series on technology demand and technology supply remains unique in the history of mortgage industry research.

Mr. Lebowitz has been a pioneer in applying computing and networking technology to financial services. He managed a team that developed the first card-based authorization and transaction processing at the gasoline pump (1976 – 1978). He was the head of Strategic Planning for Fannie Mae; created multi-country local-currency retail banking strategies for Chase Manhattan Bank International; ran an integrated mortgage technology business; managed the technology development of the first residential whole loan trading market; developed the strategy for privatizing Fannie Mae; created a demand and sales model for Freddie Mac's automated valuation model, HVE; created the strategy for a national REO management service; built plan for multi-country mortgage insurance venture.

In 2003, Mr. Lebowitz was named to Mortgage Banking Magazine's Technology All-Stars, and in 2013 he received the Steve Fraser Visionary Award, a lifetime achievement award from Mortgage Technology magazine.

CHAPTER EIGHT

AUTOMATING TOWARD THE FUTURE
JONATHON CORR | PRESIDENT AND CEO
ELLIE MAE

As I write this in 2015, it's impossible to imagine doing business today without the Internet. It's almost like imagining no automobiles, no phones, and no electricity. Today the Internet is not just ingrained in the mortgage industry, but in all of our daily lives. I dare say it is as essential to the American way of life as running water and microwave ovens. But if we are being honest, 25 years ago, very few of us in the mortgage industry could have precisely predicted the revolutionary impact of the Internet on our lives. Of course, personal computers had already begun working their way into businesses and academia. But the idea of being able to watch a movie or our favorite television show on a three-inch mobile device while riding on the subway sounded pretty ridiculous in 1990.

In 2015, however, the pace of technology innovation continues to increase. A couple of years ago, The New York Times published an article on the how long it took various innovations to achieve market penetration, starting all the way back from electricity to the Internet. After the invention of the telephone, it took more than half a century before 50 percent of all U.S. households had one. Cell phones accomplished the same feat in five years.

At such a pace, it's both exciting and dizzying to try to figure out what's around the corner. Meanwhile, the mortgage industry is facing enormous changes of its own. Whether based on economic forces, competitive pressures, or regulatory mandates, today's lenders face a never-ending barrage of new challenges. For those of us in the business of creating technology, our mission is to help lenders keep up with the increasingly difficult nature of originating and selling mortgages. It's impossible to predict with absolute certainty what our industry will look like a quarter century from now. But given what has occurred over the previous 25 years, it is safe to assume that whatever comes, we'll need automation to deal with it.

UNLIMITED POTENTIAL: A RECENT HISTORY OF MORTGAGE AUTOMATION

I wish I could say that automation has a long and storied history in the mortgage industry, but that's not the case. Any lender or mortgage professional who has been in the business since 1990 knows it, too. In fact, before automated underwriting hit the mortgage industry, sophisticated technology was seldom applied to the business of creating and packaging loans.

A quarter century ago, underwriting depended largely on subjective and, many contend, selective human decision-making. Someone had to basically hand-assemble a loan file based on their own written standards or the intricate and extensive guidelines set forth by Fannie Mae and Freddie Mae or a private investor. While guidelines existed and technology was beginning to play a role and offer some assistance, on some level every loan was directly evaluated by a human underwriter. This was problematic on many fronts, but the most concerning to observers was that loan decisions were being made, and loans were being purchased from third-party originators, by individuals with extremely diverse backgrounds and inconsistent levels of experience. Given the variety of borrower information to be processed, it was practically impossible to find any sort of uniformity within such an environment. It is little wonder that allegations of bias and discrimination have swirled around the mortgage industry for so long.

On the other hand, introducing technology into the underwriting process — proponents argued — promised to create a more level playing field, where the data took precedence over subjective and irrelevant variables about a particular borrower. Automation could also be used to analyze many different data points and combinations of data at once, which human underwriters could never do. More important perhaps, automated underwriting held the potential of more accurately assessing risk. Computerizing the mortgage process created variables and data points through which loan performance then could be measured and tracked. When loans fell into default or foreclosure, forensic efforts could be made to see the common factors that led to trouble.

In the early 1990s, before the introduction of automation, stories about mortgage discrimination and redlining were rampant. In 1994, a Gallup Poll commissioned by the MBA showed that many minority consumers who were renting housing thought they would be discriminated against based on their race or ethnic background if they sought a mortgage.

While Freddie Mac's Loan Prospector is often credited as the first automated underwriting technology in the mortgage industry, it is not as though technology use in the mortgage industry began with this particular innovation. By the mid-90s, most lenders were already using computers and some type of loan origination software to create loan files by inputting, saving, and transferring data. Some of the early pioneers in loan-origination technology were even selling personal computer equipment to lenders along with their software installed on them. Meanwhile, several large financial institutions had begun developing their own automated underwriting models, which focused heavily on LTV ratios and less so on other factors, such as credit and debt. The greatest obstacle with these early innovations was that there was very little collaboration — the many parties to mortgage transactions were rarely willing or even able to "talk" to each other from an integration standpoint; neither the technology nor any comprehensive data standard or language existed back then. The major credit-reporting companies, which built their businesses through computerization of data, were faxing credit reports to lenders well into the 1990s. However, early loan-origination technologists created many excellent concepts and industry firsts, and their influence is still being felt today.

CHAPTER EIGHT: *AUTOMATING TOWARD THE FUTURE*

Loan Prospector, released in February 1995, set a new standard for automation in the mortgage industry. By applying the same standards of credit-worthiness to all borrowers, regardless of their background, Loan Prospector virtually eliminated bias in the mortgage decision process. The data was evaluated exactly the same, regardless of an applicant's demographic or ethnic background. Default risks could now be analyzed the same way, too. By at least one estimate, the overall savings generated by Loan Prospector was believed to be $400 per loan. In June of 1995, Fannie Mae followed suit with the release of Desktop Underwriter, giving lenders another tool to measure the risk of a loan and borrower as well as the amount of documents for verification purposes. While loan approvals still depended on the review of a human underwriter tasked with evaluating loans for quality and risk outside of the parameters of automated underwriting, Loan Prospector and Desktop Underwriter became incredibly effective tools for determining the viability of conventional loans and creating a path toward fulfillment. By the end of the decade, both solutions would prove their value as effective tools for increasing efficiency, speed, and cost savings in the loan process.

Beyond the obvious, there were other benefits to automated underwriting. Because Loan Prospector and Desktop Underwriter both enabled lenders to more accurately assess risk, borrowers with good credit were rewarded with lower rates. There was also evidence that more accuracy in the underwriting process prevented certain borrowers with less than stellar credit from being classified as subprime candidates, saving them from higher costs associated with these products and significantly reducing their monthly mortgage payments. On a grander scale, automated underwriting was used to qualify a significantly higher number of people for homeownership than would normally qualify, freeing many renters. There is also evidence that lending bias decreased significantly in the years since automated underwriting took hold. Of course, automated underwriting would later be criticized for contributing to the foreclosure crisis, as were the loosening underwriting guidelines and the neglect of automated underwriting findings. But none of this was the fault of the existing technology in and of itself.

While it turned out that automating the underwriting process did make creating, selling, and servicing mortgages more efficient, it unfortunately has not made the loan process any less complex, nor any less confusing to the average borrower. In spite of the enormous wealth of information available to consumers over the Internet, and thanks to a growing number of new rules and new mortgage products created over the past 25 years, the mortgage process remains a source of mystery and confusion to many consumers, to the point at which many would-be homeowners never even attempt to achieve the American dream. Yet thanks to the pioneering work of several key industry players, the vast majority of mortgage loans originated in the U.S. today are created through some level of automation. As automation continues to grow within the mortgage industry, there is hope that buying a home will actually become easier in spite of all the obstacles being placed in the way.

THE AUTOMATION GAP

After automated underwriting took hold in the mortgage industry, efforts grew to automate other facets of lending. At the same time, the Web emerged as a tool for communicating and sharing data, casting a huge spotlight on the possibility that the many parties engaged in home finance could exchange information and facilitate loan transactions online. This began with online mortgage applications and later spread to ordering third-party services and the sharing of mortgage products and rates.

Of course, this is what the mortgage industry has historically done — information capture. By the late 1990s, the mortgage industry had not yet figured out how to apply automation to assembling all the disparate pieces of data that went into every loan file. This was in spite of the fact that the Internet had proven to be a powerful and effective tool for lenders and borrowers. This was before the advent of Software-as-a-Service solutions and the realization that the Internet could be leveraged for cloud computing business solutions. Back then, most lenders were simply trying to get a decent internet connection.

That's not to say the Internet was useless in terms of pushing automation forward. Before the year 2000, there were at least two dozen companies and startups that were embracing automation to speed up the mortgage application and origination process. These early innovators included Microsoft's HomeAdvisor, E-LOAN, iOwn and others. Ellie Mae was founded during this time, in 1997, although our approach was quite different from these consumer-facing starts. This first wave of mortgage dot-coms had a ton of ambition and hype, and several achieved rapid and significant growth, at least initially; however, most fell to earth by the new millennium.

When I joined the mortgage business more than 13 years ago, I observed that it was an industry driven by data. I saw that it was lenders' responsibility to capture a tremendous amount of information and use it to figure out what a particular borrower could afford, and to find out which products best suited the customer. Data were used to determine what the most important factors were for each borrower, given the borrower's financial profile and whether the lender was working with a refinance or purchase scenario. Once the data were collected, they were sent off to other people and other service providers, who would leverage additional data to determine whether the original data were true or not.

They may have been highly efficient tools, but Desktop Underwriter and Loan Prospector did not significantly reduce the numbers of people lenders employed to review data and approve and underwrite mortgages. The first generation of automated underwriter users still relied heavily on people to collect and review documents and third-party services like credit reports, appraisals, and flood, title, and mortgage insurance. There still existed huge gaps in automation — which, although much improvement has been made, are present to this day. But this is mostly because a mortgage is like nothing else a consumer can buy. The industry's early dot-com experiments offered proof of this.

CHAPTER EIGHT: *AUTOMATING TOWARD THE FUTURE*

The founders of many of these startups came from outside the mortgage industry, and had yet to realize just how complicated mortgage transactions were, and where the true efficiencies could be found.

Whether aided by technology or not, originating just a single residential mortgage involves the cooperation of multiple parties who participate in a series of data-centric transactions over a period of weeks. There are timetables, deadlines, disclosures, and rules that everyone must follow. When all is said and done, the loan package will consist of one thousand or more pages and contain data from more than a dozen different sources. The vast majority of information in those 1,000-page loan files had to be ordered and collected from the many different sources by fax machine, couriers, or mail.

The early online mortgage companies were mostly involved in the exchange of data at the very front end of the process in the form of application data. This was data collection, not automation. True automation was almost impossible at the turn of the century because lenders were operating with so many disparate technologies, none of which were able to talk to one other, MISMO being still in its infancy and the industry's overall technology adoption rate relatively slow. Though aided by automated underwriting and loan origination systems, almost every lender's operations were laden with redundant and wasteful effort. Paper sill reigned supreme as well, creating a hazard of its own due to the increased likelihood of privacy breaches.

This wasted time and effort in the back-end of the mortgage action doesn't include the massive amounts of communication required to request and receive the tens and thousands of data points that make up the average 1,000-page loan file. From the time the first of dozens (if not hundreds) of contacts is made between borrower and lender, the lender is tasked with ordering a credit report, providing initial disclosures, selecting and locking the rate, discussing the available loans, prices, and terms with the borrower, communicating with processing, receiving and reviewing conditions, communicating those conditions to the borrower, requesting and verifying documentation, requesting settlement services, ordering appraisals, ordering flood, title and mortgage insurance, submitting the loan package to underwriters, requesting additional information and documents from the borrower, and scheduling the closing. And these are just the communication responsibilities of the loan officer.

When we launched in 1998, it was our founder Sig Anderman's goal to automate everything in the mortgage process that could be automated, including many of the processes and tasks I've just mentioned. While that goal has not changed, our concept of how we would achieve it has indeed evolved over the years.

By 2000, Ellie Mae did not yet have an origination platform. What we had was a B2B network—the ePASS Network, which connected mortgage professionals to mortgage lenders, investors, and service providers that were critical to the origination and funding of residential mortgages. While it had its limitations, the ePASS Network turned out to be ahead of its time. We would later rename ePASS to the Ellie Mae Network in March 2010.

In 2002, in order for a loan officer to process a loan, he or she had to go to separate service providers. The Ellie Mae Network was intended to provide the industry with its own network of third parties. However, this concept didn't take off with many third parties, and we struggled as a result, though not through any fault of the technology.

What we faced were two issues — first, the network itself was not integrated with any loan origination systems, which severely limited its ability to make transactions more efficient. The second issue was that we initially had neither data buyers on the network, nor third-party data suppliers, and you didn't need a business degree to figure out how that went. Yet we were undeterred in our belief that automation made sense. What we needed was a different approach.

Fortunately, we lucked into acquiring two legacy loan origination systems. Beyond solving the first obstacle to the success of the Ellie Mae Network, this gave us the ability start creating a network of buyers and suppliers, and drive transactions. By 2001, we were beginning to gain traction, when the so-called *"dot-com implosion"* happened.

A number of companies, including those previously mentioned, had successfully leveraged the Internet to automate the mortgage application process and generated significant consumer interest, thanks in part to heavy marketing and advertising and the promise — either expressly stated or implied — that borrowers could cut out the middleman and save money by getting a mortgage online. While the vast majority of mortgage dot-coms had proven effective at capturing data online, they were not actually bringing automation to the transaction itself. In fact, the view of many observers was that they added a step in the mortgage process that didn't need to exist. Eventually the adoption rate of these services fell below their burn rates, and almost all of them eventually disappeared.

After the dot-com meltdown, the industry's attention turned to productivity — in other words, producing loans more cost effectively through automation. Progress on this front began to move ahead at a reasonable rate, although adoption left much to be desired. We felt the industry was ready for a more complete origination solution when we launched a new kind of loan origination platform, Encompass, in late 2003.

Our goal with Encompass was to provide originators with a comprehensive operating system that could handle all the key business and management functions involved in running a mortgage business. Our original version of Encompass was designed to revolutionize the traditional loan-origination system, providing software and tools that could be customized to meet the various needs of loan officers, brokers, and lenders. I said back then that the traditional LOS didn't do what lenders wanted — it couldn't scale and it didn't let users collaborate. We created different interfaces for different users, and we included contact management, marketing, and pre-qualification tools.

Encompass also served as a gateway to the Ellie Mae Network, which electronically connected mortgage professionals to the lenders, investors, and service providers who were integral to the mortgage transaction. As a result, originators could use Encompass as a single tool for loan processing, marketing, customer communication, and to interact electronically with all parties to the transaction. Encompass would also serve as the platform from which lenders could access automation to achieve efficiency in other facets of the mortgage process. This included automated preparation of loan documents borrowers must sign to obtain a loan, automated updates to borrowers regarding the status of their loans, and automated product and pricing on loans to determine the appropriate products and rates for a given borrower. Eventually Encompass would include automated reviews of loan files to check for compliance with any federal, state, and local regulations.

While lenders had the automation to originate and underwrite loans, they needed more during the early 2000's. With a rapidly changing mortgage marketplace and a housing market beginning to take off, mortgage professionals found themselves looking for increased efficiencies and ways to be more agile. As lenders expanded and began utilizing remote offices, a need grew for access to the applications and databases to originate loans without having to continually reinvest in servers and IT staffs. In response, Ellie Mae created Encompass Anywhere, a hosted solution of Encompass. Eventually Encompass Anywhere and other SaaS-based applications would enable loan officers to access their loan pipelines, appraisal orders, and other data anywhere they had a computer and an Internet connection, with no hardwired installations required.

By the way, in mentioning Ellie Mae's solutions I don't mean to minimize the contributions of leading innovators in the mortgage technology arena or discount the many quality solutions on the market today, including those of our competitors. I mention our solution primarily because they reflect the challenges lenders faced at certain times in our industry's history, and how these challenges could be overcome or at least have their negative impacts reduced through automation. But regardless of how much innovation took place in the mortgage industry, trouble lurked on the horizon that threatened to crush everything for which we had worked so hard.

THE BUBBLE BURSTS

In 2006, the housing industry was pushing all-time highs in several categories, including homeownership, purchase volume, and housing prices. Sadly, it was also approaching all-time highs in subprime, no-doc loans. While technology helped lenders and borrowers achieve great things, it would not be able to stop the impending market collapse. Something was about to give — and the results would be worse not because of what lenders did with technology, but what they could have done.

In fact, I believe the factors that contributed to the housing crisis could have been mitigated during the mid-2000's if automation had been better utilized to ensure sound lending decisions. Obviously, loan quality was not the priority it is today. But technology could have been leveraged to order, process, and review loan documents comprehensively to see if they contained information that was inaccurate or simply didn't make sense. Other factors, including weak lending practices, households that were overleveraged with debt, and the incorrect pricing of risk, could have been caught with almost no effort. The tools were there, but they just were not leveraged.

Soon the housing market was awash in new homeowners with stated-income loans that were unverified, and essentially ticking time bombs due to their poor quality. Following the mortgage crisis, the chief underwriter for one of the nation's ten largest lenders testified in Congress that more than eighty percent of the mortgages it purchased in 2007 were not underwritten to policy, and therefore defective. Eighty percent!

It is now a matter of historical record that in 2007, lenders began foreclosure proceedings on approximately 1.3 million properties, and by September of 2009, 14.4% of all U.S. mortgages outstanding were either delinquent or in foreclosure. The mortgage industry was decimated — between 2007 and 2013, more than 1,000 mortgage-related entities closed down, according to MortgageDaily.com's Mortgage Graveyard. Among the 20 largest U.S. lenders in 2007, only five are left. The effects are still being felt today.

Even Fannie Mae and Freddie Mac, who were viewed as being strong on quality compared to the industry at large when it came to underwriting standards, was impacted. They were not doing anything like they are doing now, such as Fannie Mae's Early Check or Freddie Mac's Loan Quality Advisor, or Fannie Mae's Collateral Underwriter.

I wish I could say that as a provider of software solutions that we and our clients were immune to the effects of the housing crisis. This was not the case. While much of Ellie Mae's revenues are not directly tied to mortgage volume, the basic fact was that there were fewer customers to sell to. The lenders that managed to survive this nightmare received no medals of bravery from those who sought new rules to ensure it never happened again. Their reward for staying in business was the largest regulatory action the mortgage industry has ever faced.

RIGHTING THE SHIP

As the foreclosures continued to pile up, the mortgage industry faced a massive reaction, first from investors and then from regulators. In addition to the challenges involved in processing loans, mortgage originators would now have to satisfy a multitude of federal, state, and local regulations in addition to constantly changing investor guidelines.

Of all the major trends that are currently affecting the residential mortgage industry, compliance has to be at the top in terms of importance and severity. To protect borrowers and prevent a return to the conditions that caused the housing market's collapse, regulators have introduced and enacted a number of regulatory reforms designed to ensure meaningful disclosures to borrowers, increased transparency of settlement services, and greater accountability of lenders and mortgage originators in general. Lenders had a new federal regulatory agency to deal with, as well.

CHAPTER EIGHT: *AUTOMATING TOWARD THE FUTURE*

The greatest impact came from the Dodd-Frank Wall Street Reform and Consumer Protection Act, which created the Consumer Financial Protection Bureau and contained a number of new rules that would have great impact on mortgage lending operations. For example, Regulation Z of the Truth in Lending Act of 1968 was amended to require that creditors determine a consumer's ability to repay a mortgage before making a loan, and to establish minimum mortgage underwriting standards. It also created standards for complying with the new ATR requirement by creating a *"qualified mortgage."* Other regulations lenders had to contend with during the depths of the nation's foreclosure crisis included the Home Valuation Code of Conduct, RESPA 2010, and loan officer compensation rules.

These and other regulations caused great consternation among mortgage lenders for various reasons, but mostly because of the complicated nature of mortgage loan production and the limitations of their technology. It wasn't easy for mortgage lenders to reengineer processes, especially at a time when loan volumes were so low.

On their face, the regulatory reforms required of mortgage lenders had the effect of complicating the mortgage process and increasing the amount of documentation lenders needed in order to originate and fund residential mortgages. Yet if there was any benefit to this onslaught, it was that an appropriate mind shift was taking place within the industry. Where lenders had previously left quality behind, they were now being forced to attend to it. And another silver lining to these developments was the simple fact that with every new rule came an opportunity to leverage automation, either to make the regulatory burdens disappear or, if not, easier to bear.

For example, one of the first compliance challenges after the mortgage meltdown began, the Home Valuation Code of Conduct, went into effect in 2009 and required mortgage professionals to change how they do business with appraisers. In an effort to reduce the risks associated with the appraisal process, the new rules established by Fannie Mae, Freddie Mac, and the Federal Housing Finance Agency (formerly OFHEO), set forth a series of guidelines that govern appraisal-related activity among mortgage companies for loans that are sold to the GSEs. If loans didn't measure up, Fannie and Freddie wouldn't accept them and lenders could face penalties, while brokers would be unable to submit applications to their wholesale partners. The focus was on ensuring objectivity in ordering real estate appraisals by brokers and correspondent lenders.

HVCC created a lot of concern — but it also spurred the industry to innovate. Soon, lenders began leveraging technology to facilitate HVCC-compliant ordering and delivery of appraisals from their AMCs. Additional tools were developed to help lenders gain control over which staff members could electronically order appraisals, create rules based on certain property and loan types, and create and manage their own appraisal panels. Through these solutions, lenders could order HVCC-compliant appraisals through a "blind" methodology, ensuring that no bias was involved with the process. From the perspective of AMCs, such technologies provided opportunities to get exposure to the lenders that needed their services. By providing mortgage professionals with the technology to quickly obtain HVCC-ready appraisals quickly and easily, thus alleviating the burden of compliance, they could spend greater energy doing what they are supposed to do — sell loans.

From an origination standpoint, changes in the disclosure process were the first shoe to drop following the mortgage crisis, sparking an amazing adoption rate of automation for compliance purposes. The 2010 changes to the Real Estate Settlement and Procedures Act (RESPA) created new compliance obstacles for lenders and brokers, who now had to meet certain accuracy tolerances for fees disclosed to borrowers on the GFEs and HUD-1s. Prior to these changes taking place, technology had been developed that allowed lenders to go to their loan-origination platform, select the service providers from whom they wanted to receive quotes, and obtain disclosures that contained automatically populated, accurate, real-time fees for local, state, and national closing services, all within seconds.

These innovations were made possible because technologists understood that lenders' number one concern was no longer originating as many loans as possible, but staying compliant — and controlling the costs of staying compliant — with so many new and changing regulations. For perhaps the first time, lenders began to choose technologies based on their focus on quality and compliance. For smart technology vendors, integrating new compliance features such as automated disclosures and HVCC-compliant appraisal ordering were not groundbreaking innovations on their own. Yet, among the first wave of loan-origination systems that came to market, relatively few bothered to continue investing in innovation. Most had built their software and continued to sell the same product, year after year. Perhaps it would be updated as each new computer operating system came out.

More advances arrived following the creation of the CFPB and the agency's 2014 loan compensation rules — a particularly tricky regulation that left lenders scrambling for help. Once again, technology enabled lenders to establish, manage, track, and report multiple compensation programs for brokers and loan officers, automatically applying the correct plan based on the third-party originators and other factors. Besides eliminating errors that can occur by someone's attempting to calculate the proper compensation by hand, lenders were also able to automate the creation of GFEs with the correct fees, as well as to create financial history logs in case of an audit.

Meanwhile, a number of third party processes that were not typically fulfilled electronically have benefitted from automation in recent years. For example, due to tighter underwriting guidelines and new ability-to-repay rules, more lenders began verifying their borrowers' income by ordering tax transcripts directly from the IRS. Until recently, however, the IRS would not accept electronic signatures on 4506-T IRS forms. But almost as soon as that changed, some loan originators were able send and collect signed 4506-T forms electronically from their borrowers, send them to the IRS electronically, and import the records and data directly into the loan file, all without leaving their loan origination platform.

When the CFPB's Qualified Mortgage (QM) rule came out in 2013, once again, forward-thinking lenders were ready, utilizing new tools to automatically assess QM eligibility on every loan and documenting QM compliance in the case of a request or audit. These tools continue to be used to run key ATR and QM calculations, including DTI ratios and points and fees. Loan APRs were automatically tested for safe harbor status while loan terms and features were assessed for risk. Technology also enabled lenders to verify and document a borrower's employment, income, assets and obligations—again from with a lender's mortgage origination platform. While it is true that most loans being originated when the QM rule took effect were already in compliance, lenders now had the means of demonstrating QM eligibility on any loan, with practically zero effort.

While I've been sharing a lot about regulations, advancements in mortgage automation have also helped lenders breathe easier when it comes to meeting the ever changing guidelines of their investment partners. Today, lenders have access to tools that allow them to track day-to-day changes in investor guidelines and build loans from within the loan origination platform to the exact guidelines of any entity, whether private investor or Fannie Mae and Freddie Mac. They can also check the loan file against those guidelines at any time, all the way up to the closing table. And if they don't know what loans a borrower may qualify for, all they have to do is enter the borrower's characteristics and the answers will appear—and if borrower doesn't fit a particular loan program today but will when tomorrow rolls around, the lender will know.

These advancements are all the more fascinating considering that 15 years ago, the idea of automated compliance didn't even exist. Yet driven by the fear of buybacks and fines, coupled with their basic survival instincts in a rough lending climate, lenders over the past five years embraced automation like never before, and in return it proved to be a major accelerator to their businesses. Regulators began pushing lenders to do things electronically, perhaps with the intrinsic knowledge that, when properly applied, technology can keep everyone safe. Yet in spite of all that automation has proven to accomplish in a regulatory-heavy environment, there are some industry players that fail to accept this new reality.

"HUMAN SPACKLE SYNDROME"

As the mortgage industry continued to build new technologies to keep pace with new compliance requirements, something interesting began happen. Every year, there were more new rules and regulations took place affecting lenders—not just from the CFPB, but from other federal and state agencies, even city and county ordinances involving how properties were to be maintained and conveyed. In the wake of the housing crisis, lenders first had to contend with a soaring number of buybacks and repurchase requests from investors and the GSEs. Now they had one rule after another to worry about. Meanwhile, fewer Americans were getting mortgages, many of them too jittery after watching the housing market go up in flames, others unable to quality due to stricter lending requirements. Mortgage origination volume plummeted. The lenders that had survived the crash were making hardly anything, so they had no money to waste. In the midst of all this, some lenders developed a level of concern about fines and audits that approached paranoia.

They were right to worry. In the CFPB's short history, the agency has demonstrated little patience for lenders that choose not to play by the rules. Over a recent one-year period, the agency has tagged and fined numerous mortgage lenders and servicers for redlining, failing to honor loan modifications, running deceptive ads, violating loan officer compensation rules, conducting discriminatory mortgage pricing, and steering borrowers into costlier mortgages that they didn't need. In one particular case involving a lender accused of illegally referring borrowers to mortgage insurers in exchange for kickbacks, the lender filed an appeal after a judge ordered it to pay $6.4 million in damages. The CFPB raised the lender's fine to $109 million.

Driven by such concerns, many lenders got very, very careful about the underwriting process and began to scrutinize every detail in a loan file. Yet rather than utilize the technologies that were already available to track, review, and red-flag incomplete or missing data, saving time and money, they went on a massive hiring spree. More inexplicably, some lenders actually invested in technology, yet did the same thing — they hired more people.

This was great news for all the mortgage professionals who lost their jobs in the housing crash. However, it did little for lenders when it came to their bottom lines. According to the Mortgage Bankers Association, pre-loan costs doubled between the years 2009 to 2015, rising from roughly $3,500 to $7,000. Again, the goal may have been respectable — lenders needed to serve the needs of investors or regulators, or else their businesses would face heavy losses and penalties. It also needs to be pointed out that, even when lenders leverage automation to maintain compliance, there is still value in having human expertise overseeing the process. But is there any proof that automation can actually lower a lender's compliance costs?

I had suspected that lenders would save money when they applied automation to the task of scanning loan documents for errors and incomplete or inconsistent data, just as they save money by using Desktop Underwriter or any other automated process. I wasn't sure we could put a dollar amount on it, however. With many forms of technology, analyzing the exact ROI can be difficult, but particularly difficult given the inherent complexities of the mortgage business and its dozens of moving pieces. So many factors were bound to come into play, including the differences between how one lender does business compared to another.

Ultimately, we felt that identifying the value behind automation in dollars and cents would help make the case for its adoption, which would be good for the entire industry. So we asked MarketWise Advisors LLC, a leading mortgage consulting firm based in Florida, to measure the potential ROI generated by Encompass, our all-in-one mortgage management solution. MarketWise chose to look at the activities of five different lenders, each of which used Ellie Mae's solutions in different ways. The five lenders had 2014 origination volumes that ranged between $269 million and $1.32 billion, and the number of Encompass users at each one varied from 61 users to 410. The questions were simple: Did an all-in-one solution reduce origination costs? Did it improve profits? And did it help lenders raise the quality of their loans?

MarketWise conducted extensive surveys with each lender and learned how they used Encompass. Because it is not a single system, but a suite of solutions under one platform, understanding our clients' usage was important to the study. However, a common thread among all five lenders was that each used Encompass Compliance Service. This is a service inside Encompass that runs automated compliance checks on every loan in a lender's system.

In the end, MarketWise found that the five lenders saw an average savings of $970.14 per loan, including an average savings of $446.64 in origination costs. Put another way, the lenders in the study were achieving a total average savings that was 14 percent less expensive than the current average cost to produce a loan. To be clear, this was not a full-scale study of the entire mortgage industry's use of automation, only one provider and five lenders. But at least we were able to confirm that automation saves money.

In spite of such evidence, many lenders are continuing to pile on loan processes and underwriters, believing that this is the key to avoiding hefty fines and jail time. The reality is that they are actually increasing these risks by clinging to manual processes, which amplify the likelihood that mistakes will be made. In fact, in some ways, the mortgage industry went from a world in which electronic, paperless mortgages seemed like a viable, near-future reality 15 years ago, to one that is now filled with what I call *"human spackle."*

Calling human beings *"spackle"* may sound harsh, but that is the basic function they serve. Spackle doesn't fix anything; it's used for patching holes. Adding bodies is simply adding manual processes, and when you have more manual processes, you invariably have more mistakes.

Once again, I don't believe technology holds all the answers. In fact, Ellie Mae is not only a technology provider. We also provide consulting services through AllRegs to mortgage lenders, and have made it a goal to build the best and brightest team of mortgage compliance experts in the industry. In a post-Dodd-Frank era, we wanted our clients to have access to the education and resources they need to conduct business safely. But not every mortgage lender can build a top-notch compliance team, so they add warm bodies. As a result, there are more underwriters working on loan files today, more processors, more back office staff and more "double-checkers" in our industry than ever.

But the worse thing about human spackle is that it's not helping lenders with the biggest regulatory challenge to hit the industry in many years.

CLIMBING MT. RESPA-TILA

Over the past 20 years since Fannie Mae and Freddie Mac brought the mortgage industry into the world of automation, the business of selling loans has come to resemble an automobile assembly line. Every year, based on what new regulation or market need lenders are trying to address, tweaks are made in the production cycle. Year after year, as the assembly line grew more complex, lenders added automation wherever possible to build loans with greater speed and efficiency. But in this mad dash to streamline the mortgage process, quality got left by the roadside, leading to disastrous events.

Today, however, automation is helping lenders build loans of greater quality than ever. Yet of all the new rules that automation has been able to tackle, the latest one poses the greatest challenge, simply because lenders cannot totally automate their way around it.

The TILA-RESPA Integrated Disclosure rule (TRID) or RESPA-TILA, as we call it, easily dwarfs in scope the RESPA 2010 changes and any other regulation of the past two decades. It has affected the mortgage operations of every lender far beyond the primary goal of introducing new Loan Estimate and Closing Statement disclosures; it has forced lenders to review and make changes to their compliance testing, reporting requirements, staff training, third party relationships, and much more.

Shortly after TRID took effect on October 3, 2015, it became clear that a number of technology vendors had neither the expertise nor bandwidth to help their clients comply with the new disclosure rule. They failed to coordinate and collaborate with their clients and other industry experts to put the necessary changes in place, and as a result, their clients — who are ultimately responsible for complying — have struggled. I understand that some vendors are still trying to figure out how to comply with TRID while also helping their clients comply with other regulations. Apparently they are experiencing conflicts because they haven't spent the time or the resources to properly research the issue.

While it remains to be seen what the broad industry impacts will be, more than a month after TRID took effect, about three-quarters of mortgage lenders seemed to be moving ahead smoothly while the rest remained unsure whether they were in compliance or not. I am relatively certain there are still companies out there scrambling and trying to figure things out. For example, many lenders are unclear about the fact that the creditor is the entity in control over the Closing Statement. The creditors, of course, are the ones who are fully liable for everything on the disclosures. Some lenders are waking up to the hard lesson that not only could their vendors not provide them with proper training or advice, they weren't ready themselves.

As a whole, the mortgage industry spent an incredible amount of time and effort getting ready for TRID, and yet it was still not completely ready. Most lenders do their best to comply with new regulations and make adjustments along the way. However, in this case, lenders had more than a year and a half to prepare — including a two-month extension. The team at Ellie Mae spent about 18 months developing the software, creating the workflows and business rules, and coordinating with our clients to prepare for RESPA-TILA. That's not all we did, either. Because we see ourselves as our customers' business partners, we spent days, weeks, and sometimes months providing our clients with education and training on the rules. We even took our training on the road, hosting regional events around the country.

Automation alone cannot solve lenders' compliance hurdles; this much has become clear. But it's my belief that lenders can no longer handle compliance without it. Regulations like TRID, for example, are too complex to handle manually, and are impossible to adhere to without some type of automation guiding the way. Every new regulation is a little like this — adding some new wrinkle to the mortgage production process, or disrupting a company's current procedures. In these cases, automation has proven to be the safest, most practical, and certainly most efficient method for adjusting to these changes.

ACCELERATING INTO THE FUTURE

We talked about the savings that lenders can achieve by applying automation to solve their compliance challenges. But there is another, overarching benefit looming on the horizon.

RESPA-TILA and every other regulatory requirement that has come before or will come after are not only driving up costs and increasing the demand for automation. They are leading lenders to embrace paperless technology and electronic signatures like never before. For this reason, I believe our industry is today closer than ever to producing fully electronic, compliant mortgages, the benefits of which are innumerable. Consider all the communications that occur between real estate agents, borrowers, loan officers, underwriters, processors, title companies, third-party service providers, and the secondary market on every transaction, along with the considerable (and growing) volume of data that goes along with it — bank statements, property details, insurance, appraisals, disclosures, credit reports, W2s, tax transcripts, and on and on. Lenders are bombarded with so much data that it can take a week for someone to sift through by hand. However, a fully electronic transaction has the potential to boil down every mortgage decision that does not include some human element to a matter of seconds, simply by using the technologies and tools that are currently available today.

As every new wave of lenders utilizes automation to deal with a new regulation like TRID, they are creating more converts to this paperless way of thinking. One of our newer clients, AJ Franchi, CIO of Gold Star Finance, a multi-state mortgage lender, said his company until recently kept all of its files on paper. But since switching to automated e-disclosures to manage TRID compliance, he isn't looking back. *"It took a lot of the onus off us to maintain some of the state disclosures, and it also gives us the peace of mind of knowing that the disclosures go out on every loan,"* Franchi told us. *"In this market, where volumes have come down a little bit, the cost to do a loan has only gone up. The more you can automate, the better your service offering is to your client, the better price you can offer, and the more efficiently you can run."*

Jeff Douglass, CEO of Wyndham Capital Mortgage, was already on board with paperless loans before he began utilizing our services to automate compliance. He estimates his company has saved *"hundreds of thousands of dollars,"* telling us, *"We are in the direct-to-consumer channel and we derive most of our business from the Internet, which is a lower margin channel, so we have to focus on the technology piece and getting a loan through as quickly as possibly,"* he said. *"We're a paperless environment, and all the work flows through the compliance milestones, so there is no duplication of entry anywhere through the process."*

TRID isn't the first massive regulatory change that the mortgage industry has faced, and I'm sure it won't be the last. In fact, as I write this, the CFPB has just rolled out 800 pages of new rules updating the Home Mortgage Disclosure Act (HMDA). This is not going to affect lenders nearly as much as RESPA-TILA, but it will still create a great deal of work. This time, the CFPB is giving the industry more time to prepare — perhaps the agency saw that it took longer for the industry to handle RESPA-TILA than anyone expected. But as soon as lenders have finished getting through RESPA-TILA, they will have another hill to climb. It never really ends.

While some lenders don't yet *"get it"* — the ones that are still using human spackle, for instance — I think that the state of automation in the mortgage industry has jumped tenfold in the years since the housing crisis, and we have all these new regulations to thank for it. Each new rule facing lenders since the housing crisis was a perfect target for automation. At the same time, quality is now in the spotlight, where it belongs, and where it will be forced to stay.

The near future bodes extremely well for continued innovation. At Ellie Mae, we're very aware of what's happening in the market at any point in time. In fact, we apply automation ourselves to create a monthly Origination Insight Report that takes a large sample of our clients' loan volume and provides a fairly intricate snapshot of mortgage rates, credit scores, LTV ratios, and other data. I prefer not to make predictions, but it's my sincere hope that we are entering a healthier housing market that is structured more normally in terms of purchase and refi volume. The long-term picture taking shape before us is pretty favorable. The economy is fairly strong, there is significant pent-up demand for first-time homeownership, and mortgage rates should remain attractive for some time, even if they rise a little.

I also believe that lenders which want to succeed in this future will need to broaden the areas in which they use automation. Based on what consumers want today, lenders will need cloud-based, mobile-friendly, and customer-facing solutions that help them connect and engage borrowers with greater speed and effectiveness. Lenders that can't keep up aren't going to last.

Already, we're seeing smaller mortgage companies that cannot compete, cannot stay compliant, or cannot bring down costs being bought up by larger fish, and these are typically the companies that are not using automation to save money, so their problems are now getting worse with TRID on the books and no effective strategy for dealing with it. I believe quite a lot of lenders are in this predicament that we don't know about, but eventually things will get flushed out.

I don't believe automation is going to push the human element out of the loan quality equation, or even reduce their numbers. Mortgage lending at the level and intricacy at which it is done today still involves human expertise, especially at the borrower level. A mortgage is such a big and important transaction — it's not like buying and selling stocks. Someone needs to engage with consumers and help them understand the process. Consumers will likely need help finding the right loan product, and loan officers are in the best position to help push the transaction along, coordinate with real estate agencies, and explain things, like the need to do a reappraisal, or to offer guidance on what language can be allowed on a contract.

However, I can see loan processors, for example, being squeezed by automation. We're approaching a world in which lenders can pull all the information they need to originate a loan automatically, such as bank account and income data, and validate it against other data that's in the file. This is essentially what a lot of processors do today. I think the bigger issue is what will happen to the industry landscape, because it will change.

I believe cloud-based computing and SaaS-based solutions continue to gain popularity, but these issues will open up new challenges as well. For example, one of the biggest issues facing lenders today is data security. We've seen an increasing number of high-profile data breaches of U.S. banks, and mortgage lenders are natural targets since they collect and maintain huge amounts of consumer information. Every lender will need access to security experts and learn to develop best practices, because security is an issue that everyone is going to face.

In spite of the industry's recent accomplishments, Ellie Mae's goal to automate everything that can be automated in the mortgage transaction may seem like quite a leap. But I do believe that everything in the mortgage process is going to be automated, and that we will see a growing share of digital mortgages sooner rather than later. The industry is still facing friction on the back end of the transaction — recording is still done largely the same way it was done over 100 years ago, for example. But as far as the consumer is concerned, I think we will see a fully electronic transaction from the front end of the process all the way through closing. And basically, it will happen by necessity.

Over the past several years, on top of every regulatory hurdle thrown at them, lenders saw their gross production costs double. A considerable amount of this additional cost is directly attributable to the *"human spackle"* element. With TRID now in effect, I believe we're going to see those numbers rise in the near term. The only hope for reversing this trend permanently while at the same time improving the borrower experience and producing compliant, high quality loans, is for lenders to make a fundamental change and embrace automation. I believe they can do it, too. And they are about to get a lot of help.

The next wave of first-time homebuyers is coming, and the majority of them are younger consumers who will prefer an electronic experience. Maybe they won't buy homes this year, or even next year in significant volume, but they are coming. Given what we know about how they engage the providers of goods and services, and what their behaviors are, it's safe to say that the vast majority of first-time homebuyers have a data-centric perspective and will want to shop for mortgages online to get the best deal. Lenders that want to capture the next wave of home buyers would be wise to transition along with them, and market themselves as providers of quality, compliant mortgage loans, lenders that know how to operate efficiently and cost-effectively.

And considering what we know about the pace of innovation — consider again the contrasts in telephone and smart phone adoption — I believe that in five years, there is a very good chance mortgages will routinely be done electronically. Does that mean all mortgages? No. But we have gone past a certain point, and I think the momentum now is only going to speed up. Over the next two years, barring some type of market disruption, Millennial home buyers will begin to wield their influence on technology adoption. And the better the economy does, the more likely we will see Millennials buying homes — and pushing automation to its most exciting milestone yet.

ABOUT THE AUTHOR

Jonathan H. Corr, President & CEO of Ellie Mae, has served as the Company's chief executive officer since February 2015 and president since February 2013. Mr. Corr has also served as a member of Ellie Mae's Board of Directors since February 2015. Previously, Mr. Corr served as the Company's chief operating officer from November 2011 to February 2015, executive vice president and chief strategy officer from November 2009 to November 2011, as chief strategy officer from August 2005 to November 2009 and as the Company's senior vice president of product management from October 2002 to August 2005.

Prior to joining the Company, Mr. Corr held executive and management positions at PeopleSoft, Inc., KANA, BroadBase Software, and Netscape Communications. Mr. Corr holds a Bachelor of Science degree in Engineering from Columbia University and a Master of Business Administration degree from Stanford University.

CHAPTER NINE

eCLOSINGS AND eMORTGAGES
HARRY GARDNER | VICE PRESIDENT, ESTRATEGIES
ELLIE MAE

Today's broad use of the internet and online technologies has helped to drive many aspects of our daily lives toward electronic signatures and paperless processes. But the mortgage industry has been slow to shed itself of the traditional paper-based closing process, despite the potential benefits and cost savings of eMortgages. From 2001 – 2009, I worked at the Mortgage Bankers Association and was directly involved in the growth of MISMO® and the development of industry standards and guidance around eMortgages. In that role I was fortunate to have met, worked with, and call friends many smart, talented volunteers from across the industry. This chapter describes the foundational aspects of eClosings and eMortgages, then delves into some important related issues like industry standards, the value proposition, and security, and finally looks at the state of industry adoption, today and looking toward the future.

FOUNDATIONS: THE COMPONENTS OF AN ECLOSING

What exactly is an eMortgage, and how does it differ from eClosing? An eClosing is fairly self-explanatory: A mortgage closing where at least some, and preferably all, of the closing documents are presented, reviewed, and signed in electronic format rather than on paper. Industry participants have varying views on what defines an eMortgage, however. From the investor point of view, Fannie Mae and Freddie Mac define an eMortgage as a mortgage loan where, at a minimum, the promissory note is electronic, because that is the one critical document for investor loan purchase. I tend to think of the term eMortgage more broadly, as a loan where the majority of the documents (including disclosures) are created and signed electronically.

The holy grail of eMortgages will be reached when we have widespread adoption of mortgage loans where all of the disclosures and closing documents are created and signed entirely in electronic format — truly paperless, compared to today's implementations that only achieve *"less paper."*

LEGAL FRAMEWORK

ESIGN and UETA form the broad legal framework for all eSignature processes today. UETA (the Uniform Electronic Transaction Act) was released by the National Conference of Commissioners on Uniform State Laws (NCCUSL) in 1999, and is a model law for states to adopt as they see fit. In the following year, seeing slow initial adoption of UETA by states, the Clinton administration passed ESIGN, the Electronic Signatures in Global and National Commerce Act, in order to spur adoption and use of eSignatures by providing a legal safety net. In states that had not yet passed a version of UETA, ESIGN would take effect, thus making eSignatures valid in all 50 states and ensuring that they could be used in interstate commerce.

Both laws essentially state that electronic signatures are legally valid, if they are performed with the proper processes and disclosures. The first section of ESIGN states that a contract or signature "may not be denied legal effect, validity, or enforceability solely because it is in electronic form." The next section makes it clear that an individual has the right to not use electronic signatures if he or she doesn't want to, for any reason. Finally, the section after that spells out the requirement for the consumer to *"consent electronically, in a manner that reasonably demonstrates that the consumer can access information in the electronic form that will be used to provide the information that is the subject of the consent."*

ESIGN also says that if a business is required to retain a record of a transaction, it can retain those records in electronic format as long as they are accessible to those entitled to access them, and can be *"accurately reproduced for later reference, whether by transmission, printing or otherwise."*

In summary, a borrower must consent to the use of eSignatures, and can opt out for any reason and at any point in the process. The system that captures their consent must do so by using the same technology that the actual signing ceremony will use, in order to demonstrate the consumer's ability to access that technology (say, a web browser or PDF viewer). And the lender or investor can retain the electronic documents in their electronic form, as long as they can be accessed later, if needed.

On June 30, 2010, ten years after ESIGN was passed, Congress passed a resolution recognizing June 30 as *"National ESIGN Day."*

INDUSTRY STANDARDS

MISMO, the Mortgage Industry Standards Maintenance Organization, was formed by the MBA in 1999 after a group of mortgage technology firms had come together under the name *"XML Mortgage Partners"* and demonstrated the need for broader mortgage industry data standards. MISMO did not specify technology platforms or processes, but published XML (eXtensible Markup Language) data transaction templates that allowed business partners to communicate information between each other in a standardized format, greatly reducing the effort and time required to develop each new data interface.

In 2001, MISMO expanded beyond process-area workgroups like Origination, Tax, Title, Flood, and Property Valuation to form the eMortgage Workgroup, which was chartered to develop standards and guidelines for the nascent concept of an electronic mortgage. From 2001-2005 or so, the eMortgage Workgroup operated almost as a parallel group equal in size to all of MISMO, holding its own separate interim meetings between the MISMO Trimester meetings of January, May, and September. There was so much interest and work to be developed that the eMortgage Workgroup spawned a number of individual subgroups to focus on specific aspects of eMortgages like the SMART Doc® electronic document specification.

On the property recording side of the industry, also in the late 1990s, two national groups of county recorders came together to form the first industry-wide task force to develop common standards and guidelines for the property-recording world. The National Association of County Recorders, Election Officials & Clerks (NACRC) and the International Association of Clerks, Recorders, Election Officials & Treasurers (IACREOT), joined forces to create PRIJTF, the Property Records Industry Joint Task Force. Some of the participants in PRIJTF also attended the early MISMO meetings, and as the work of PRIJTF continued to expand, they came together to form PRIA, the Property Records Industry Association, with a structure and development model patterned after MISMO. PRIA publishes XML data standards for eRecording and eNotarization.

ESIGNATURES

Electronic signatures can take a variety of forms. ESIGN and UETA are technologically neutral — they don't prescribe any specific form of eSignatures. Both allow for broad acceptance of *"an electronic sound, symbol or process, attached to or logically associated with a contract or other record and executed or adopted by a person with the intent to sign the record"* as an eSignature, as long as other requirements are met. Limits of acceptance may be set by investor purchase policy — Fannie Mae does not accept electronic signatures using sound, for example.

The most common forms of eSignatures are click-sign (clicking on an icon or button, like the *"I Agree"* button often used to sign the end-user license agreement when installing software), and signature pads that capture an image of the borrower's signature and apply that to the document. Those signature images are sometimes called holographic signatures, although they don't actually use laser holographic technology. There is also a more complex form of signature pad that captures thousands of real-time data points on pen pressure and velocity as the borrower signs, rather than just a simple image of the signature. This is called a biometric signature, and is thought to add an additional layer of protection against forgery, since pen pressure and velocity are very difficult to duplicate, even if a forger can create an accurate rendition of someone's signature.

Today's eMortgage implementations use either click-sign, signing pads, or signature images captured on a tablet computer with a stylus pen. Some efforts have been made to move toward digital signatures for borrowers, but have not been successful due to the added cost and complexity. Lawyers might say that click-sign is the weakest form of eSignature and might recommend that a stronger signature technology be used for the most critical mortgage documents, like the Note and the Security Instrument, but to date no mortgage loans have been deemed invalid or not legal just because they used a click-sign solution.

The differences between electronic signatures and digital signatures are widely misunderstood, and often the term *"digital signature"* is used incorrectly. A digital signature is the most complex or advanced form of eSignature. While a digital signature is a form of eSignature, an eSignature (click-sign, signing pad, etc) is typically NOT a digital signature. Digital signatures are often applied by systems, for things like the tamper-evident seal (described below), rather than being used by individuals for applying a legal signature to a document. Some technology providers may have contributed to this confusion by making claims for a *"digital mortgage"* when in fact they use electronic signatures in their solution, like everyone else.

EDOCUMENTS

Electronic documents can be implemented in a variety of ways using mainstream file formats like Microsoft Word and Adobe PDF, but PDF is by far the most commonly used in the mortgage industry. Software tools are readily available, and the PDF format itself is now an open ISO (International Organization for Standardization, www.iso.org) standard rather than a proprietary format controlled by Adobe. In addition, the PDF/A (PDF *"Archive"*) specification defines an electronic document structure designed to be reproducible for many years into the future, regardless of changes in operating systems and computer hardware.

The MISMO® SMART Doc® specification developed out of an early technical framework that originated within Fannie Mae. Designed specifically for the eNote, its structure contains a document VIEW section (what the borrower sees and signs), a DATA section containing XML data for system validation, and a system for linking each item of data in the VIEW to a corresponding XML data point in the DATA section.

The SMART Doc Version 1.02 specification is the version currently accepted by Fannie Mae and Freddie Mac for eNote delivery. Its functionality is somewhat inflexible (in terms of being able to add data elements required for documents other than the eNote), and it is a technical specification separate and distinct from the early MISMO XML standards themselves.

In the MISMO 3.x Reference Model, the Document structure is an inherent part of the overall standard, and provides far more flexibility and capability than Version 1.02. The term *"SMART Doc Version 3"* is used to refer to this Document structure in Version 3.x — it has the potential to be an industry-wide standard for all electronic mortgage documents, which would provide a level of eDocument standardization and interoperability that does not currently exist.

CHAPTER NINE: eCLOSINGS AND eMORTGAGES

TAMPER-EVIDENT SEAL

As the vision for broad industry adoption of eMortgage technology grew, it became evident that the eClosing documents would need to be transferred between various systems as loans were originated and then sold to investors, or as servicing rights were subsequently transferred. Within MISMO we developed the concept of the Tamper-Evident Seal, to ensure that document integrity could be re-validated at any point downstream, especially for investors like Fannie Mae and Freddie Mac, who wanted a way to ensure that an eNote had not been altered since it was signed.

A tamper-evident seal is the slang name for a hash value calculated on a single electronic document. The hash value is a long number that results from running a specific hashing algorithm on that eDocument. I like to describe it as a *"digital thumbprint"* because it's easy to visualize that way — a complex number that is unique to that document. Because of the way hashing algorithms work, even a tiny change to the document will result in a completely different hash value.

Once the hash value is calculated, it is encrypted and stored within the eDocument. The encryption is important because, if it were not encrypted, anyone could edit the document, re-run the hash function, and then replace the original hash value with the new hash value to cover their tracks.

This is where PKI comes in: PKI is an asymmetric encryption system, with a Public/Private key pair. Anything that is encrypted with a private key can only be decrypted with the public key, and vice-versa. So, if you're sending someone a file, you would encrypt it with their public key that anyone can access, and only your recipient can decrypt your file at their end, using the private key that only they possess. Likewise, if they want to send you something, they encrypt it with your public key, and only you can decrypt it with your private key.

By encrypting the hash value with a private key from the eClosing system and storing that encrypted hash value and the corresponding public key with the document, any other system can revalidate the document by running the same hashing algorithm on it and comparing the resulting hash value to the decrypted hash value from the document. They will match precisely if no tampering has occurred. Note that the tamper-evident seal only tells you if tampering has occurred, but cannot identify exactly what was changed on the document.

ENOTES — IDENTIFYING OWNERSHIP

One major challenge in the development of eMortgage infrastructure was the issue of eNote ownership. Because the paper Note is a Negotiable Instrument as defined in the Uniform Commercial Code, the legal ownership of a paper note is defined by the physical possession of the original copy having ink signatures on it. There can only be one original paper Note, and copies can be easily identified as such. Industry old-timers will recall the *"smudge test,"* where a moistened fingertip was used to verify that the signature was an original ink signature and not a high-quality photocopy.

ESIGN defines new terminology for the electronic world: A paper Negotiable Instrument is called an electronic Transferable Record, and possession (legal ownership of the paper note) is now called Control of the Transferable Record. The concept of having an original copy of the Note becomes more challenging, because any copy of an electronic Note is digitally identical to the original — there simply isn't a way to mark the original eNote to make it different from any subsequent copies.

So how can we identify the *"original"* eNote, and even more important, keep track of who owns it? One solution would be to hold all of the industry's eNotes in a single electronic vault, which could then keep the originals in one place and add some sort of watermark or stamp to any copies. This idea was vetted in the early days of eMortgage development, but was deemed too difficult and impractical to put into operation. Who would be given the responsibility to be the holder of every eNote? What about the Doc Custody providers — would that new entity compete with their business model, as eMortgages gained mainstream adoption? Would all originators and investors be willing to put their trust into that single entity to hold their valuable eNotes?

The concept of a *"national eNote registry"* began to develop, and at MBA we hosted an industry task force of about 40 participants, representatives from the GSEs, private investors, lenders, warehouse lenders, MERS, and more, who met several times during 2002 to hammer out the details. Ultimately, that task force published a business requirements document defining what a National eNote Registry would need to do. Its primary function would be to act as a master index to identify the owner (Controller) and location of each eNote, and to track changes in ownership (Transfers of Control), such as when an originator sold an eNote to an investor. For this scheme to work, the eNote would need to have an additional piece of text that is not present in a paper Note, a clause which essentially says *"To find out who owns me and where I'm located, look me up in the National eNote Registry."*

When the National eNote Registry Business Requirements document was released to the industry at the MBA Technology Conference in March 2003, MERS immediately announced that they would build such a registry as an adjunct to the existing MERS system. The new registry went into production operation in mid-2004 as the MERS® eRegistry. It's important to note that the MERS eRegistry is separate from the original MERS system, which primarily tracks the changes in servicing rights and beneficial ownership interests in mortgage loans that are registered on that system. The MERS eRegistry is solely focused on identifying the Controller of each electronic Note.

After about a year of production operation, MERSCORP Holdings announced that they were also going to field a system that leveraged the existing connectivity of lenders, investors, and eClosing providers into the MERS eRegistry, in order to provide a central *"mailbox"* for electronic documents to be transferred. Dubbed MERS® eDelivery, it would allow a sender (say, the lender's eClosing platform) to send in a set of eDocuments with a standardized XML package format that contains instructions for delivery to one or more recipients (who must also be connected to the system). MERS eDelivery does not store or process the package contents, but simply receives them into the centralized hub and then forwards them out to the recipient, with automated messaging to confirm delivery and receipt. This eliminated the potential need for each lender's eClosing system to implement point-to-point integrations with every other electronic vaulting system that might be running for investors, servicers, and custodians in the industry.

ELECTRONIC VAULTING

Obviously, secure storage and long-term management of the electronic documents in an eMortgage is a critical factor, just as we need reliable, secure custodial services for paper mortgage documents. All eClosing systems include an electronic vault capability to perform this function. But in the eMortgage world, the electronic vault must not only store and secure the documents, it takes on a special meaning by also providing the connectivity to the MERS® eRegistry and eDelivery in order to perform key functions like the eNote Registration, Transfers of Control, and of course eDocument delivery to other parties.

The term *"EVAULT"®* was trademarked long ago by EVAULT, Inc., a company providing data backup and recovery services, despite the fact that the term *"eVault"* had been widely used in the mortgage industry for several years at that point by myself and many others involved in the development of the standards and guidelines. The company is still in business today as *"EVault Managed Services"* and is now owned by Seagate. Interestingly, the same *"EVAULT"* term was also filed for trademark in February 2012 by Granite Security Products to refer to their metal safes. Part of the trademark filing includes the claim that the *"First Use Anywhere Date"* was *"2006-10-00,"* or October 2006. Today we generally refer to electronic vaulting instead of *"EVault"* to avoid any trademark infringement or copyright issues.

ENOTARIZATION

Electronic notarization has been the topic of much debate over the past 15 years, as various mortgage industry entities and notary organizations tried to define the role of a Notary in the eMortgage world. Notary laws are promulgated at the state level, by the Secretary of State's office in each U.S. state. The current situation is a patchwork of rules and laws — some states have published a defined set of rules for eNotarization, some have simply said that it is *"allowed"* without elaborating further, and some have essentially said nothing one way or the other.

In the paper world, the role of a notary public is fairly straightforward: Check the identity of the signer(s), witness the actual signing ceremony, and affix the stamp and seal information to the signed documents to attest that the signers were not under duress and signed their closing documents of their own free will.

Many parties hold the opinion that *"a notary is a notary is a notary"* and that eNotarization is simply a different way for the notary to sign the documents, just like the transition from quill pens to ballpoint ink pens many years ago. Thus, in an eClosing, the notary should perform the exact same functions, and simply needs to be able to notarize the eDocuments with an electronic signature. This requires a particular change in mindset in regard to the classic notary stamp, which creates an embossed imprint onto a paper document — obviously impossible to do on an electronic document.

Others, including one major notary trade association, felt that notaries could take on a greater role in the eMortgage world by using a PKI digital signature to ensure document integrity after eNotarization had taken place. But this places a burden of responsibility on the notary public that does not exist in the paper world — no one would think of summoning a notary into a courtroom and asking them to testify that they can assure the court that a paper document they had notarized months ago had not been changed in any way since then.

When considering a move toward electronic signatures and processes, it's always important to ask if the new process is being held to a higher standard in some way than what was readily accepted in the paper world. This eNotarization issue is a classic example of the complexities that might arise from adding new and different processes in an eMortgage world, compared to the widely-accepted role of a notary in the paper world today.

There is a new and somewhat controversial development in eNotarization — the ability for a notary to witness a signing ceremony over a remote video link, rather than being in the same room as the borrower. The Commonwealth of Virginia passed a law allowing for remote notarization a few years ago, and more recently Montana followed suit with their own version. Virginia's law allows a Virginia notary to remotely witness a signing ceremony anywhere in the U.S, relying on the long history of state to state reciprocity in recognizing the validity of notarized documents. In other words, if a person from California happened to be in Virginia and needed to sign a paper document that required notarization, they could go to a Virginia notary, have the document witnessed and notarized, and California would accept that as a legally-notarized document upon their return home. By extending that concept out under the video notarization law, a Virginia notary could be in Virginia, witness a mortgage closing in California via remote video link over the internet, and eNotarize the documents. The Montana law is more restrictive, limited to residents, property and notaries of Montana — a way to make notarization easier in a state where a borrower might be a hundred miles from the nearest notary.

The Virginia model generated a bit of backlash from other states, some saying they wouldn't recognize such notarizations, but it's unclear how they would know whether an eNotarization took place remotely or in person, after the closing ceremony was complete (other than the fact that it was a Virginia notary that notarized closing documents in some other state). Many industry observers are waiting for a legal challenge to establish a case-law precedent.

ERECORDING

Just as certain closing documents require notarization, some closing documents must be recorded in the county land-records systems in the U.S., most notably the Deed of Trust or Security Instrument. County recorders are elected or appointed officials, and there are 3,585 counties and recording jurisdictions in the United States. Some are large, populous counties like Los Angeles, while many are small, rural jurisdictions with a small office and little technology. As of this writing, 1,349 counties are now eRecording out of 3,585 — while that is only about one-third, the good news is that those counties cover over 72% of the U.S. population, so about three-fourths of all mortgages have the potential to be eRecorded today.

PRIA, the Property Records Industry Association, develops and maintains data standards and guidelines for eRecording. They have defined three levels of eRecording to address the continuum of document types that could be sent to the County Recorder, from paper, to images, to intelligent eDocuments:

- *Model 1:* Paper documents with ink signatures that are scanned by a Submitter, who then transmits the images to the County Recorder's office. The Recorder views those images and manually enters data into the recording system for recordation of the images.

- *Model 2:* Image file plus separate XML recording data. The image file can come from either a true electronic document (say, eSigned PDF) or a scanned paper document. The XML recording data does not have a direct relationship or connection to the data represented in the image file, so it must be manually validated for accuracy.

- *Model 3:* Intelligent electronic documents with View and Data sections that are linked, as they are in a Version 1.02 Category 1 SMART® document. The Data section contains recording information to be used by the eRecording system.

There is ongoing, steady progress in county by county adoption of eRecording, so the numbers and population coverage will continue to grow moving forward.

IMPORTANT ISSUES RELATED TO EMORTGAGES

Value Proposition: Cost Savings, Efficiencies, and More

eMortgages can bring a variety of both tangible and intangible cost savings to the mortgage origination and investor delivery processes. The tangible savings are relatively obvious: the elimination of paper printing, copying, handling, shipping, storage, and similar aspects can save lenders many hard costs in supplies and overhead, which come right off the bottom line. And remember — at a 10% profit level, $100 in bottom-line cost savings is equivalent to increasing revenue by $1,000. Boring, but still important.

Intangible savings are more difficult to quantify, but are also much more exciting and significant. In the most optimal eMortgage scenario, all documents are created, signed and managed entirely in electronic form, from loan application, to closing, to investor delivery and servicing. In addition, all of the meaningful documents would use a standardized intelligent eDocument format like the SMART Doc, with the legal view and underlying data elements wrapped together in a single file.

Imagine all the areas of newfound process efficiency and streamlining that are possible. Start with the disclosures — lenders know exactly when a borrower logged into their system to view each disclosure document, how long they spent reading them, and of course when they signed them. This is particularly valuable for ensuring that the Closing Disclosure was received by the borrower three days prior to closing, and having a clear audit trail showing evidence of compliance. But the lender can also issue the rest of the closing package to the borrower's secure online eClosing portal prior to the closing date — borrowers can review their closing docs from home and notify their loan officers if they spot any errors or have questions, so that the closing docs will always be error-free at closing. Lenders can also opt to allow the borrowers to eSign the non-notarized documents prior to the actual closing ceremony, to streamline the closing ceremony even further.

At the closing table, borrowers feel more comfortable because they're not viewing a big stack of paper closing-documents for the very first time and feeling pressured to speed-read through them and then sign the bottom line on the biggest loan most of them will ever commit to. The eClosing platform ensures that all signature points are signed, and can provide online links to supporting information about each specific closing document, should the borrower have a question about one. Some technology vendors have even thought about providing a *"lender concierge"* capability, providing a real-time video link to a lender's remote representative during closing. This would mitigate the common borrower frustration of sitting at the closing table wondering exactly what one specific document or fee is for, and the mobile notary saying *"I don't know, that's a question for your lender, but if you want to get this loan you need to sign everything today because your rate lock expires tomorrow."*

What if a serious error is still not discovered until the borrower is sitting at the closing table? With an eClosing, it can be corrected on the fly, and a new electronic document package can be redrawn and placed into the eClosing portal to replace the problem docs, within minutes.

With data and document as a single standardized unit, systems can perform automated post-closing reviews on every closing (not just a small sampling), eliminating the infamous *"stare and compare"* process to reconcile paper docs with the system of record after the package returns to the lender's shop.

Lost notes become a dim memory of the paper-based mortgage process. Multiple backup copies of a given eNote will always exist, as well as reference copies potentially residing with the originator, the title company, the investor, and the warehouse lender if one was involved. The MERS eRegistry provides an independent record of control or ownership, so that if the Authoritative Copy of the eNote was somehow lost or destroyed, a backup copy can easily be validated against the tamper-evident seal to prove that it is digitally identical to the original eNote, and it can then become the Authoritative Copy.

eMortgage Security

Many organizations, especially their legal staff, express general concern over the security of the eMortgage process. Online data breaches have become a fact of life in our modern world, and most people now have extensive amounts of personal information stored in many different commercial cloud-based online data systems — bank accounts, credit cards, utility bills, and personal account logins.

Concern and caution is always healthy when considering any new electronic process. Fortunately, eMortgage technology provides a number of significant security improvements compared to what we readily accept in today's paper-based processes, and does not introduce any new vulnerabilities. Let's examine several specific areas:

Personal data stored in cloud-based systems: Data storage and backup systems are always potentially vulnerable to hacking attacks, but this is a fact of life in all mortgage-technology systems. Whether you're doing a paper-based closing or an eClosing today, all of the data used to produce that set of closing documents, and all of the post-closing process (which often includes scanning the paper docs back into electronic images), must be kept secure against hacking attacks and are equally at risk whether ink or electronic signatures are used to sign the documents.

Shotgunning: Deliberate fraud committed by a borrower and closing agent in collusion to close on the same property with multiple lenders in one day is effectively eliminated by lenders using eClosings. The fraudsters would be caught red-handed at the second closing, because the first eNote would already be registered with the MERS eRegistry, so the second eNote registration would return an error.

Lost Notes: As described above, lost Notes are a thing of the past in the eMortgage world. The MERS eRegistry always identifies the Controller of the Authoritative Copy of the eNote, so legal ownership cannot be compromised or threatened the way it can in the paper world, where there is only one copy of the wet-ink-signed paper Note that can be lost or destroyed.

Borrower Authentication: For most paper closings today, the closing agent or mobile notary checks the borrower's driver's license as legal identification, and the closing proceeds. Borrowers attempting to fraudulently close a mortgage can easily obtain a false driver's license to get past this minor hurdle. But many eClosing systems include the ability to further authenticate the borrower's identity using *"out of wallet"* questions generated from credit records and similar databases. In one anecdotal case, a husband and wife were attempting to perform an eClosing, but the *"wife"* failed several iterations of the authentication questions, and she turned out to be the husband's mistress and not his actual wife.

Foreclosures: Some eMortgages (about 8,800 of the 300,000+ total registered on the MERS eRegistry to date) have been foreclosed upon over the years since 2005, and to date there have been no reports of any loans where the foreclosure process was prevented or infringed upon because the loan was an eMortgage instead of on paper.

IMPLEMENTATION AND ADOPTION

How it Works: Real-World Implementation

We've talked about the hypothetical *"perfect"* eClosing process and all of the benefits it can entail. But the eMortgage landscape is far from perfect at this point in its evolution. We've covered some of the most common implementation compromises already — paper Notes to avoid the complexity of a full electronic vault with MERS eRegistry transactions (or for FHA loans, because FHA does not yet accept eNotes, though they do accept other documents in electronic format), paper Security Instrument and other recordable documents in counties that don't yet support eRecording, and paper Notarized documents where eNotarization presents an obstacle.

Combinations of electronic and paper documents like this are called hybrid eClosings, and comprise the vast majority of the 300,000+ eClosings that have occurred since the MERS eRegistry went live in 2005. But a small number of true eClosings have occurred in locales where eRecording and eNotarization were both supported and the eNotes were in SMART Doc format for delivery to Fannie Mae or Freddie Mac.

Similarly, pools of loans that include both paper and electronic Notes have become relatively commonplace in recent years, requiring servicers to add electronic vault capability to their systems in order to accept delivery of the eNotes in such hybrid pools.

Technology implementations of eClosing systems have taken a variety of approaches. The key components include the closing data feed from the Loan Origination System or LOS, the generation of the closing documents from that data feed, the tagging of the closing docs for eSignatures, the eSigning engine that ingests the documents and presents them for electronic signing, and the electronic vault that manages the specialized eSigning of the SMART Doc eNote as well as the MERS eRegistry transactions for initial registration, transfers of control, and more.

Some eClosing providers have started with an existing mortgage document library capability and added the eSigning and vaulting components to that, either by building their own or by licensing a third-party engine like eSign Systems (now owned by DocMagic). Others have developed their own standalone eClosing capability (some without the SMART Doc eNote functionality), and then partnered with one or more doc providers so that a set of closing docs is generated by the doc provider and transmitted to the eClosing system for the actual electronic closing event.

Some observers feel that the most effective and logical place for the eClosing and electronic vault functions to reside are with the LOS provider, especially if the LOS includes its own full doc library that most of their customers use. This would provide tighter linking between docs and eClosing, since both components are controlled by the same entity. If the LOS, doc provider, and eClosing system are separate entities, then multiple interfaces are required: LOS data feeds to the doc provider(s), eDocument delivery from the doc provider into the eClosing systems (tagged for electronic signature points using whatever technology the eClosing system requires — one might use Adobe Form Fields, while another could use X-Y coordinates to locate the signature points), and reverse connections to return the signed, executed eClosing docs back to the LOS.

Moving forward, we will continue to see standalone eClosing technology providers partnered with document vendors, and will likely see growth in embedded LOS solutions. Ellie Mae's Encompass LOS platform currently performs very large production of eDisclosures each month, and the company's product roadmap contains an integrated eClosing platform intended to enable their lender customers to move to a completely paperless loan process.

Title and settlement agents are faced with learning and supporting multiple eClosing systems and their User Interfaces because of this industry reality, and so eClosing providers realize that it is incumbent upon them to ensure that their process flows and screen designs are as completely self-explanatory and easy to use as possible.

Industry Adoption
Overall industry adoption has been slow and somewhat difficult, for a variety of reasons. Lenders want more investor acceptance in order to broaden their options for best execution beyond the mainstream of Fannie Mae and Freddie Mac. Investors say that they haven't heard their lenders asking for eMortgage acceptance, and their legal teams typically raise an abundance of caution over the perceived risks that were described above, so they have been slow to move forward.

One challenge for broader adoption has been the perennial Catch-22 of the mortgage industry's cyclical nature: During a boom cycle, originators are so busy making loans and keeping up with production pipelines that they don't have time to implement a new system and process flow for eClosings. Yet when the cycle dips and production is slow, lenders are concerned with cost management and reluctant to invest in new technologies.

Industry adoption seemed to be gaining some real momentum back in 2007, two years into the MERS eRegistry production operation, but the foreclosure crisis was developing and hit the entire industry hard for the next four years. All momentum toward eClosings ground to a halt as lenders struggled to survive. Now, in 2016 and beyond, we are seeing renewed interest in eClosing, and slow but steady growth.

One hurdle that some participants identify is the fact that the eNote requires an exception process, being in MISMO SMART Doc format, compared to the rest of the eSignable PDF closing documents. Again, the new SMART Doc Version 3 format has the potential to resolve this, by providing a universal intelligent-electronic-document structure that is equally useful for all documents.

WAREHOUSE LENDING

One area of particular interest recently has been in the warehouse lending process. eWarehouse lending has the potential to eliminate specific areas of risk for warehouse lenders and accelerate the overall process. For example, in the paper process, the warehouse lender extends funds to the correspondent originator for closing, but their legal interest in the Note is not perfected until they have received the ink-signed original paper Note with the blank endorsement, at best in an overnight shipment. With an eClosing, Control of the eNote can be transferred to the warehouse lender within seconds after it is signed, reducing their risk period from 24-48 hours down to a few seconds.

Correspondent originators can also benefit from the eWarehouse process. In the paper world, a correspondent can *"turn"* their warehouse line (originate loans that use up the full value of their warehouse line of credit) typically about every 10-14 days. So, with a warehouse line of $10 million, and 2-3 turns per month, they can originate $20-30 million in production each month. If that correspondent has the potential to do more production, they can become capital constrained by their warehouse line. But with the increased velocity in the eWarehouse process — instant electronic delivery to the warehouse lender and then on to the end investor — a correspondent originator might now turn their warehouse line 5-7 times a month, so that same $10 million warehouse line would then support $50-70 million in loan production per month.

Warehouse lenders were initially cautious about the eWarehouse process, in part because with eNotes there is no direct equivalent to the paper Note / Bailee letter investor delivery process. A Bailee letter is defined in the Uniform Commercial Code specifically for real tangible property, so the concept doesn't translate over to an electronic Transferable Record, the technical term for the eNote. But by receiving Control of the eNote on the MERS eRegistry, their legal rights are fully protected. As they become more comfortable with the process, understand the potential benefits, and see other warehouse investors moving forward, the momentum is growing for broader adoption.

LOOKING TO THE FUTURE

Many believe, as I do, that broad adoption of eClosings is inevitable, because the cost savings, process efficiencies, and improved security and compliance aspects are too compelling to ignore. There will come a tipping point of mainstream adoption — as more investors start accepting eNotes and originating lenders continue to grow in their adoption of eClosing as a competitive advantage, overall adoption will curve upward as the majority of lenders realize that they must also offer eClosing to retain parity.

In panel sessions and industry presentations, I've said many times that mainstream adoption was *"only three to five years away."* Those predictions from the mid-2000s turned out to be overly optimistic, and were further impacted by the foreclosure crisis. But with new momentum building as a result of the Consumer Financial Protection Bureau's recent eClosing Pilot project, new technology providers entering the space, and steadily-growing interest from lenders, warehouse lenders, and investors, I believe that we will see the growth curve ramp sharply upward well before 2020.

ABOUT THE AUTHOR

Harry Gardner is the Vice President of eStrategies for Ellie Mae®, a leading provider of enterprise level, on-demand automated solutions for the residential mortgage industry. Ellie Mae hosts Encompass®, an end-to-end solution providing the core operating system for mortgage originators that spans customer relationship management, loan origination and business management.

Gardner was formerly President of SigniaDocs, a national eMortgage solutions provider. He is a frequent speaker and writer on eMortgages, mortgage technology, industry standards and enterprise data management issues. Mr. Gardner was previously the Vice President of Industry Technology for the Mortgage Bankers Association, and was the President of MISMO, Inc.

In October 2012, Gardner received the Steve Fraser Visionary Award at the Mortgage Technology Magazine annual awards ceremony. The award is "a lifetime achievement award that recognizes the accomplishments of an outstanding mortgage technology innovator, visionary or evangelizer." Gardner was also named one of Mortgage Banking magazine's 2009 eMortgage All-Stars.

Gardner is a graduate of the University of Virginia, with a bachelor's degree in electrical engineering. He can be reached at harry.gardner@elliemae.com or 202-409-5903.

CHAPTER TEN

REVERSE MORTGAGE LOAN ORIGINATION SOFTWARE TECHNOLOGY

JOHN BUTTON | PRESIDENT AND CEO

REVERSEVISION

Not unlike the traditional "forward" mortgage space, the majority of the reverse mortgage industry relies on technology from point of sale to closing loans. The right technology assists lenders with checks and safeguards to ensure loans are compliant and error free, while at the same time aiding the loan officer with sales tools like simulators, graphs, charts, and proposals that make it easy for borrowers to understand the loan. Technology for both forward and reverse are designed to fulfill their users' business needs and workflow, but the sales process, loan structure, and origination workflow are fundamentally different, which is why each loan type has dedicated software.

WHAT IS SAAS?

Most loan origination software (LOS) products are available as Software as a Service (SaaS), a software distribution model in which applications are hosted by a vendor or service provider and made available to customers over a network, typically the Internet. This approach has grown attractive for most software categories, because the provider is able to deliver a complete turn-key operating environment to the user for substantially less total cost than on-premises install software is able to provide.

SaaS is particularly attractive with LOS solutions, given that a working solution must include not only a software program, but also numerous interfaces and data feeds. Rate updates, address verification data, regulator connections, property appraisal services, credit reports, and fraud detection are but a few of the many required touch points that are required to make LOS software into a solution.

Security is another area where SaaS excels. The nature of cyber threats and the growing complexity of technology systems require equally powerful and specialized tools operated by skilled, dedicated staff to maintain security. It is difficult and expensive for individual firms to satisfy these needs. A SaaS solution uses a shared resource which substantially reduces the cost for the individual company or user. Such solutions include costly but necessary data-center and operational certifications like Information Security Policy (InfoSec) and Statement on Standards for Attestation Engagements (SSAE) No. 16 (SSAE 16), which is a report on controls at a service organization.

Finally, SaaS enables mobility for the user as it is inherently a service at a distance accessed via an available anywhere network.

SHARED LOAN ACCESS

Throughout most of the lending industry, whenever two or more firms are joint participants in the lending process — such as mortgage brokers and lenders — information standards are adopted to move data and loans between the companies. In mortgage lending, standard forms have included Fannie Mae Desktop Originator and Desktop Underwriter 3.2 Format (aka "DU 3.2 files"), and more recently MISMO Uniform Loan Delivery Data Specification v2.6 or v3.x (e.g., "MISMO 2.6 files"). While such standards solve an important problem, and have been very useful, there are fundamentally alternative methods to meet this intercompany sharing need.

In industries that are more mature technologically, such as manufacturing and logistics, such needs to coordinate a transaction between firms have been met with a class of software systems known as Supply Chain Management. These systems interlink the firms on common systems rather than using standard formats for the transfer of data. File transfer is completely eliminated. Information is shared in a common system between the companies involved in the transaction. This avoids delays, versioning issues, and data translation errors. The companies operate on one version of the factual information at all times. Appropriate access to the information is based on user roles enabling them to read and edit as appropriate for their role and the stage of the transaction.

In reverse lending, this same advanced concept is implemented via a loan exchange where two or more firms can share a common system. Each performs their appropriate actions on a shared loan record. This approach speeds the transaction, reduces errors, and improves compliance. SaaS solutions lend themselves to implementing this shared-solution concept. Such a solution is rare in traditional mortgage lending but commonly available to the reverse mortgage industry.

In comparison to the traditional forward mortgage industry, the youth of reverse lending permits this advanced rethink of solving the essential intercompany sharing need.

WHOLESALE PARTNER SUPPORT

In the specific case of shared loan access between the lender and partner companies in their third party originations channel (e.g., brokers), a powerful technology feature is a licensing arrangement that enables the lender to provide LOS technology to their partner at low to no additional cost. For the lender, being able to provide an LOS solution to the partner both strengthens the partnership and improves performance by ensuing both parties operate in a common system. For the partner firm, receiving access to an LOS as a component of the relationship is a clear cost benefit.

COMPLIANCE AND LOAN QUALITY

Technology plays a key role in ensuring loans meet compliance standards. LOS capabilities can ensure loan quality by: catching incorrect or missing data values as they are entered, blocking loan officers from submitting an application in states in which they are not licensed, inhibiting application stage changes when aggregate data is incorrect, re-calculating critical rates and amounts at each usage point, blocking the use of previously generated forms like GFEs when loan characteristics change, and automatically driving loan document selections and content on loan characteristics.

These are a few examples of important capabilities that serve lending professions in making a complex process more error-free.

DOCUMENT PREPARATION

Ultimately, documents are the fundamental output of the lending process. From proposals to applications and closing, the documents that are generated in the lending process will require complex use of the data gathered during the process. The optimum technology solution will be accomplished with a tight coupling between the LOS and the document generation system.

This is an area where a single provider should be considered. A single technology provider can take full advantage of the LOS's logic to drive document generation and speed updates to users when regulations change.

FULFILLMENT SERVICES INTEGRATION

Numerous services are required to close a loan application. These include credit reports, property appraisals, tax reviews, title insurance, flood insurance, and others. All require some information from the loan record, and return both field level data and documents. LOS technology that can order such services, provide fulfillment status, and insert response data directly into the loan record is of considerable value to the lender.

In reverse lending, an important example of the value of service integration is *credit*. Unlike some forms of lending where only a FICO score or similar individual value is required from the credit check, reverse underwriting requires a review of all credit trade-lines as part of the Financial Assessment of the borrower's ability to pay property tax and insurance. As a result, credit services feed a large amount of data into the LOS to support underwriting. While possible, manual entry of this information is both time-consuming and highly likely to introduce defects into the process.

Advanced technology solutions will fully integrate such services — both request and response — directly into the LOS to speed delivery and reduce errors.

REPORTING AND ANALYTICS

As with any data-driven activity, reporting is an important capability to measure and drive the process. In addition, mortgage lending has a number of regulatory reporting requirements such as Home Mortgage Disclosure Act (HMDA) and NMLS Mortgage Call Report (MCR). Any technology solution must meet these fundamental needs.

Often included in the general topic of "reporting" are more general data access and exports. The ability to export the data behind any report is a significant time-saver and service to users.

Direct access to the underlying data that drives originations technology is increasingly key to supporting high-performance lenders. Getting directly to the data as it changes throughout the process enables company-unique reporting and even more critical integration. No system provides every possible capability a lender might need. Having the ability to attach directly to the LOS data and create information-driven extensions is the difference between a tool that enables success and frustration.

Uses for such data-access include linking data from originations to sales, CRM, or other marketing tools. This capability is also key to interrelating a traditional forward-lending system with reverse lending within a single enterprise.

ROLES

The ability to control loan-and-system access is crucial within an LOS. A natural mechanism to accomplish this is to establish access based on user roles. Technology can do the job of matching and maintaining appropriate access to data, features, and actions in the LOS, based on the role assigned to the user.

Further, in a shared-loan-exchange LOS solution, roles also determine how a lender's wholesale partners are managed. This includes all the same capabilities as the lender's users, but also implementing policies like the delegation of user administration to the partner.

SALES

Until industry loan volume grows appreciably, marketing and sales will continue to be the most fundamental business issue in reverse mortgage lending. As the central business challenge, this area could most benefit from technology solutions.

At a minimum, classic sales tools like contact and campaign management are fundamental. Each loan officer — the sales person of the loan industry — must be enabled with basic contact management that includes information and action tracking. Information should include the prospective borrower's address, phone, email, relationships, and notes capturing unique facts about the borrower and their needs. Action reminders like next follow-up call or email should also be available.

Industry specialization then builds on basic contact management by adding shared data between the contact management system and the LOS to avoid re-entry of borrower information.

Given the critical role that awareness-building via education plays in growing this market, adding campaign-management features to the contact-management suite enables important mass email and mail marketing to increase the value of ordered contact information. Bringing easy-to-use tools around campaigns to loan officers in scale has a substantial impact on industry growth.

Fact-based persuasive tools can then be used to take full advantage of these basic contact management capabilities. This should include graphical tools to better explain the features and effects of the reverse loan to a prospective borrower via loan simulations and "what if" scenarios. *This area is the highest value component of sales tools and the least developed throughout the reverse lending industry.* Substantial potential exists in making complex financial situations clear using graphical depictions of the effect over time of a reverse mortgage.

SUCCESS-BASED PRICING

The mortgage industry can be volatile. High volume could be experienced one month and then not so much the next. An LOS where pricing that is closely coupled with volume removes at least some of the fixed-cost technology burden. Possibly more important, this form of pricing creates a true partnership between the technology provider and the lender. In this way, both are measured and rewarded on the same success objective: closing loans.

THE FUTURE

While products that bring together most of the technology enablers described above exist now, we can expect considerable advancement in the future. LOS products like ReverseVision's RV Exchange encompass nearly all of the key capabilities, including most important of all the shared loan concept via an Exchange linking firms together in a single transaction.

While LOS tools will continue to improve in the future by implementing regulatory changes, additional integrations, and other features designed to speed transactions with fewer errors, sales tools will be the strategically important area of technology advancement.

Currently, the reverse-lending industry is not limited by fulfillment or cost but by a lack of borrowers from a relatively enormous prospect pool that could benefit from the product. Marketing (i.e., awareness and interest-building) and sales (i.e., closing on borrower-specific benefits) are the keys to industry growth, and thus should be the focal point of future technology development efforts.

In particular, the reverse loan is complex and unfamiliar to most prospective borrowers. Academic research has shown that the loan can be highly beneficial in retirement financial scenarios that are complex to explain. The key to unlocking widespread use of the loan in these effective retirement plans will be sales technology that makes the complex easy to understand and quick to execute. The near future will include such tools in broad use around the reverse-lending industry.

ABOUT THE AUTHOR

John Button, President & CEO of ReverseVision, is a business-to-business executive, investor, and entrepreneur with more than 30 years of diverse experience concentrated in technology and the cultivation of business development strategies.

Before joining ReverseVision as president, John had been focused on a series of business ventures including serving as president of an information sharing technology provider, an investor in two businesses and a consultant to a business incubator. Previously, John served as Chief Operating Officer for Del Mar DataTrac (DMD) – a leading innovator in mortgage lending automation, including the well-regarded mortgage loan origination system (LOS) DataTrac. His role with DMD included overall business operations responsibility, direct responsibility for product management, customer support, professional services and information technology.

Prior to that, John has held senior executive positions with IPS Sendero, RF/Spectrum Decision Science Corporation, and IBM.

John was an employee of the U.S. Navy, where he served as a systems engineer and attended both Drexel University and Rensselaer Polytechnic Institute.

He is a motorcycle enthusiast and enjoys going on rides in Baja and the US as often as possible.

CHAPTER ELEVEN

THE PENDULUM OF REGULATION

CHRIS APPIE | VICE PRESIDENT AND COUNSEL
COMPLIANCE SYSTEMS

In the years following the upheaval of the 2008 financial crisis, the financial services industry continues to grapple with new laws and regulations intended to prevent a similar event from occurring without freezing access to credit or crippling the economy. Critics of the federal government's response to this crisis, The Dodd-Frank Wall Street Reform and Consumer Protection Act, argue the law solves problems that no longer exist, creates an agency without adequate congressional control, and requires new burdensome regulation that is inconsistent with the proper role of the federal government. Supporters argue that the law will prevent taxpayer dollars from being used to prop up big banks again, and will protect consumers from lenders that, unregulated, will put their individual profits above all else and cause another economic calamity. As one studies the requirements placed on lenders to ensure compliance with the law, it becomes increasingly clear that what really matters is the analysis of complete, consistent, compliant loan data. Systems that ensure and safeguard data integrity are of paramount importance and can be used to drive software applications that produce compliant documents and disclosures, defend against complaints and lawsuits, provide information to regulators and the secondary market, and position lenders to properly address the next wave of compliance requirements that regulators have yet to write.

Writing about regulation and compliance is tough because laws tend to change quickly, regulations and case law even more so. We are in a period of rapid regulatory change, where printed information can quickly become stale and is best left to actively maintained websites. For example, the Consumer Financial Protection Bureau publishes its excellent examination manuals in plain English on its website and any tactical detail on how to comply with federal financial law is detailed there; there is little sense in reinventing that work.[1] Therefore, while this chapter touches on the newer industry acronyms resulting from the Dodd-Frank Act, such as QM, QRM, ATR, TIP, UDAAP, etc., it is intended to focus on overall industry trends and provide the historical context necessary to understand trends in government regulation of the mortgage and banking industry. This includes a look at early American banks, 20th-century financial crises, the creation of government-sponsored enterprises, the ongoing push for consumer protection, and new laws intended to safeguard the economy.

The fact that the economic meltdown of 2008 caused the regulatory pendulum to swing toward more regulation is obvious and expected. The more subtle observation is that

---

[1] The CFPB Supervision and Examination Manual, available at: http://www.consumerfinance.gov/guidance/supervision/manual/

the more this pendulum swings, the more the pivot point itself is forced to slide, causing the entire system to shift in such a way that even a swing toward less regulation comes from a place where more regulation is already the norm.

Breaches of trust between the financial industry and the public it serves—or even the perception of such breaches—are corrected or overcorrected by pushes for regulatory reform, just as periods of relative tranquility become the impetus for lowering regulatory barriers which, every so often, result in unintended consequences and harm to the economy. The industry may unwind threads, but it cannot unwind the tapestry of U.S. financial laws that have grown since the beginning of our nation.

HISTORY PRIOR TO 1900

First and Second Banks of the United States: A Constitutional Watershed

Barely two years after ratification of the Constitution in 1789, Congress passed the Bank Bill of 1791, creating the First Bank of the United States. A majority of the Congress believed such an institution *"will be very conducive to the successful conducting of the national finance; will tend to give facility to the obtaining of loans, for the use of the government, in sudden emergencies; and will be productive of considerable advantages to trade and industry in general."*[2] This feeling was, however, not universal. Both Thomas Jefferson and James Madison opposed the Bank Bill as unconstitutional. The bank's charter lasted 20 years and when the charter ran out it was not renewed.[3] Seven years later, in 1816, Congress passed "An Act to Incorporate the Subscribers to the Bank of the United States," which chartered the Second Bank of the United States. It, too, was short lived, and in 1836 under President Andrew Jackson the charter of the Second National Bank, like that of the First National Bank, was allowed to expire.[4]

The government's attempt to create a banking industry was thus a mixed bag. However, before its charter ran out the Second National Bank would provide a backdrop for one of the most significant Supreme Court cases in the history of the nation.

McCulloch v Maryland: Federal Preemption of State Banking Law and Implied Federal Power

The Second Bank of America was controversial, so much so that the Maryland legislature passed a law attempting to tax it out of existence by requiring a tax to be paid on all notes issued by a bank not chartered in Maryland.[5] A lawsuit ensued when

---

2 Journals of the Continental Congress, 1774-1789 (34 vols.; Washington, 1904-37.), XX, 546-48; XXI, 1187-90.
3 Bowden, Elbert V. (1989). Money, Banking, and the Financial System. St. Paul, MN: West Publishing Company. p. 97 Bowden, Elbert V, Money, Banking, and the Financial System, (West, 1989), p. 97
4 Hixson, William F., Triumph of the Bankers: Money and Banking in the Eighteenth and Nineteenth Centuries, London: Praeger, 1993. P. 14-15
5 McCulloch v Maryland, 17 U.S. 316 (1819), Syllabus at 317McCulloch v Maryland Syllabus at 317

James McCulloch, a representative of the Bank of the United States, refused to pay the tax. McCulloch lost in Maryland state court but appealed to the Supreme Court of the United States.

We now know this lawsuit as *McCulloch v. Maryland,* 17 U.S. 316 (1819). In deciding the case the court first tackled the question of whether Congress had the power to create a national bank. The Constitution clearly gave Congress the power *"to lay and collect taxes, duties, imposts and excises, to pay the debts and provide for the common defense and general welfare of the United States."*[6] Equally clear was that the Constitution did not specifically give Congress the power to create a bank. The court noted: *"Among the enumerated powers, we do not find that of establishing a bank or creating a corporation. But there is no phrase in the instrument which, like the articles of confederation, excludes incidental or implied powers; and which requires that everything granted shall be expressly and minutely described."*[7]

Having found silence in the Constitution, the court looked to whether it was reasonable to believe that the law was in furtherance of an explicit power granted to the federal government, namely, the power to collect and distribute revenue. In dicta, the implications of which the court may not have fully understood, it turned a deferential tone to the other two co-equal branches of government: Congress that had passed the bill and the President who had signed it into law. In the view of the court, it stood to reason that those two institutions acted in good faith, and by their action in passing and signing the bill must have believed it was within their authority to do so. The court was compelled by this and noted: *"The bill for incorporating the Bank of the United States did not steal upon an unsuspecting legislature, and pass unobserved. Its principle was completely understood, and was opposed with equal zeal and ability. After being resisted, first, in the fair and open field of debate, and afterwards, in the executive cabinet, with as much persevering talent as any measure has ever experienced, and being supported by arguments which convinced minds as pure and as intelligent as this country can boast, it became a law."*

The court held the act of creating a bank was within the implied powers of Congress under the Necessary and Proper Clause: *"It is never the end for which other powers are exercised, but a means by which other objects are accomplished… [t]he power of creating a corporation is never used for its own sake, but for the purpose of effecting something else."*[8] In this case the 'something else' were the explicitly permitted *"great powers, to lay and collect taxes; to borrow money; to regulate commerce; to declare and conduct a war; and to raise and support armies and navies. The sword and the purse, all the external relations, and no inconsiderable portion of the industry of the nation are entrusted to its Government. It can never be pretended that these vast powers draw after them others of inferior importance merely because they are inferior. Such an idea can never be advanced. But it may with great reason be contended that a Government entrusted with such ample powers, on the due execution of which the happiness and prosperity of the Nation so vitally depends, must also be entrusted with ample means for their execution."*[9]

---

6 U.S. Const. art. I, § 8, cl. 1Article 1 section 8
7 McCulloch v. Maryland, 17 U.S. 316, 406 (1819)McCulloch v. Maryland, 17 U.S. 316 (1819)
8 Ibid, at 411Id. At 411
9 Ibid, at 407-408Id 407-408

With this holding, the power of the federal government to act outside the strict grants of powers in the Constitution had been enshrined. Chief Justice Marshall, writing for the court, famously declared: *"Let the end be legitimate, let it be within the scope of the constitution, and all means which are appropriate, which are plainly adapted to that end, which are not prohibited, but consist with the letter and spirit of the constitution, are constitutional."*

Having decided the federal law was valid, what was to become of the Maryland law? On its face, the Constitution provides a response: *"Laws of the United States which shall be made in pursuance thereof…shall be the supreme law of the land."*[10] The Constitution does not, however, state that the law of the United States can be the only law of the land on a given subject.

Maryland contended that even if the National Bank was validly created under the Constitution, the Maryland law was likewise a valid exercise of Maryland's sovereignty; the national bank could exist but it still needed to pay the tax in Maryland required by Maryland law. The Supreme Court decision concluded otherwise. *"If we apply the principle for which the State of Maryland contends, to the Constitution generally, we shall find it capable of changing totally the character of that instrument. We shall find it capable of arresting all the measures of the Government, and of prostrating it at the foot of the States. The American people have declared their Constitution and the laws made in pursuance thereof to be supreme, but this principle would transfer the supremacy, in fact, to the States."*[11]

The Maryland law was thus preempted by federal law. In this particular instance the law was voided outright, but over the next almost 200 years this principal would be a cornerstone of constitutional law in the United States.

McCulloch, with its holding that federal law need not be explicitly delineated in the Constitution to be valid, and that it is supreme over state law, is in great degree the genesis of all federal law that impacts the mortgage and banking industries. From the Truth-in Lending Act[12] and The Real Estate Settlement Procedures Act[13] to Dodd-Frank and its implementing regulations, all roads for federal intervention into the industry can be traced back to the principles of *McCulloch v Maryland*.

Banking During a Civil War: The Federal Government Tries Again
After the Second National Bank was shuttered, the federal government largely shied away from intervention in the banking system in the years leading up to the Civil War. In this era where slavery, couched as a state's-rights issue, permeated every aspect of American society, one can certainly understand that proponents of a strong federal role in banking sat on the sidelines and avoided fanning the flames of another perceived federal governmental intrusion into the affairs of a state. This détente clearly changed with the hostilities of 1861 and the tremendous bloodshed that followed. Emboldened

---

10 U.S. Const. art. 6, cl. 2U.S. Constitution Article 6, Clause 2
11 McCulloch, at 432McCulloch at 432
12 15 USC §1601, et seq.
13 12 USC §2601, et seq.

by the cause, the government sought to pass legislation not only to help finance the war, but also to bring some uniformity to the state-centered banking patchwork that extended through the financial markets.

To account for these challenges, Congress passed the National Bank Acts of 1863-1866.[14] Under these laws, federally chartered institutions were permitted to issue notes backed by the U.S. Treasury itself. This power, coupled with a tax on all notes issued by state-chartered banks, had the effect of both creating a uniform national currency and increasing the number of nationally chartered banks, as state-chartered banks switched charter to avoid the tax. Additionally, these laws established the Office of Comptroller of the Currency (OCC) and tasked it with examining and supervising nationally chartered institutions. By creating federally charted banks, Congress created the dual system of state and national chartered banks we know today.

TWENTIETH CENTURY PENDULUM SWINGS

It took a national financial calamity to create the next big change in the banking system. In 1907, the stock market was falling fast and a series of questionable trades caused a run on the banks that had financed these deals. Eventually, the Knickerbocker Trust Company, the third-largest trust in New York, failed. Not dissimilar to the failure of Lehman Brothers in 2008, the Knickerbocker failure caused panic throughout the financial system. Fearing their own banks would also fail, depositors began to demand their money held in their deposit accounts. Institutions did not have the liquid assets to fulfill these demands, and panic spread. Fearing the fallout to the larger economy of the United States, a group of private financiers led by J.P. Morgan loaned incredibly large amounts of their own capital to banks to allow them to continue operations and meet the needs of depositors. It was private money that saved the banking system, not the government. Congress took note and calls began for the creation of a central 'bank of last resort' to lend money under such extraordinary circumstances.

In response to the panic (and likely calls from rich political donors who didn't want their personal money to get tied up like that again), Congress passed the Federal Reserve Act of 1913.[15] This act created the Federal Reserve, a semi-governmental agency with a Board of Governors appointed by the President and approved by the Senate. The Act created a number of regional Federal Reserve Banks to carry out the operations of the Federal Reserve; all nationally chartered banks were required to become members of the Federal Reserve System and buy stock in their respective Federal Reserve banks. The Federal Reserve was given responsibility for issuing a standard national currency (the Federal Reserve Note) as well as providing financial stability to the economy of the United States by setting monetary policy, including the Target Federal Funds Rate. This is the interest rate at which depository institutions lend reserve balances to other depository institutions overnight, and is really the basis for interest rates for products

---

14 Congress passed three separate Bank Acts on February 25, 1863; June 3, 1864; and July 13; 1866 (ch. 58, 12 Stat. 665; February 25, 1863), (ch. 106, 13 Stat. 99; June 3, 1864)

15 Federal Reserve Act, December 23, 1913. https://fraser.stlouisfed.org/title/?id=966

ranging from consumer loans to mortgages. The Federal Reserve supervises and monitors state-chartered banks that are members of the Federal Reserve System via Safety and Soundness examinations. Interestingly, the Federal Reserve is not directly funded by Congress and therefore not subject to the appropriations process. A similar funding mechanism has been set up to fund the CFPB, which has drawn sharp criticism and is discussed in greater detail later.

The Great Depression

It is difficult to overstate the impact of the Great Depression and subsequent New Deal legislation on the banking and finance systems of the United States. In the four years between the 1929 stock market crash and the first swearing in of Franklin Roosevelt in 1933, 40% of all banks had failed,[16] the unemployment rate was 23.6%,[17] and nearly a quarter of all mortgage debt was in default.[18] Within days of his inauguration, Roosevelt began pushing legislation designed to get the economy moving and to lay the groundwork intended to prevent another depression. As evidenced by his three subsequent elections to the presidency, many were pleased with the laws pushed through Congress by Roosevelt, but others were concerned that the federal government was drastically overstepping its constitutional powers. The critics would see their concerns realized when the courts relied on the Commerce Clause to uphold a number of New-Deal era laws. This liberal reading of the Commerce Clause set the stage for the federal government to become involved with all matter of financial laws intended to protect consumers. When considering the proper role of the government in these areas, we must remember that with the expansion of laws passed under the Commerce Clause, the pivot point of the regulatory pendulum had shifted drastically toward increased federal governmental intervention in areas of banking and finance.

1930's: The Commerce Clause and New Deal Activism

In the late 1930's Congress believed that fluctuation in wheat prices was causing harm to the economy and passed a law[19] to regulate prices by limiting the amount of land farmers used for wheat production. The authority by which Congress acted was the power granted under the Commerce Clause (Article 1, section 8 of the Constitution).[20] In *Wickard v. Filburn*, Roscoe Filburn argued that the wheat he produced was only used to feed his own cattle; therefore, Congress had no power to pass a law limiting his ability to grow wheat that would not be transported interstate. The court disagreed and held that when an activity *"exerts a substantial economic effect on interstate commerce"*[21] it is within the power of Congress to regulate that activity. To paraphrase the court's position: if everyone produced his own wheat, demand would decrease and drive prices down.

---

16 R. W. Hafer, The Federal Reserve System (Greenwood, 2005) p 18
17 VanGiezen, Robert and Schwenk, Albert E., "Compensation from Before World War I through the Great Depression," www.bls.gov/opub/cwc/cm20030124ar03p1.htm
18 Senate Committee on Banking and Currency, Subcommittee on Home Mortgages, Etc., "Testimony of Horace Russell," General Counsel, Federal Home Loan Bank Board of Atlanta, Home Owners Loan Act, 73rd Congress, at 6, 9 (April 20 and 22, 1933)
19 The Agricultural Adjustment Act of 1938 Pub.L. 75–430, 7 USC Chapter 35 § 1281
20 U.S. Const. art. 1, § 8 cl. 3
21 Wickard v. Filburn, 317 U.S. 111 (1942)

Over the course of time there have been some limitations on the Commerce Clause authority, but even those did not substantially change the authority of Congress to act with almost unfettered latitude under the Commerce Clause.

1930's: A Shift to Consumer Protection with Glass-Steagall

In the 1930s legislative changes affecting banking were driven by a significant shift to the left in American politics, where the role of government was not only to protect the American people from foreign aggression, but to protect the American people from big business and in some cases, from themselves. This political shift led to the passage of The Banking Act of 1933, commonly referred to as the Glass-Steagall Act. This law drew a line in the sand between commercial and investment banking. Commercial banks were generally prohibited from engaging in the securities business; investment banks were prohibited from taking deposits. The law reflected the mood of the time and is representative of a number of policies that critics believed was an unprecedented intrusion into the private market. *"An important motivation for the Act was the desire to restrict the use of bank credit for speculation and to direct bank credit into what Glass and others thought to be more productive uses, such as industry, commerce, and agriculture."*[22]

Congress created the Federal Deposit Insurance Corporation (FDIC) in the same law as the 1933 Glass-Steagall Act. The FDIC is not funded by tax dollars but requires all institutions to pay premiums that are used to fund its operations, including an insurance program whereby member banks are backed by the full faith and credit of the United States government. A similar scheme was set up in 1934 to insure deposits of savings and loan associations,[23] and in 1970 for credit unions.[24] The effect of deposit insurance on the American financial system is profound. *"Since the start of FDIC insurance on January 1, 1934, no depositor has lost a single cent of insured funds as a result of a failure."*[25] An interesting side effect of this deposit insurance was to not only make depositors feel secure but to also help control mortgage lending rates and keep them relatively low. Because banks and S&Ls knew their assets (deposits) were insured and backed by the federal government, they could loan money at modest rates. In addition to guaranteeing deposits, the FDIC also *"directly examines and supervises more than 4,500 banks and savings banks for operational safety and soundness."* The FDIC is the primary federal regulator of banks that are chartered by the states that do not join the Federal Reserve System.[26]

1930's: Credit Unions, Savings and Loan Associations, and Federal Home Loan Banks

In an earlier attempt to lower the cost of home mortgages, Congress passed and President Hoover signed the Federal Home Loan Bank Act in 1932. This act created the Federal Home Loan Bank System to allow the Federal Home Loan Banks to

---

22 Maues, Julia, "Banking Act of 1933, commonly called Glass-Steagall": http://www.federalreservehistory.org/Events/DetailView/25
23 National Housing Act of 1934, Pub.L. 84–345, 48 Stat. 847
24 12 U.S.C. §§ 1781–1790(c)v
25 Who is the FDiC?" https://www.fdic.gov/about/learn/symbol/index.html
26 Ibid.

advance loan funds to savings and loan associations, building associations, depository institutions, etc.,[27] so that those institutions could make mortgage loans to consumers. Member institutions purchasing stock in the Federal Home Loan Bank in return were qualified for advances from the FHLB for purposes of making mortgage loans to consumers. In the years following World War II these banks became a major force in funding mortgage loans in the Unites States. As part of the Housing and Economic Recovery Act of 2008, the Federal Housing Finance Agency (FHFA) was charged with overseeing the FHL banks.[28] According to the FHFA, around 80% of U.S. lending institutions rely on the FHL banks as a source of funds.[29]

The Great Depression caused Congress to seek out new ways to provide deposit and loan services for consumers, and as a result created the federally chartered credit union.[30] While functionally similar to banks, the credit union charter to provide services to a certain field of membership as not-for-profit entities exempt from some federal taxes[31] caused many banks to strongly oppose their creation.

1930's: The Mortgage, Transformed
Before the Great Depression, the single-family home mortgage was a very different instrument than the 30-year fixed-rate mortgage we know today. Typically, residential mortgages in the United States were available only for a short term (5–10 years) and featured "bullet" payments of principal at term. Unless borrowers could find the means to refinance these loans when they came due, they would have to pay off the outstanding loan balance. In addition, most loans carried a variable interest rate. [32]

Despite President Hoover's attempt to introduce liquidity into the mortgage market via the Home Loan Bank System, home prices continued to fall with the economy. Mortgage loans were short-term loans that required frequent refinancing and because home prices were falling, lenders became fearful that their collateral position would continue to erode, leaving them upside down if they refinanced the loan. The refusal to refinance created a vicious economic cycle where borrowers defaulted, homes went into foreclosure, housing prices continued to fall, and the economy plunged into turmoil.

In a particularly successful piece of the New Deal legislation, Roosevelt pushed the Home Owners Loan Act of 1933 through Congress. It created the Home Owner's Loan Corporation (HOLC) *"[t]o provide emergency relief with respect to home mortgage indebtedness, to refinance home mortgages, to extend relief to the owners of homes occupied by them and who are unable to amortize their debt elsewhere…"*[33]

---

27 Federal Home Loan Bank Act of 1932, Pub.L. 72–304, 47 Stat. 725, §4a
28 "Governance and Regulation" http://www.fhlbanks.com/governance-and-regulation.html
29 "The Federal Home Loan Bank System" http://www.fhfa.gov/SupervisionRegulation/FederalHomeLoanBanks/Pages/About-FHL-Banks.aspx
30 Federal Credit Union Act 12 U.S.C. ch. 14
31 26 USC Sec. 501(c)
32 Richard K. Green, Susan M. Wachter The American Mortgage in Historical and International Context, Journal of Economic Perspectives, Volume 19, Issue 4, Fall 2005, pages 93-114.
33 Home Owners Loan Act of 1933 Pub.L. 73–43, 48 Stat. 128.

The HOLC was successful by two important measures. First, by the mid-1930s, it provided refinancing for nearly 20% of urban homes in the country,[34] saving those homeowners from losing their homes while keeping lenders whole and preventing a further deterioration in home prices.

Second, these loans were not simply refinancing into the short-term, variable rate balloon loans of the past. These mortgage loans, roughly one million of them, were converted into fixed-rate, long-term (20-year) fully amortizing mortgages, fundamentally changing home-ownership in the United States and ushering in the modern era of mortgage finance.[35] In an unusual turn of events for a governmental agency whose purpose had been achieved, HOLC was wound down, netting a small profit for the government.[36]

1930's: The Federal Housing Administration (FHA)
The government intervened in the market via the HOLC to prevent the further collapse of the economy, but in doing so created a system where government was directly involved in the holding of these long-term mortgages. In the midst of the Great Depression, private-market participants would not purchase mortgages without some type of guaranty that the principal obligation would be repaid in full and on time. The challenge, then, was to introduce private money back into the system and get the government out of the mortgage business.

Congress attempted to address this problem with the National Housing Act of 1934.[37] This law created the Federal Housing Administration (FHA), which was tasked with providing mortgage insurance so that private money could be reintroduced into the market both in mortgage originations and in the secondary market.

Realizing that the old mortgage paradigm of short-term, balloon mortgages had helped lead to the Great Depression, the FHA kept the longer-term, amortizing mortgage originally used by the HOLC as a requirement for its mortgage insurance. The mortgage in America was forever changed.

As a condition precedent to making a loan with insurance from the FHA, a lender was and still is required to become an FHA-approved lender. The FHA is self-funded by premiums paid by borrowers for mortgage insurance, which allows borrowers to purchase homes with low down-payments[38] and provides the lender with certainty that they will be made whole should the borrower default.

---

34 Calder, L. (2009). Financing the American Dream: A Cultural History of Consumer Credit. Princeton University Press. p. 280
35 Green & Wachter, p 93-114
36 Rose, Jonathan D., "The Incredible HOLC? Mortgage Relief during the Great Depression," (January 15, 2010), www.uncg.edu/bae/econ/seminars/2010/Rose.pdf
37 National Housing Act of 1934 Pub.L. 84–345, 48 Stat. 847
38 Servicemen's Readjustment Act of 1944 (P.L. 78-346, 58 Stat. 284m)

1930's: Fannie Mae

Shortly after the creation of the FHA, Congress realized that liquidity in the mortgage markets was of paramount importance to continue the flow of loans to eligible borrowers. If lenders were required to hold their FHA-insured mortgages on their books for 20 years, their ability to lend new money would be drastically curtailed. As a result, the National Housing Act was amended in 1938 to create the Federal National Mortgage Association (FNMA), commonly called Fannie Mae. Fannie Mae purchased FHA insured mortgages from the originating lender, thereby freeing up the lenders capital to make additional loans.

1940's: Loans Specifically for Veterans

Following World War II, Congress passed the Servicemen's Readjustment Act of 1944, commonly called the G.I. Bill.[39] As a benefit of military service, veterans were eligible for VA loans, a portion of which are guaranteed by the government itself (the Department of Veterans Affairs). VA loan terms were (and are) often more generous than other loan options and include programs with no down-payments, no mortgage insurance, and no prepayment penalties.[40]

1950's and 1960's: Fannie Mae, Consumer Protection, and Compliance

In 1954 Congress again tried to extricate the government from the mortgage business and transitioned Fannie Mae into a semi-public company where shareholders could purchase common stock, with the government holding preferred stock.[41]

The Housing and Urban Development Act of 1968 split Fannie Mae into two organizations. One was a governmental agency named Ginnie Mae, set up to guarantee timely payment of principal and interest on privately issued mortgage-backed securities (MBS) collateralized by FHA, VA, or other government-insured or guaranteed mortgages, while the other half of the company kept the name Fannie Mae and was made fully private.[42]

As with the FHA, Fannie Mae became a reliable part of the mortgag-finance system. Home ownership was on the rise and the expansion of programs like private mortgage insurance further opened access to credit. Private mortgage insurance allowed borrowers to obtain a mortgage loan with less than the traditional 20% down payment by essentially duplicating the FHA mortgage insurance program, but in a non-governmental context and without the FHA loan limits. This insurance is designed to ensure that, should the borrower default, the lender would be made whole.

Next, with a fairly stable and complete mortgage-finance system, the government turned its attention to consumer protection, and as a result drastically expanded the need for lenders to develop programs to ensure compliance with new, consumer-focused laws.

---

39 Servicemen's Readjustment Act of 1944 (P.L. 78-346, 58 Stat. 284m)
40 "Purchase & Cash-Out Refinance Home Loans" http://www.benefits.va.gov/homeloans/purchasecashout.asp
41 12 USC Ch 13, Subch. III, §§1716-1723i

Borrowers have always received some type of documentation when they took out a mortgage loan. The promissory note tells borrowers what they owe, their payment amount, interest rate, and what remedies are available to the lender if borrowers stop paying. The mortgage or deed of trust tells borrowers how lenders can foreclose and take their home back if they stop paying. Of course, there is more to a mortgage transaction than just these legal documents. How does a borrower know the details of loan fees, fees paid to title companies, and fees paid to an attorney? How much will the borrower have paid in total principal and interest in 30 years? How do borrowers compare loans from multiple lenders when documents and terminology are not consistent?

Congress attempted to address these questions with The Truth in Lending Act (TILA) of 1968. This law was intended to promote the informed use of consumer credit by standardizing the disclosure of interest rates and other costs associated with borrowing. Likely the most well-known TILA disclosure is the mandated disclosure of an Annual Percentage Rate (APR), or the total cost of credit (e.g., interest, fees, etc.) expressed as a percentage.[43] This rate is required to be prominently disclosed and is intended to eliminate misleading interest-rate calculations.

TILA also provides one of the most powerful consumer-protection rights under law: the Right of Rescission. Rescission is designed to prevent borrowers from pledging their principal dwelling (e.g., non-purchase-money loan) without adequate time to consider all factors. In such cases, TILA provides a three-business-day cooling-off period with a right to cancel, so that the borrower can evaluate whether the money they will be lent is really worth the potential loss of their home.[44]

TILA is implemented by Regulation Z, which contains various model disclosures designed to ensure compliance with the law. When reviewing the requirements of any federal law, it is essential to understand and not overlook the importance of the Regulations and even Official Staff Interpretations vis-a-vis the underlying law. For example, TILA provides that if a lender uses a model form or follows Regulation Z, it has a safe harbor from violations of the law.

1970-80's: Freddie Mac, Expanded Consumer Protection and Unintended Consequences

Since the spin-off of Fannie Mae as a private entity in 1968, Congress believed it had a de-facto monopoly on the secondary mortgage market and thus sought to balance it by creating another entity to compete with Fannie Mae. And in 1970, it did that by creating the Federal Home Loan Mortgage Corporation (FHLMC), commonly called Freddie Mac.

Congress also believed that the agencies providing consumer data to lenders needed stronger rules to ensure consumer interests were protected. Congress passed The Fair

---

42 The Housing and Urban Development Act of 1968, Pub.L. 90–448, 82 Stat. 476
43 12 CFR 1026.6(b)(4)(i)
44 12 CFR 1026.15 & 1026.23

CHAPTER ELEVEN: *THE PENDULUM OF REGULATION* 157

Credit Reporting Act (FCRA) of 1970.[45] This law, implemented by Regulation V[46], was enacted to promote the accuracy, fairness, and privacy of consumer information collected by consumer reporting agencies. It was intended to protect consumers from willful or negligent inclusion of inaccurate information in their credit reports. To that end, FCRA sets standards for the collection, communication, and use of consumer credit information.

Continuing the trend of increasing consumer protections, Congress passed The Equal Credit Opportunity Act (ECOA) of 1974.[47] Implemented by Regulation B, it intends to secure equal credit availability to all creditworthy customers by prohibiting lenders from improperly discriminating when extending credit. Regulation B covers creditor activities before, during, and after any potential extension of credit. Creditors are prohibited from relying on factors such as race, color, religion, national origin, sex, reliance upon public assistance, or a prior good faith exercise of any right under the Consumer Credit Protection Act.[48]

In the same year, Congress addressed a troubling pattern of undisclosed kickbacks between agents, builders, insurers, and lenders involved in consumer real estate transactions with the passage of The Real Estate Settlement Procedures Act (RESPA) of 1974.[49] Originally implemented by HUD's Regulation X, RESPA was enacted to end these kickbacks and requires disclosure of all fees paid to the lender or a third party at or prior to loan closing. RESPA required lenders to provide a Good Faith Estimate (GFE) for all of a loan's approximate costs and an additional Settlement Statement (HUD-1) for loan closing.

With the passage of the consumer protection laws of the 1960's and 1970's one gets the impression that Congress realized some unsavory practices were occurring, but that they were unsure to what degree these practices permeated the mortgage market or whether there were other unscrupulous behavior about which they were simply not aware. To help collect more data on industry activity, Congress passed The Home Mortgage Disclosure Act (HMDA) of 1975.[50] Implemented by Regulation C,[51] the law is intended to provide the public and regulators with information and disclosures regarding the availability of housing credit. More specifically, it is used to identify potential discriminatory lending patterns in home loans, community-specific financial institution effectiveness, and optimal uses of public-sector investments.

HMDA requires most financial institutions to maintain a Loan/Application Register (LAR) and annually turn over the LAR to their supervising agency (e.g. Federal Reserve Board, National Credit Union Administration, or Office of Currency Comptroller).

---

45 15 USC §1681, et seq.
46 12 CFR §1022, et seq.
47 15 USC §1691, et seq.
48 See 12 CFR 202.4 and 12 CFR 102.4.
49 12 USC §2601, et seq.
50 12 USC §2801, et seq.
51 12 CFR §1003, et seq.

The LAR must include information about applications and completed loans for home improvements, home purchases, pre-approvals, and refinances for one- to four-unit dwellings. The data to be collected includes typical underwriting information, such as a borrower's income and the location of the home, as well as demographic information, such as the borrower's race and sex. The supervising agencies turn over the data to the Federal Financial Institutions Examination Council, which analyzes and publishes the results.

Having established a fairly sophisticated disclosure scheme, Congress turned its attention to the back-end of the mortgage lifecycle and to protecting debtors who fail to make loan payments. The Fair Debt Collection Practices Act (FDCPA) of 1977,[52] implemented by Regulation F,[53] established legal protection from abusive debt-collection practices, promoted fair debt-collection, and provided consumers with an avenue for disputing and obtaining validation of debt information in order to ensure the information's accuracy. It amended the Consumer Credit Protection Act and is sometimes used in conjunction with the Fair Credit Reporting Act.[54] The FDCPA creates guidelines under which debt collectors may conduct business, defines rights of consumers involved with debt collectors, and prescribes penalties and remedies for violations of the Act. Among other acts, debt collectors are prohibited from harassing, deceiving, threatening, abusing, or publishing a consumer's information.[55]

During this time, as Congress continued to pass laws regulating consumer financial services, the steadily increasing rates of the 1970's-80's produced an economic challenge which resulted in the massive closing of Savings and Loan Associations (S&L's). The increasing-rate environment impacted all aspects of the economy, but S&L's were particularly susceptible to the increases because they were primarily focused on making long-term fixed-rate mortgages. In order to help fund these mortgages, S&L's were reliant on deposits and when the interest rates that they needed to pay to get new deposits increased and the rates they were earning on these long-term mortgages did not, the S&L's began to rapidly lose money. The governmental response was to de-regulate these institutions with the hope that with more unfettered access to makes loans the S&L's would save themselves. Congress therefore passed the Garn–St Germain Depository Institutions Act of 1982, which permitted S&L's to make loans they previously had not been able to, such as nonresidential and variable-rate mortgages. These changes led to severe unintended consequences when S&L's, inexperienced with underwriting these products, expanded their portfolios into risky loans that eventually went bad and took the S&L's along with them.[56] While there were many additional factors contributing to the crisis, deregulation generally proved unsuccessful, and the consequence of this action was that the American taxpayer bailed out the industry.[57]

---

52 15 USC §1692, et seq.
53 12 CFR §1006, et seq.
54 15 USC 1681, et seq.
55 15 USC 1692 §§805-812
56 Robinson, K. J. (2013). The Savings and Loan Crisis.
   http://www.federalreservehistory.org/Events/DetailView/4
57 Financial Institutions Reform Recovery and Enforcement Act of 1989, Pub.L. 101–73

During the S&L crisis, 1,043 institutions holding $519 billion in assets were closed and from "January 1, 1986, through year-end 1995, the number of federally insured thrift institutions in the United States declined from 3,234 to 1,645, or by approximately 50 percent".[58]

1990's: Regulatory Seesaw

In 1990, the National Affordable Housing Act required additional detailed disclosures concerning the transfer, sale, or assignment of mortgage servicing and mortgage escrow accounts.

The 1990's also saw the introduction of the Home Ownership and Equity Protection Act (HOEPA), resulting in new disclosures for higher-cost, closed-end, and reverse mortgages. Tolerances for real-estate-secured loans and lender-liability limitations for disclosure errors were also introduced by HOEPA.

Coming full circle back to the private mortgage programs that helped increase homeownership, Congress passed the Homeowners Protection Act of 1998, providing borrowers with the right to request termination of their private mortgage insurance when their loan-to-value (LTV) ratio reaches 80%, and require the lender to terminate the insurance automatically when the LTV reaches 78%.[59]

It is important to note that the Glass-Steagall separation of commercial and investment banks was always controversial, and over the course of the century, support for the separation waned. This particular swing of the regulatory pendulum culminated with the Financial Services Modernization Act of 1999, commonly referred to as the Gramm-Leach-Bliley Act (GBLA). Among other things, GBLA repealed the Glass-Steagall prohibition on commercial banks participating in investment activities. This, too, would prove to be a controversial decision. Critics argued that the Gramm-Leach-Bliley Act, allowing commercial banks to invest in stocks, derivatives, and the insurance markets, caused institutions to form a massive conglomeration of financial services companies that were too big to fail, leading to the unintended consequence of the 2008 economic crisis.

THE 21ST CENTURY AND THE MORTGAGE MELTDOWN

In 2008 the economy faced the worst downturn since the Great Depression. All of the consumer-protection laws passed in the last 30 years did not prevent borrowers from obtaining, and lenders from making, loans that borrowers could not repay. Not surprisingly, the government reacted in a manner consistent with its history and intervened heavily, injecting enormous sums of money into the financial markets, even going so far as to become the majority shareholder in General Motors.[60] There are

---

58 Curry, T., & Shibut, L. (2000). The Cost of the Savings and Loan Crisis. FDIC Banking Review, 13(2), 26-35
59 12 USC 4902
60 Neil King Jr., Sharon Terlep, "GM Collapses Into Government's Arms" (Wall Street Journal, June 2, 2009) http://www.wsj.com/articles/SB124385428627671889

plenty of good summaries as to what happened and to attempt to recite those here is not practical. The Senate Banking Committee provided its own succinct summary when passing the Dodd–Frank Wall Street Reform and Consumer Protection Act:

"Two years ago today, Bear Stearns was collapsing. In the time since, Americans have faced the worst financial crisis since the Great Depression. Millions have lost their jobs, businesses have failed, housing prices have dropped, and savings were wiped out."[61]

There was no shortage of blame or critics to dispense it, with both regulation and deregulation held up as root causes of the 2008 financial crisis. Many argued that because of their status as government-sponsored entities, Fannie Mae and Freddie Mac had the implicit backing of the federal government. Proponents held that this was a good thing for the American people and the economy because it allowed Fannie/Freddie some freedom to craft aggressive programs to expand homeownership that would not have been otherwise possible. Critics, however, identified this implicit guaranty as key in the over-leveraging that contributed to financial crisis of 2008.

In a surprise to almost no one, the government executed on its implicit guaranty of Fannie Mae and Freddie Mac. Congress passed The Housing and Economic Recovery Act of 2008,[62] which placed both Fannie Mae and Freddie Mac into conservatorships under the direction of the Federal Housing Finance Authority. (As of 2015, neither Fannie nor Freddie has exited conservancy and the government has found itself back in the mortgage business.)

Dodd-Frank in General

In 2010 Congress passed what many call the most sweeping financial reform bill in the history of the United States: The Dodd-Frank Wall Street Reform and Consumer Protection Act of 2010. The massive law (over 2400 pages) is divided into 16 titles of U.S. Code. The legislative intent of the law was *"To promote the financial stability of the United States by improving accountability and transparency in the financial system, to end "too big to fail", to protect the American taxpayer by ending bailouts, to protect consumers from abusive financial services practices, and for other purposes."*[63]

The law attempts to accomplish this by modifying rules in vast areas of the financial system, including hedge funds, derivatives, credit default swaps, mortgage brokers, payday lenders, credit rating agencies, the insurance industry, and mortgage-backed securities. Interestingly, the law expresses the "Sense of the Congress" that reform will not be complete without addressing Fannie/Freddie, but there are no substantive modifications to those agencies in the Act.

Believing that a major cause of the collapse was too many uncoordinated federal agencies, the law created the Financial Services Oversight Council (FSOC) and

---

61 "Factsheet: Senate Financial-Regulation Bill" (Wall Street Journal, March 15, 2010)
   http://blogs.wsj.com/economics/2010/03/15/factsheet-senate-financial-regulation-bill/
62 HOUSING AND ECONOMIC RECOVERY ACT OF 2008, P.L. 110-289
63 DODD-FRANK WALL STREET REFORM AND CONSUMER PROTECTION ACT, PL 111-203, July 21, 2010, 124 Stat 1376

charged it with ensuring that threats to the economy are not siloed in multiple agencies and that data is shared, collectively understood by regulators and Congress, and acted upon when necessary. The Council is chaired by the Secretary of the Treasury, with membership from the major federal financial agencies (OCC, FDIC, SEC, etc.). In one of its more controversial provisions, Dodd-Frank provides a mechanism to break up large banks or other companies that *"would pose a grave threat to the financial stability of the United States"*[64] were they to fail. Upon recommendation of the Federal Reserve Board and a 2/3 vote of the council, these large companies can be required *"to sell or otherwise transfer assets or off-balance-sheet items to unaffiliated entities."*[65] This authority permits the governmental dissolution of companies, regardless of whether the company is a monopoly under the antitrust laws.[66] In cases where banks fail on their own, Dodd-Frank created the Office of Dissolution within the FDIC to wind down under-capitalized banks and created a mechanism to liquidate failed financial firms.

Dodd-Frank Specifically
Of the 16 titles of federal law created by Dodd-Frank, two specifically deserve special attention for their impact on the mortgage industry: Title XIV, The Mortgage Reform and Anti-Predatory Lending Act, which substantively modified many consumer protection laws, including major changes to TILA and RESPA (which are discussed in detail below) and Title X, The Consumer Financial Protection Act of 2010 which created the Consumer Financial Protection Bureau, or CFPB, and gave it **exclusive rulemaking authority** for any federal consumer financial law. These enumerated laws include almost any law that requires disclosures to consumers in a mortgage transaction such as TILA, HMDA, HOEPA, RESPA, ECOA, FCRA, etc.

In addition to its wide rulemaking authority for all federal consumer financial laws, the CFPB also has specific supervisory and enforcement power over depository institutions with assets over $10 billion and over their affiliates. The CFPB has noted that these *"institutions collectively hold more than 80 percent of the banking industry's assets."*[67]

In addition to traditional banks over $10 billion in assets, the CFPB was also given authority to oversee nonbank compliance for entities such as mortgage companies, brokers, servicers, payday lenders, etc., regardless of the size of these entities. Additionally, the CFPB has authority to define by rule other "larger participants" it wishes to pull under its supervisory umbrella.[68]

It is important to note that in the drafting of regulations, supervision of banks and non-bank entities, and the enforcement of consumer financial protection laws, the CFPB has taken a decidedly consumer-focused approach in contrast to the "safety and soundness" approach of other supervising agencies. This approach is evident in the numerous consumer focus-groups that the CFPB used in designing the new Loan Estimate and

---

64 12 USC 5331(a)(5)
65 Ibid.
66 12 USC 5331 et. seq.
67 "What the Division Does" http://www.consumerfinance.gov/jobs/supervision/
68 12 USC §§5511-5519

Closing Disclosure documents, and, the consumer-compliance database the CFPB has created. On July 21, 2011, the day the CFPB officially took over enforcement authority for federal consumer finance laws under Dodd-Frank, the Special Advisor to the Secretary of the Treasury, (and now Senator from Massachusetts) Elizabeth Warren, sent a letter to the CEOs of all banks with assets over $10 billion succinctly stating the vision of the new Bureau:

> "*Focus on Consumers:* The CFPB will focus on risks to consumers, and compliance with the Federal consumer financial laws, when it evaluates the policies and practices of a financial institution. We expect that institutions will offer consumer financial products and services in accordance with Federal consumer financial laws, and will maintain effective systems and controls to manage their compliance responsibilities. As we conduct our reviews, we will focus on an institution's ability to detect, prevent, and correct practices that present a significant risk of violating the law and causing consumer harm."[69]

Some commentators argue that the CFPB has focused on the consumer to the detriment of the mortgage industry, requiring changes that are impractical or burdensomely expensive with little practical benefit to borrowers, which have the unintended consequence of increasing time to close loans and reducing availability of credit.

Separation of Powers: The Funding and Structure of the CFPB

The Dodd-Frank Act was not a true bipartisan bill and consequently has polarized opinion as to the efficacy and constitutionality of the law. Only three Republican senators voted for the bill.[70] Things were even more polarized in the House where no Republican representative voted for it.[71] Supporters of the law argue the previous regulatory structure provided far too many federal agencies with overlapping responsibilities, which led to conflicting rules and a general incoordination of information that heavily contributed to the economic crisis of 2008. Some of the strongest criticism of the law comes not from the fact that one agency writes regulations for such a large body of law, but rather that the funding and structure of the CFPB is inconsistent with meaningful congressional oversight.

The Constitution provides that "*[n]o money shall be drawn from the treasury, but in consequence of appropriations made by law; and a regular statement and account of receipts and expenditures of all public money shall be published from time to time.*"[72] In attempting to understand the back story and thought process the founders used in drafting the Constitution, scholars often turn to the Federalist Papers, a series of articles by Alexander Hamilton, John Jay, and James Madison advocating for its adoption. In

---

[69] "CFPB Supervision CEO Letter No. 1" (July 21, 2011)
   http://files.consumerfinance.gov/f/2011/07/20110721_CFPBSupervisionCEOLetter1.pdf
[70] H.R. 4173(11th): Dodd-Frank Wall Street Reform and Consumer Protection Act
   https://www.govtrack.us/congress/votes/111-2010/s208
[71] H.R. 4173(11th): Dodd-Frank Wall Street Reform and Consumer Protection Act
   https://www.govtrack.us/congress/votes/111-2009/h968
[72] 72 U.S. Const. art. 1 §9, cl. 7

CHAPTER ELEVEN: *THE PENDULUM OF REGULATION* 163

Federalist 58, Madison reasons that this power, the power to withhold funds, is the paramount power entrusted to government and particularly the House. *"The House of Representatives cannot only refuse, but they alone can propose, the supplies requisite for the support of government. They, in a word, hold the purse that powerful instrument by which we behold.... [t]his power over the purse may, in fact, be regarded as the most complete and effectual weapon with which any constitution can arm the immediate representatives of the people, for obtaining a redress of every grievance, and for carrying into effect every just and salutary measure."* [73] Many argue that this principle, fundamental to the Constitution, has been violated by the Dodd-Frank Act.

Section 1017 of Dodd-Frank created the CFPB as a sub-department of the Federal Reserve Board with one director, appointed by the President and confirmed by the Senate. In what can only be described as a highly controversial provision, the law explicitly funds the CFPB not through the normal appropriations process, but through the Federal Reserve Board, which according to the law must transfer to the CFPB *"the amount determined by the Director to be reasonably necessary to carry out the authorities of the Bureau under Federal consumer financial law."* [74] While this is funding is limited to 12% of the operating budget of the Federal Reserve Board, the actual dollars are higher than many lawmakers would prefer. The CFPB estimates that for fiscal year 2016 the cap will be $631.7 million.[75] The kicker for the opponents of the law is that it goes on to state that *"[n]otwithstanding any other provision in this title, the funds derived from the Federal Reserve System pursuant to this subsection* **shall not be subject to review by the Committees on Appropriations of the House of Representatives and the Senate** (emphasis added)."[76] The law specifically removes from Congress the power to fund or review the funding of the CFPB.

The power of the Director to determine his or her own budget and then have that budget transferred from the Federal Reserve Board without any congressional approval places substantial, relatively unchecked power with one person. What would the founders think of such a law? It takes some mental gymnastics to harmonize this funding scheme with Madison's views that the overriding power of the purse must be specifically placed with the branch of government closest to the people. It is not difficult to imagine the indignation some feel at the structure of the CFPB. Efforts to modify it so that it has a board of governors versus a single director and to bring its funding under the purview of Congress have been introduced numerous times, and even passed the House. However, the bill was not brought up for a vote in the Senate.[77]

The Volker Rule GBLA Reversed? Glass-Steagall Reinstated?
With the passage of GBLA in 1999, commercial banks were once again allowed to

---

73 The Federalist Papers No. 58
74 12 USC 5497
75 The CFPB Strategic Plan, Budget, and Performance Plan and Report, Available:
   http://files.consumerfinance.gov/f/201502_cfpb_report_strategic-plan-budget-and-performance-plan_FY2014-2016.pdf
76 12 USC 5497
77 https://www.govtrack.us/congress/bills/113/hr3193

participate in investment markets. Some argued that this conglomeration of interests created institutions that were too big to fail and led to the unprecedented governmental intervention in the market during the 2008 financial crisis. One of these critics was Paul Volker, former Chairman of the Federal Reserve Board. Volker argued that depository intuitions involvement in investment markets had been a major component of the financial crisis. President Obama agreed and when introducing the so-called Volker Rule said: *"Banks will no longer be allowed to own, invest, or sponsor hedge funds, private equity funds, or proprietary trading operations for their own profit, unrelated to serving their customers. If financial firms want to trade for profit, that's something they're free to do. Indeed, doing so — responsibly — is a good thing for the markets and the economy. But these firms should not be allowed to run these hedge funds and private equities funds while running a bank backed by the American people."*[78] The President only partially won this battle, and a watered-down Volker Rule was codified as Section 619 of the Dodd-Frank Act. Recall that Glass-Steagall once required separation of investment and commercial banking, which was reversed by GLBA. While the toned down Volker Rule did not completely take us back to the Glass-Steagall era, it does restrict institutions from investing more than 3% of their Tier 1 capital into the security markets.[79]

Federal Preemption and Changes in Dodd-Frank
Federal preemption of state law comes from the Supremacy Clause[80] of the Constitution and is illuminated by Supreme Court in prominent cases like *McCulloch v. Maryland*, discussed at some length previously in this article.

With preemption, courts have held that in some areas Congress intended to fully occupy a field, and therefore any state law on the subject matter is preempted. Courts have also held that in other areas, federal law has only set the floor, and a state may pass additional laws so long as those do not conflict with the federal law. As an example, the Truth in Lending Act requires various, specific disclosures to loan borrowers,[81] but borrowers in Michigan are also required by state law to receive a "Borrowers Bill of Rights."[82] On its face, this law is not unconstitutional because Congress did not intend to prevent additional information from being provided to borrowers and the state law simply provides an additional disclosure that is not in conflict with the federal law. A state law like this would clearly apply to a state-chartered institution, but what about a bank chartered under federal law? This is where preemption analysis can get difficult because a federally chartered bank is afforded some level of protection from state banking laws.

During the Civil War, Congress passed the National Bank Act (NBA), which provided that nationally chartered banks would have all powers *"as shall be necessary to carry on*

---

78 Remarks by the President on Financial Reform, January 21, 2010. Available:
    https://www.whitehouse.gov/the-press-office/remarks-president-financial-reform
79 12 USC. 1851
80 U.S. const. Art. 6, §2
81 15 U.S.C. ch. 41 § 1601
82 M.C.L.A. 445.1636

the business of banking." [83] Soon thereafter the Supreme Court held that state banking laws in conflict with the NBA were preempted.[84] In another case, the court held that national banks could charge higher interest than permitted under state law for state-chartered banks.[85] When the Office of the Comptroller of the Currency (OCC) was created, it was given authority to draft regulations interpreting the NBA, and has taken a fairly strong position that banks chartered under federal law are, except in some limited cases, exempt from state-law requirements and restrictions.

As an example of the extensive nature of preemption for national banks, in *Barnett Bank of Marion County, N.A. v. Nelson, Florida Insurance Commissioner,* the Supreme Court put a fine point on the issue and held that state laws are preempted when they *"prevent or significantly interfere with the national bank's exercise of its powers."*[86] In 2004, the OCC took preemption a step further and issued a rule based on the Barnett holding that provided state laws were preempted then they *"obstruct, impair or condition"* the ability of a national bank to carry out its purpose. The wave of preemption was further expanded in Watters v. Wachovia Bank, N.A. when the Court held that state-chartered subsidiaries of national banks were also preempted from state law.[87] After Watters, many observers believed that federal banks were almost completely out of the reach of any state legislature. In 2009, the Court did slightly move the needle back when it held that a state could, in fact, enforce their own fair-lending laws against a national bank, noting that *"general supervision and control' and 'oversight' are worlds apart from law enforcement."* [88]

Some argue that the mortgage crisis of 2008 can be directly traced back to the Civil War period and the preemption from state law afforded nationally chartered banks by the National Bank Act. This preemption, it is argued, allowed 'too big to fail' national banks to be shielded from investigation by state attorneys general some 150 years later. These arguments maintain that the OCC was too slow to rein in these national institutions, and, using preemption as a sword, the OCC prevented state attorneys general from intervening. At the same time, state-chartered institutions, fearing they would be at a competitive disadvantage, resisted any attempts to pass laws preventing them from making the same risky loans as the national banks — which they argue caused the global recession.

Dodd-Frank addresses the preemption issue in a number of ways. First, it essentially codifies the standards in *Barnett* as the go-forward standard for determining preemption, thereby removing the ability of the courts to use a more liberal standard. Some argue that this Barnett rule is less deferential to national banks than the 2004 OCC rules on preemption, but others disagree with this conclusion. Interestingly, Dodd-Frank limits

---

83 12 U.S.C. § 24
84 National Exchange Bank v. Moore, 17 F. Case. 1211 (1868)
85 Tiffany v. National Bank of Missouri, 85 U.S. 409 (1874).
86 Barnett Bank of Marion County, N.A. v. Nelson, Florida Insurance Commissioner, et al., 517 U.S. 25 (1996)
87 Watters v. Wachovia Bank, N.A. 550 U.S. 1 127 S.Ct. 1559 (2007)
88 Cuomo v. Clearing House Ass'n., 129 S.Ct. 2710 (2009)

the OCC's power to declare that a state law is preempted, by requiring consultation with the CFPB prior to a preemption determination. The law also codifies the holding in *Cuomo* that certain consumer financial laws can be enforced against national banks. Finally, the law overturns the Watters decision and provides that state-chartered subsidiaries of national banks are not entitled to federal preemption. The jury is still out as to whether the OCC regulations implementing the Dodd-Frank standards have been issued in such a way as to have rendered the law functionally equivalent to pre-Dodd-Frank standards. In any event, it does seem unlikely that federal banks will be afforded a wider field of preemption in the future under Dodd-Frank.[89]

Attempts to Prevent Future Governmental Intervention in the Mortgage Market (ATR/QM/QRM)

In the Dodd-Frank Act, Congress clearly placed a fair amount of blame on what it saw as unscrupulous lenders. As the argument went, lenders made loans and as quickly as possible sold those loans to Fannie Mae or Freddie Mac. That system worked so long as the pool of qualified borrowers continued to outpace the loan volumes to which these lenders had become accustomed. The problem, of course, was that once these qualified borrowers received their mortgages, they were no longer available to take out mortgages and the pool of qualified borrowers began to dry up. Lenders who built their businesses on these loan volumes and the associated profits began to slowly lower their underwriting standards until they were making loans with little or no regard as to whether the borrower had the ability to repay the loan. As long as they could still sell these loans to Fannie or Freddie, the system still seemed to work — until it didn't.

To address this perceived issue, Dodd-Frank required that lenders make a reasonable, good-faith determination that borrowers can repay their loan. If a borrower's loan is foreclosed, the borrower can raise as an affirmative defense to the foreclosure that the lender did not consider their ability to repay when making the loan. Recognizing that this scenario created the prospect of lenders being hauled into court to defend themselves against almost any loan in foreclosure, the law created a so-called Qualified Mortgage (QM). The QM rule creates a safe harbor for the lender against a claim from borrowers that they did not have the ability to repay the loan. The new QM rule is fairly extensive. For example, loans with negative amortization are not permitted, nor are loans with terms over thirty years or scenarios where the borrower's total debt-to-income ratio exceeds 43%.[90]

Lenders making a QM that is considered higher-priced do not receive a safe harbor, but are entitled to a rebuttable presumption that the borrower had the ability to repay. This presumption shifts the burden on the borrower to prove that they did not have the ability to repay. It is important to note that QM loans are not a necessity. So long as the borrower has passed the ATR test, a lender is free to make the loan, but may later have to prove the borrower had the ability to repay, because they will not be afforded a safe harbor for these loans.

---

89 12 USC 5551 et. seq.
90 12 CFR 1026.43(e)(2)(vi)

In addition to the Qualified Mortgage, Dodd-Frank attempted to address the problem of lenders selling bad loans to Fannie and Freddie by creating another category of mortgage, the Qualified Residential Mortgage (QRM). The idea of the QRM is that if a lender subjects itself to delineated underwriting standards, it can sell the mortgage outright on the secondary market. If, however, the lender chooses to make a mortgage that does not meet this criteria, it must retain a 5% stake in the mortgage being sold. This requirement means that while lenders can make riskier loans, they must have some skin in the game and cannot simply transfer that risk to Fannie or Freddie. Fortunately for the industry, the definition of a QRM closely matches that of a QM, drastically simplifying underwriting standards for loans that will be potentially salable.

The ATR/QM/QRM rules are designed to introduce a level of transparency and commonality to the market without preventing lenders from making loans that fit their risk profile. For lenders with a healthy appetite for risk, they only need to confirm the borrower has a reasonable ability to repay — an argument against which would be futile. On the other hand, lenders can jump through some additional underwriting hoops if their risk profile points towards the security of a safe harbor and the flexibility to sell off 100% of the loan. In any event, the government is now more involved than ever in the mortgage underwriting market — the regulatory pendulum has swung and caused the pivot point to move with it. Government involvement in underwriting standards may in the future decrease, but likely will never go away.

Attempt to Simplify Consumer Disclosures: TRID
When Congress originally divided up regulatory responsibility for laws impacting the mortgage industry, they placed rulemaking authority for the Truth-in-Lending Act with the Federal Reserve Board and the Real Estate Settlement Procedures Act with the Department of Housing and Urban Development. Consequently, two different major disclosure schemes emerged, with the Federal Reserve Board writing regulations requiring early and final Truth in Lending Disclosures and HUD writing regulations requiring a Good Faith Estimate of Settlement Costs and a final Settlement Statement. While these different disclosures did not outright contradict each other, they did provide different level of details that many felt contributed to confusion as to the terms and cost of loans. In an attempt to combat this confusion, Dodd-Frank moved regulatory authority for both laws to the CFPB and required the agency to issue rules combining disclosures.

After much deliberation and consumer and industry feedback, on November 20, 2013 the CFPB released a 1,888-page final rule mandating the integration of the disclosures currently required by RESPA and TILA, specifically the Truth-In-Lending Disclosures (Early and Final TIL), the Good Faith Estimate (GFE), and the HUD-1 Settlement Statement (HUD-1). Under the TILA-RESPA Integrated Disclosure (TRID) Rule, the GFE and Early TIL are combined to form the Loan Estimate. The final rule combines the Final TIL and HUD-1 into a single Closing Disclosure. The new rule took effect on October 3, 2015, meaning that the new disclosure documents must be used for any transaction in which the loan application was received on or after that day.

The first new form, the Loan Estimate, is designed to provide disclosures that will be helpful to consumers in understanding the key features, costs, and risks of the mortgage for which they are applying, and to encourage and facilitate loan shopping. The form must be provided to consumers within three business days after they submit a loan application, and seven business days prior to consummation. The second form, the Closing Disclosure, is designed to provide information that will be helpful to consumers in understanding all of the costs and risks associated with the transaction. This form must be provided to consumers at least three business days before they close on the loan.[91]

The forms are designed to use clear language and make it easier for consumers to locate key information, such as interest rates, monthly payments, and costs to close the loan. The forms also provide more information to help consumers decide if they can afford the loan and compare the costs of different loan products.[92]

The TRID Rule added new disclosures designed to help consumers understand the costs associated with their loan, including the Total Interest Percentage amount and separate "In 5 Years" amounts to capture the total principal and total principal, interest, mortgage insurance, and loan costs paid through the end of the 60th month of the loan. The new disclosures also required alphabetizing of fees and rounding of certain fee amounts in attempt to make the information easily understandable.

Long-Term Implications
The CFPB developed the TRID Rule as part of its Know Before You Owe (KBYO) initiative to make it easier for consumers to understand and compare mortgage loans. The CFPB involved consumers and industry participants in the creation of the new forms by soliciting feedback and engaging in consumer testing. KBYO is not just about mortgages, however. The CFPB has already launched into other consumer financial product segments with its KBYO initiative, creating a model credit-card agreement and a student-loan shopping sheet (and encouraging universities to use it).

While the TRID Rule was the first major regulatory change under KBYO, it likely will not be the last. As part of KBYO, the CFPB will continue to gather data on consumers' financial experience pain points. If those pain points pose significant risks to consumers, the CFPB may go beyond "encouraging" use of model consumer disclosures by proposing regulations that require new disclosures or modification to existing ones.

Data-Driven Disclosures and Transactions
The TRID Rule brought to fruition something many in the mortgage industry have been long seeking: a common industry dataset. Prior to the TRID Rule taking effect, Fannie Mae and Freddie Mac published a common dataset to implement the CFPB's Closing Disclosure. The new Uniform Closing Dataset (UCD) is based on MISMO

---

91 Integrated Mortgage Disclosures under the Real Estate Settlement Procedures Act (Regulation X) and the Truth In Lending Act (Regulation Z), Preamble, p. 3
92 Ibid.

(Mortgage Industry Standards Maintenance Organization) data standards. Sometime after the TRID Rule takes effect, Fannie and Freddie will be requiring the UCD from lenders.

Adoption of the UCD has wide-ranging implications for the mortgage industry. The benefits of having data available in a standard, commonly understood format will make it easier to exchange and analyze data. Once the UCD is implemented and these benefits are realized, the movement toward a common dataset may gain traction for other disclosures and transactions.

The CFPB Goes for Data: HMDA Modified

Contemporaneous with the transfer of rulemaking authority for HMDA from the Federal Reserve Board to the CFPB, Dodd-Frank modified the types of institutions and transactions subject to HMDA. In October 2015, the CFPB adopted rules that significantly increased the amount of data institutions must provide from each applicable transaction, including both applications and completed loans. Some of the data required are descriptors of the transaction, such as whether the lien securing a loan is in first place or is subordinate, or whether the transaction involves a manufactured home.

The 2015 regulations also expanded the list of demographic information that must be requested from borrowers in the form of "government monitoring information." The information sought includes age, sex, race, and ethnicity but, applicants are given complete discretion to self-identify their ethnicity and race classifications. If applicants decline to self-identify, lenders must identify race classifications in face-to-face situations with applicants, based on applicant surname and visual observation. [93]

The regulations changed the definitions of home-improvement loans and refinancings to standardize the data reported, and expanded the amount of information from the terms and conditions of closed loans that must be provided to regulators. Lenders must now disclose the loan rate-spreads for originations of home-purchase loans, secured home-improvement loans, and refinancings. Loan-rate-spread is the difference between the annual percentage rate (APR) on a loan and the yield on comparable Treasury securities.

Lenders must now reveal to their regulator all closed loans that have points or fees in excess of specific thresholds defined in the Truth in Lending Act and Regulation Z, as well as whether a loan is subject to the Home Ownership and Equity Protection Act (HOEPA). These are considered "high-cost loans" because either interest rates or loan points and fees exceed certain pre-defined levels. Lenders are additionally required to report (1) denials of requests for preapproval; and (2) approvals of "requests for preapprovals" that result in originations.[94] With these substantive revisions it is clear the CFPB is focused not only on protecting the consumer, but protecting the consumer

---

93 12 CFR 203.4(a)(iv)(B)(3) and official comment
94 15 USC 1639

CFPB Continues to Focus on Consumer: UDAAP

Of all the expansions of consumer protection law, none concerns lenders more than the ban on financial businesses and their service providers from engaging in any "unfair, deceptive, or abusive act or practice."[95] The regulations apply to many parts of the financial services industry, including lending, deposits, mortgage servicing, debt collection, and marketing.

This is a particularly worrisome requirement for lenders, not because they intend to carry on their business by abusing or deceiving their customers, but because there is an inherently subjective component in determining what is unfair. Unlike other regulations, it is difficult to know for sure if you are complying with the law. The disclosed Annual Percentage Rate is either right or wrong; fees disclosed are either right or wrong. These are clear and objective facts. Figuring out whether a lender treated someone unfairly? That's much tougher. Especially in the absence of an established body of case law to guide the industry on what "is" and what "isn't".

The law applies to both particular transactions or events ("acts") and ongoing business policies and procedures ("practices"). An act or practice that is abusive could also be characterized as unfair or deceptive. The three categories are not mutually exclusive, and an act that fits in one category may have characteristics of one or both of the other categories.

Unfair Acts or Practices

An act or practice is unfair when it causes or is likely to cause substantial injury to consumers; the injury is not reasonably avoidable by consumers; and the injury is not outweighed by countervailing benefits to consumers or to competition.[96]

Unfortunately, lenders and service providers will need to subjectively judge if their way of doing business is likely to harm consumers, and if consumers can avoid that harm without excessive cost or consequence to themselves. The main, although not exclusive, type of harm at issue is monetary. How much is this term or provision in the agreement costing borrowers, and are they getting some benefit from it? Can a reasonable consumer avoid this cost? The CFPB states in its examination manual that it will likely find acts unfair if they either cause a significant amount of harm to a small number of people or a small amount of harm to a large number of people. The facts of the situation will be central in determining if some act is unfair.

Deceptive Acts or Practices

A few months ago, I was forwarded a curious email demonstrating that a sentence as

---

95 12 USC §5536(a)(1)(B)
96 12 USC §§ 5531, 5536.

simple as *"I never said she stole my money"* has seven very different reasonable meanings depending on which word is stressed. How are lenders to ensure their employees do not deceive borrowers when communicating in a language with such nuances? The law does provide some guidance by providing that statements or actions which would mislead an ordinary consumer about important terms of an agreement will be seen as deceptive acts, but the subjectivity of the English language understandably scares many lenders.[97]

The CFPB looks to existing interpretations from the Fair Debt Collection Practices Act and the Federal Trade Commission (FTC) enforcement decisions for clarification on how it will likely interpret allegedly deceptive acts. The FTC's "four Ps" test can be helpful in judging whether a representation, act, omission, or practice is likely to be deceptive or misleading: Is the statement *prominent* enough for the consumer to notice? Is the information *presented* in an easy-to-understand format that does not contradict other information in the package and at a time when the consumer's attention is not distracted elsewhere? Is the *placement* of the information in a location where consumers can be expected to look or hear? Finally, is the information in close *proximity* to the claim it qualifies?

Abusive Acts or Practices

Abusive acts are those that either actively hinder a person from knowing what he or she is agreeing to or taking advantage of the person's lack of knowledge. An abusive act could be one that: materially interferes with the ability of a consumer to understand a term or condition of a financial product or service; takes unreasonable advantage of a consumer's lack of understanding of the material risks, costs, or conditions of the product or service; uses the consumer's inability to protect his or her interests in selecting or using a consumer financial product or service; or takes advantage of a consumer's reasonable reliance on a lender's employee or contractor to act in the interests of the consumer.

We all know that there are bad apples in any organization who bend or break the policies of the organization when it suits their own needs. Even if a specific employee deceives a customer, it is imperative to show the regulators that it was an isolated act and not part of a larger practice of the organization as a whole. Therefore, a lender must ensure there are documented processes and procedures for communicating with borrowers, commonly understood training materials that are continually refreshed for all relevant employees, and a policy of maintaining all consumer correspondence. This data will prove invaluable in enabling the lender to show that a good-faith, serious plan exists to prevent the commission of unfair, deceptive, or abusive acts.

Looking Forward: Data Will Be King

Governmental action impacting the financial-services industry is seldom proactive and therefore to fully understand financial regulations one must understand the historical and economic forces leading to those regulations. This is a major reason why the

---

97 12 USC § 5531(c)(2)

regulatory process is inherently flawed: regulations are backward-looking and attempt to predict bad things that may happen in the future based on things that happened in the past. Compounding the matter, these changes are often made in the fog of war, where well-intended regulations have unintended consequences. The industry should not forget how the well-intentioned modification of banking powers in the reversal of Glass-Steagall and the deregulation of savings and loans contributed to economic calamity in their respective eras. There is reason to be hopeful, however, that this will not continue to be the case. New systems that can quickly access loan data that are complete, consistent, and compliant are becoming the industry norm. Protecting consumers through analysis of this data is what the CFPB cares about. On the day the Bureau sprang into existence, it sent a letter to all banks with assets over $10 billion and laid this out:

Data Driven. Like all CFPB activities, the supervision function rests firmly on analysis of available data about the activities of entities it supervises, the markets in which they operate, and risks to consumers posed by activities in these markets."[98]

The CFPB is getting this data from a variety of sources and using it in a variety of ways. First, consider what the Bureau is doing with data regarding complaints against lenders. It has made it available in a publically searchable database that is driving market participants into action. It is simply bad for business to have prospective customers browse complaints about how a lender treated its existing customers. This leads to a self-service type of enforcement where the lender makes things right without governmental enforcement, simply because of the risk that public shame has on future business. Second, consider the increased data payload required under HMDA for things like lien position, manufactured home loans, and the borrower's self-identified race. Other data will come from the new Uniform Closing Data, which will make it easier to exchange and analyze loan-specific closing data. The CFPB isn't just collecting this data; they are using it to identify problems in the market and to draft and enforce regulations before the next crisis hits the headlines.

Precisely for this reason, systems that ensure and safeguard data integrity are of paramount importance. Such technology can be used to drive software applications that produce compliant documents and disclosures, defend against complaints and lawsuits, and to provide information to regulators and the secondary market. While many lenders do not have the resources or expertise to build these systems, it is logical for them to look to third parties for this expertise. Lenders should be cautioned, however, that the CFPB will be looking hard at third-party service-provider relationships. In an industry bulletin in 2013, the CFPB reminded the industry that: "Depending on the circumstances, legal responsibility may lie with the supervised bank or nonbank as well as with the supervised service provider."[99]

---

[98] "CFPB Supervision CEO Letter No. 1" (July 21, 2011)
   http://files.consumerfinance.gov/f/2011/07/20110721_CFPBSupervisionCEOLetter1.pdf
[99] CFPB Bulletin 2012-13

As an organization wades through regulations, it is imperative to thoroughly vet third-party service providers and to partner with organizations that have proven track records and vetted expertise for ensuring compliance with federal financial law.

Big data is changing the regulatory paradigm. As real-time data increasingly drives all aspects of American life, so too will it drive the participants in the banking industry. Banking regulators will be able to receive a wealth of information in almost real time — this speed would have been unheard of just a few years ago and will allow the focus of the CFPB to remain on protecting the consumer through the use of reliable data.

Finally, in presenting this data to consumers we must not forget that we are living in a world where paper is going away and the medium by which lenders disclose information to borrowers is likely to change. The comprehensible exchange of data to consumers is what matters. The mechanism of communicating data should be tailored based on the information to be conveyed, not the other way around. The medium by which we disclose will likely change, and that's a good thing. Visitors to the Jefferson Memorial in Washington, D.C., will recall the quote carved on the interior of the monument:

> *I am not an advocate for frequent changes in laws and constitutions. But laws and institutions must go hand in hand with the progress of the human mind. As that becomes more developed, more enlightened, as new discoveries are made, new truths discovered and manners and opinions change, with the change of circumstances, institutions must advance also to keep pace with the times. We might as well require a man to wear still the coat which fitted him when a boy as civilized society to remain ever under the regimen of their barbarous ancestors.*

Financial products, contracts, and disclosures rooted in a paper-based, non-electronic world is the functional equivalent of forcing a grown man to wear the coat that fit him as a boy. Let's advance to keep pace with the times and get some clothes that fit us.

ABOUT THE AUTHOR

Chris Appie is Vice President & Counsel at Compliance Systems, Inc. (CSi). Chris earned a B.A. with honors in Political Science from Oakland University and a J.D. from The University of Detroit Mercy School of Law. He is a member of the State Bar of Michigan, including the Business Law and Real Property sections. Chris leverages years of specialization in financial regulatory compliance and close working relationships with CSi's partners to ensure best-in-class solutions and services. When he's not busy with work, he's busy trying to keep his five kids under control in grocery stores and other public places.

CSi is a provider of best-in-class financial transaction technology and expertise that allows lenders and financial institutions across the United States to compliantly document financial transactions including mortgage, home equity, consumer, and commercial loans as well as deposit and retirement accounts. CSi specializes in analyzing the data around these transactions resulting in documentation that mitigates risks thus allowing institutions to better target resources on activities that help their bottom line.

Chris wishes to express his very special thanks to the great folks at CSi for their help and contributions to this article: Dennis Adama, Sandy Nietling, Manish Joshi, Greg Bierl, Joel Haitz, and Dan Poling.

CHAPTER TWELVE

FAIR LENDING

STEPHEN M. MCGURL | MANAGING DIRECTOR

MCGURL RISK ADVISORS LLC

In order to know what fair lending is, it would be useful to know the definition of "unfair lending." Unfair lending or as it is better known by the term, discriminatory lending, is the practice of banks, governments (local, state or federal agencies), or other lending institutions denying credit, in the form of housing loans, to one or more groups of people, primarily on the basis of their race, ethnic origin, sex, or religion.

The definition of fair lending, as described by the Dodd–Frank Wall Street Reform and Consumer Protection Act (commonly referred to as Dodd-Frank), states that "fair lending" consists of "fair, equitable, and nondiscriminatory access to credit for consumers." The primary legislation behind fair lending is the Fair Housing Act (FHAct) and Equal Credit Opportunity Act (ECOA). I will reference other legislation that can be used to support fair lending a little later in the chapter.

In 2010, Dodd–Frank was signed into federal law by President Barack Obama and had an overriding effect on FHAct and ECOA, because they appeared to not have a definition of fair lending. The Dodd-Frank Act granted very broad oversight for fair lending to the Consumer Financial Protection Bureau ("CFPB"). The lack of a clear definition within either the FHAct and ECOA in conjunction with the above definition from the Dodd-Frank Act leads the lending community to believe that the CFPB has a broad mandate for them to enforce the legislation.

Dodd-Frank established the CFPB as the first federal agency with a mission focused solely on consumer financial protection and making consumer financial markets work for American consumers, responsible businesses, and the economy as a whole. Dodd-Frank also established the Office of Fair Lending and Equal Opportunity, known as the Office of Fair Lending, within the CFPB. The Office of Fair Lending was responsible for "providing oversight and enforcement of Federal laws intended to ensure the fair, equitable, and nondiscriminatory access to credit for both individuals and communities that are enforced by the Bureau," including ECOA and HMDA. The Office of Fair Lending also coordinates "fair-lending efforts of the Bureau with other Federal and State regulators to promote consistent, efficient, and effective enforcement of federal fair lending laws." They, as a result of their mandate, have an obligation to work with private industry, fair lending, civil rights, and consumer and community advocates on the promotion of fair lending compliance and education.

Fair lending is still needed in the United States. Equal access is still needed in the United States. To be clear, banks, government agencies, and other lenders need the continued guidance and enforcement of our federal and state laws to monitor them to ensure their policies, procedures, and practices provide equal access to credit on a fair basis.

A HISTORY OF FAIR LENDING

When the Civil War ended in April of 1865, and the abolition of slavery was ratified by Congress in December of 1865, Jim Crow laws were introduced. These laws led to the discrimination of racial and ethnic minorities, especially African-Americans. Fifteen state courts obeyed ordinances that enforced the denial of housing to African American and other minority groups in white-zoned areas. It wasn't until 1917 that these ordinances became illegal through the Supreme Court case, Buchanan v. Warley. Following the court's decision, however, nineteen states legally supported "covenants," or agreements, between property owners to not rent or sell any homes to racial or ethnic minorities. These covenants too were made illegal in 1948.

The National Housing Act of 1934, also known as the Capehart Act, was enacted June 28, 1934. The Capehart Act was part of FDR's New Deal passed during the Great Depression in order to make housing and home mortgages more affordable. It created the Federal Housing Administration (FHA), which is still in existence today, and the Federal Savings and Loan Insurance Corporation, which ceased to exist after 1989, when its assets were transferred to a fund under the Federal Deposit Insurance Corporation (FDIC) authority. Both the FHA and the Federal Savings and Loan Insurance Corporation worked to create the backbone of the mortgage and home-building industries.

The Housing Act of 1937, formally the "United States Housing Act of 1937," and sometimes called the Wagner-Steagall Act, provided for subsidies to be paid from the U.S. government to local public housing agencies (LHAs) to improve living conditions for low-income families. The sponsoring legislators were Representative Henry B. Steagall, Democrat of Alabama, and Senator Robert F. Wagner, Democrat of New York.

The act created the United States Housing Authority within the United States Department of the Interior. The act builds on the National Housing Act of 1934, which created the Federal Housing Administration. Both the 1934 Act and the 1937 Act were influenced by American housing reformers of the period, particularly Catherine Bauer.

These acts were initially controversial, but eventually gained national acceptance, and some provisions of the Act have remained, but in amended form. The Housing Act of 1949, enacted during the Truman administration, set new post-war national goals for decent living environments; it also funded "slum clearance" and the urban renewal projects, and created many national public housing programs. In 1965 the Public Housing Administration, the U.S. Housing Authority, and the House and Home Financing Agency were all swept into the newly formed and re-organized United States Department of Housing and Urban Development (HUD).

Though these acts of national legislation were aimed at the worthy goals of improving housing conditions, clearing slums, forming agencies that would do good works in the future by creating many national housing programs, and forming the beginning of a national housing policy, there was no clear policy that gave guidance to fair lending.

It was not until the Civil Rights Act of 1968, popularly known as the Fair Housing Act, that the federal government made any and all types of housing discrimination unconstitutional. The act explicitly prohibits housing discrimination practices common at the time, but still active today, including filtering information about a home's availability, racial steering, blockbusting, and redlining. Today, we have seen enforcement actions that counter "reverse redlining," which may closely reflect racial steering.

The Housing and Community Development Act of 1974 was a United States federal law that amended the Housing Act of 1937 to create Section 8 housing, authorized "Entitlement Communities Grants" to be awarded by HUD, and created the National Institute of Building Sciences.

The Equal Credit Opportunity Act (ECOA) was added to the federal Consumer Credit Protection Act in 1974. The ECOA, known as Regulation B, contains two basic and comprehensive prohibitions against discriminatory lending practices:

- A creditor shall not discriminate against an applicant on a prohibited basis regarding any aspect of a credit transaction.

- A creditor shall not make any oral or written statement, in advertising or otherwise, to applicants or prospective applicants that would discourage, on a prohibited basis, a reasonable person from making or pursuing an application.

As you can see, the history of fair lending as it relates to the mortgage industry was a progressive notion. The beginning of legislation in the New Deal helped create the backbone of a housing industry, but didn't specifically address fair lending. As the laws of the United States started to address housing issues as a whole and the impact of housing on the economy, fair lending became a concept that was both necessary and a matter of good business practice.

HOW FAIR LENDING HAS HELPED THE LENDING INDUSTRY AND CONSUMERS

Fair lending has undoubtedly helped the lending industry improve its practices towards lending overall, and its policies and procedures as well. What bank is now not aware of the concepts of overt evidence of disparate treatment, comparative evidence of disparate treatment, or evidence of disparate impact?

Lending institutions are now required to address certain issues that will help them stay in compliance with all state and federal laws. This is good policy and it is good business. The institutions will only benefit from doing the following:

- Reviewing its lending policies and practices to ensure that they are reaching the most customers possible within their natural footprint
- Reviewing its compliance-management systems so that they are in compliance with local, state, and federal laws, and consequently reduce their costs of responding to complaints from customers and regulators
- Reviewing new products in the development stage; the lenders should be aware of what their competitors are offering and what their customers are asking for in their marketplace
- Regularly reviewing and enhancing its fair lending training program to develop consistency in its interactions with its customers
- Identifying aspects of the pricing/underwriting process that involve discretion, which is most of underwriting and pricing; monitoring the lending practices of its brokers and other agents; and comparing its geographical lending profile with those of similar lenders to avoid allegations of redlining

Monitoring sales and service practices helps the lender ensure that it is in compliance with the law and regulatory guidelines. Indirectly, a *self-test* designed specifically to measure adherence to the law (e.g. Fair Housing Act, Equal Credit Opportunity Act and Fair Trade Act) will also provide valuable information about the sales and service process and suggest areas where the financial institution can improve.

By regularly monitoring the experiences encountered by consumers, the lender can detect and then resolve issues that may represent violations of the law before they result in complaints and allegations that can negatively impact reputation and sales. A plan that systematically tests sales and service practices will be viewed positively by third parties, government regulators, and enforcement agencies. It is a proactive step to help ensure customers are treated fairly and honestly. Hence it has been viewed as a mitigating factor by regulators and enforcement agencies when reviewing issues uncovered during a fair lending examination or investigation.

For the consumer, it means a process that provides the information needed to choose the right loan at the most appropriate rates and terms. The data or information generated through self-testing designed specifically to measure discrimination is privileged under the Equal Credit Opportunity Act ("ECOA") and the Fair Housing Act ("FHA"). In order to encourage self-testing, Congress in 1996 created a legal privilege for data gathered on a voluntary basis to specifically assess compliance with ECOA and the FHA.

The regulators defined self-testing as voluntary activities carried out by a third party that collect information assessing compliance, that is not readily available or collected in loan files, applicant records, or through everyday normal business practices. The purpose was to encourage financial institutions to use more creative types of activities — Mystery Shopping, Post 6 Application Surveys, and Customer Feedback — to help detect those issues that cannot readily be identified through file reviews and on-site inspections by field auditors. Since then, the definition of a self-test has been expanded to include activities to classify protected and non-protected classes of consumers applying for non-mortgage loan products in order to specifically assess compliance with ECOA. Civil-rights groups, community activists, government regulators, and enforcement agencies regularly use mystery shopping and post application surveys to help detect violations of the law and acts against public policy.

Recognizing that fair lending is good business, the "Closing the Gap" study states that lenders, and their regulators, should look for ways to eliminate the unjustified lending disparities that have been documented over the years. A series of questions from it are included here to assist lenders in evaluating fair-lending performance. When hiring, do you seek cultural diversity which reflects the demographics of your community? When hiring lending staff, do you take into account possible racial, religious or other prejudices of job applicants? Do you train all staff in the area of fair lending? Do you have any mechanisms through which unfair lending practices, policies, or procedures may be detected? If so, are you able to determine the effectiveness of those mechanisms? Do you inform all potential borrowers, regardless of their race or ethnic background or the location of the property, about all of your lending programs so they may decide which best fits their needs? Do you deliberately steer minority applicants to federally insured programs because you assume that minorities are less credit-worthy? Do you have mortgage lending practices that include location of property as a risk factor? Does your mortgage pre-qualifying procedure tend to encourage or discourage minority applicants? Do you offer home-buyer education programs for potential applicants who are unfamiliar with the mortgage lending process? Do you regularly review your advertising to see if the choice of illustrations or models suggests a customer preference based on race? Are you as assertive in attracting minority applicants as you are in attracting non-minority applicants? Are you familiar with the practices of the real estate and mortgage brokers with whom you do business? Do you encourage the brokers and appraisers with whom you do business to be constructively active in minority communities? All things being equal, do non-minority and minority credit applicants have the same chance of getting a loan from this financial institution?

A lender should have the goal of serving everyone who wants to become a homeowner. We are committed to treating all of our customers fairly and equally in every neighborhood where we do business. This commitment is part of our mission to provide quality financial services to our customers. Our commitment to treating all customers fairly is also in agreement with all related laws. We price our mortgages fairly, and we believe our current practices prevent discrimination against individuals. We take fair lending very seriously, and are committed to working with industry and community groups to stamp out discrimination.

MITIGATING FAIR LENDING RISKS

Exceptions that deviate from standards or best practices created by a lender, such as pricing or credit scores, are not always a bad thing. They can help to generate business for a mortgage lender by allowing consumers to be approved for a loan. However, as much as exceptions can aid a consumer, they can also cause a nightmare for mortgage lenders by subjecting them to increased examination scrutiny, fair lending enforcement actions, or supervisory observations.

To achieve fair-lending compliance with exceptions by way of exception management and policies, mortgage lenders should understand that exception management generally requires more monitoring than other areas of management, specifically to ensure that comparable individuals are being treated similarly. Proper monitoring can help a mortgage lender avoid violations and keep them off the radar of regulatory agencies. Exceptions and discretions are not illegal when it comes to mortgage loan origination; they do, however, draw additional regulator attention to fair-lending compliance.

Framework to Ensure Compliance with Exception Management and Fair Lending

First, there is the big-picture framework that can also be translated to multiple areas of a company, and is not isolated to just fair lending and exceptions management. A lender should have a strong compliance-management system (CMS) in place. A successful compliance management system will consist of a lending-compliance program, which should include policies and procedures to govern the lending process. Next, there should be a consumer-compliant management program. This program should respond to individual matters and identify major issues and/or trends that may foreshadow a possible fair-lending violation. In addition, a compliance audit should be conducted by an independent entity on a yearly basis at minimum. Finally, there needs to be active management from the executive leadership team, as well as Board of Director oversight, to establish clear lines of accountability in the lending process. It is not difficult to imagine how these characteristics of a strong compliance-management system can easily translate to other areas of concern for a company, such as additional oversight requirements related to board governance.

Best Practices to Ensure Compliance with Exception Management and Fair Lending

There are several steps in the loan process that are typically subject to exceptions of established company policies, making them attributable to discrimination risk factors. These particular steps need to be methodically managed. The exceptions often involve underwriting, pricing guidelines, marketing plans, servicing, and loan application forms. These exceptions lead to the need for a second tier of compliance that focuses on a more direct framework to help manage the exceptions. An effective framework will ensure that the lender will not face any violations of discrimination when exercising discretion in the loan-approval process.

Managing these exceptions will involve using the following best practices:

Have defined policies and approaches for exceptions. Defined policies of special circumstances will demonstrate discipline around treating similarly-situated individuals. For example, if a lender has a standard threshold of a 620 credit score, a loan officer may be permitted to reduce to 600 when certain factors exist. If a potential borrower has an even lower credit score of 580, a manager's approval would be required, and, finally, for a score below 580, review and approval would be required from a company executive, such as a Chief Risk Officer.

Mortgage lenders should implement a reporting system in which the frequency of exceptions can be documented. The frequency reports could include items such as the given number of exceptions, or a trend encountered when they are used. This will allow for policy adjustments to decrease the need of exceptions.

Lenders should analyze why exceptions are being made, specifically looking at what triggers the exception, including, for instance, threshold requirements or accommodating a client who frequently uses the lender to obtain mortgage loans.

The exception-approval process should be well documented through a chain-of-command structure, commencing with the first time the exception is documented and through to the final individual with approval authority. Depending on the severity of the exception, there should be various tiers of approval authority required. Each individual file containing exceptions should be documented and should be able to stand alone in the event an issue arises requiring review of such an exception.

Probably the most important step in exception management is a comparative review. It is imperative that companies have a framework to monitor underwriting exceptions to ensure comparable individuals are being treated similarly to help avoid discriminatory impacts. Implementation of the framework and these types of best practices can help to ensure that, when lenders issue exceptions to loans, whether by credit score, price, or some other factor, the company is mitigating risks that may arise from investigations by regulatory agencies as they relate to fair-lending violations. In addition to this framework, a lender can take further steps to combat fair-lending violations by acting in a completely transparent manner in its dealing with consumers.

THE CURRENT LAWS THAT SUPPORT FAIR LENDING

The two federal fair-lending laws — the Equal Credit Opportunity Act and the Fair Housing Act — prohibit discrimination in credit transactions, including transactions related to residential real estate.

Equal Credit Opportunity Act (ECOA) – Regulation B
The Equal Credit Opportunity Act (ECOA), Regulation B, prohibits

discrimination in any aspect of a credit transaction. It applies to any extension of credit, including residential real estate lending.

Regulation B prohibits discrimination based on eight measurable factors: race or color, religion, national origin, sex, marital status, age (provided the applicant has the capacity to contract), the applicant's receipt of income derived from any public assistance program, and the applicant's exercising, in good faith, of any right under the Consumer Credit Protection Act (exercising their right to complain).

The regulation is concerned not only with the treatment of persons who have initiated the application process, but also with lender behavior before the application is even taken. Lending officers and employees must be careful to take no action that would, on a prohibited basis, discourage a reasonable person from applying for a loan. This is the area quite often where a bank runs into trouble, when the sales management structure is not aware of the practices of its front-line sales force.

For example, a loan officer may not intentionally (or unintentionally) advertise its credit services or practices in ways that would tend to encourage some types of borrowers and discourage others on a prohibited basis. To take this one step further, your practices can not have an "adverse impact" on any one of the protected classes under Regulation B. This is known as *disparate impact*. Additionally, a loan officer may not use prescreening tactics likely to discourage potential applicants on a prohibited basis. Instructions to loan officers or brokers to use scripts, rate quotes, or other means to discourage applicants from applying for credit on a prohibited basis are also prohibited.

In January 2015, in a much anticipated case, the U.S. Supreme Court heard oral arguments that challenged whether disparate impact will remain a safeguard against discrimination in housing regardless of intent. In June of 2015, the Supreme Court returned its ruling. It stated that disparate impact claims are cognizable under the Fair Housing Act after considering the Act's "results-oriented language," the Court's interpretation of similar language in title VII of the Civil Rights Act of 1964, and the Age Discrimination in Employment Act (ADEA), Congress' ratification of disparate-impact claims in 1988 against the backdrop of the unanimous view of nine Courts of Appeals, and the statutory purpose.

The Supreme Court's decision upholds HUD's disparate-impact rule which establishes a burden-shifting framework for addressing disparate-impact claims. HUD issued its rule in February 2013 to establish a standard by which disparate-impact cases were, and will continue to be, adjudicated. The Court recognized that discrimination is not always overt and that disparate impact is an important tool to permit "plaintiffs to counteract unconscious prejudices and disguised animus that escape easy classification as disparate treatment."

Fair Housing Act

The Fair Housing Act (FHAct) which is implemented by HUD regulations, prohibits discrimination in all aspects of residential real estate–related transactions, including, but not limited to, making loans to buy, build, repair, or improve a dwelling, purchasing real estate loans, selling, brokering, or appraising residential real estate selling, or renting a dwelling.

The FHAct prohibits discrimination based on race or color, religion, national origin, sex, familial status (households having children under the age of 18 living with a parent/legal custodian, pregnant women, or persons with legal custody of children under 18), or handicap; discouraging or selectively encouraging applicants with respect to inquiries about or applications for credit, refusing to extend credit, or using different standards in determining whether to extend credit, varying the terms of credit offered, including the amount, interest rate, duration, and type of loan, using different standards to evaluate collateral, treating a borrower differently in servicing a loan or invoking default remedies, using different standards for pooling or packaging a loan in the secondary market; and a lender may not express, orally or in writing, a preference that is based on a prohibited factor or indicate that it will treat applicants differently on the basis of a prohibited factor.

Moreover, a lender may not discriminate on a prohibited basis because of the characteristics of an applicant, prospective applicant, or borrower, a person associated with an applicant, prospective applicant, or borrower (for example, a co-applicant, spouse, business partner, or live-in aide), the present or prospective occupants of either the property to be financed or the neighborhood, or other area in which the property to be financed is located.

Finally, the FHAct requires lenders to make reasonable accommodations for a person with disabilities when such accommodations are necessary to afford the person an equal opportunity to apply for credit.

Home Mortgage Disclosure Act – Regulation C

The Home Mortgage Disclosure Act (HMDA) was enacted by Congress in 1975 and was originally implemented by the Federal Reserve Board's "Regulation C". On July 21 2011, rule-writing authority for HMDA transferred from the Federal Reserve Board to the Consumer Financial Protection Bureau (CFPB). The CFPB's Regulation C, which now implements HMDA, requires lending institutions to report public loan data.

HMDA mandates that certain lenders, usually designated by size, shall report certain information to their regulator so that the regulator can make determinations on the lender's fair lending performance. Currently, the rule regarding the asset-size exemption threshold for banks, savings associations, and credit unions under Regulation C is at $44 million for 2016. Institutions with assets of $44 million or less as of December 31, 2015 are exempt from collecting HMDA data in 2016.

HMDA and the CFPB's Regulation C require most mortgage lenders located in metropolitan areas to collect, report, and disclose data about mortgage loan applications, originations, and purchases. The data cover home-purchase loans, home-improvement loans, and refinance transactions. There are 48 data points that lenders must report, as of October 2015. The data reported include the type, purpose, and amount of the loan; the race, ethnicity, sex, and income of the loan applicant; the location of the property; and loan-pricing information for some loans. HMDA data is used to help determine whether banks are serving the housing needs of their communities. The information is also used to assist in identifying possible discriminatory lending patterns. If CFPB determines that an institution is showing a pattern of discriminatory practices, it is obligated to refer the lender to the Department of Justice (DOJ).

Almost immediately, the data collected by HMDA has enabled researchers, community groups, and others to understand the fundamental relationship between mortgage lending and community development. In other words, HMDA data shows evidence of location discrimination. However, HMDA could not yet fulfill its statutory goal of ensuring fair-lending practices, since HMDA data represents lending at the community level and not the demand for mortgage credit or creditworthiness at the individual level. The available data was not specific enough to draw conclusions about community fair lending. And banks simply argued that HMDA data only revealed disparity where there were relatively few applications or where applicants were disproportionately lacking in creditworthiness.

As part of its response to the savings and loan crisis of the late 1980's, Congress amended HMDA in 1988 to expand the types of institutions it covered. And in 1989, the Financial Institutions Reform Recovery and Enforcement Act (FIRREA) required HMDA to include transaction-level data, including data on race, gender, and income. With these amendments, HMDA data was now detailed enough for regulatory agencies to identify potential discrimination in mortgage application denial decisions.

TYPES OF LENDING DISCRIMINATION

The courts have recognized three types of proof of lending discrimination under the ECOA and the FHAct:

- Overt evidence of disparate treatment
- Comparative evidence of disparate treatment
- Evidence of disparate impact

Disparate Treatment
The existence of illegal disparate treatment may be established either by statements revealing that a lender explicitly considered prohibited factors (overt evidence), or by differences in treatment that are not fully explained by legitimate nondiscriminatory factors (comparative evidence).

Overt Evidence of Disparate Treatment
Overt evidence of discrimination exists when a lender openly discriminates on a prohibited basis. For example, a lender offers a mortgage product with a lower loan-to-value ratio (more restrictive) for applicants age 21–30, and a higher loan-to-value (more favorable) for applicants over 30. This policy violates the ECOA's prohibition on discrimination on the basis of age.

Overt evidence of discrimination also exists even when a lender expresses — but does not act on — a discriminatory preference. For example, a loan officer tells a customer, "our bank does not like to make home mortgages to Pacific Islanders, but the law says we may not discriminate, and we have to comply with the law." If an employee of a bank makes this statement, it violates the FHAct's prohibition against statements expressing a discriminatory preference (prohibiting the discouraging of applicants on a prohibited basis).

Comparative Evidence of Disparate Treatment
Disparate treatment occurs when a lender treats a credit applicant differently on the basis of one of the prohibited factors. It is not necessary to show that, beyond the difference in treatment, the treatment was motivated by prejudice or by conscious intention to discriminate against a person. Different treatment is considered by courts to be intentional discrimination because the difference in treatment on a prohibited basis has no credible, nondiscriminatory explanation.

Disparate treatment may be more likely to occur in the treatment of applicants who are neither clearly well qualified nor clearly unqualified. Discrimination may more readily affect applicants in this middle group for two reasons. First, applications that are "close cases" have more room and need for lender discretion. Second, whether or not an applicant qualifies may depend on the level of assistance provided by the lender in completing an application. The lender may, for example, propose solutions to credit or other problems relevant to an application, identify compensating factors, and provide encouragement to the applicant. Lenders are under no obligation to provide such assistance, but to the extent that they do, the assistance must be provided in a nondiscriminatory way.

Example: A nonminority couple applies for an home loan. The lender finds adverse information in the couple's credit report. The lender discusses the credit report with the couple and determines that the adverse information, a judgment against the couple, was incorrect, as the judgment had been vacated. The nonminority couple was granted a loan. A minority couple applied for a similar loan with the same lender. Upon discovering adverse information in the minority couple's credit report, the lender denies the loan application on the basis of the adverse information without giving the couple an opportunity to discuss the report.

The foregoing is an example of disparate treatment of similarly situated applicants, apparently on the basis of a prohibited factor, in the amount of assistance and information provided. If a lender has apparently treated similar applicants differently on the basis of a prohibited factor, it must explain the difference. If the explanation is not found to be credible, the Federal Reserve may conclude that the lender intentionally discriminated.

Redlining is a form of illegal disparate treatment whereby a lender provides unequal access to credit, or unequal terms of credit, because of the race, color, national origin, or other prohibited characteristic(s) of the residents of the area in which the credit-seeker resides or will reside or in which the residential property to be mortgaged is located. Redlining may violate both the FHAct and the ECOA.

Disparate Impact
A disparate impact occurs when a lender applies a racially (or otherwise) neutral policy or practice equally to all credit applicants, but the policy or practice disproportionately excludes or burdens certain persons on a prohibited basis. *Example:* A lender's policy is to deny loan applications for single-family residences for less than $60,000. The policy has been in effect for ten years. This minimum loan amount policy is shown to disproportionately exclude potential minority applicants from consideration because of their income levels or the value of the houses in the areas in which they live. Although the law on disparate impact as it applies to lending discrimination continues to develop, it has been clearly established that a policy or practice that creates a disparity on a prohibited basis is not, by itself, proof of a violation.

Community Reinvestment Act (CRA) – Regulation BB
The Community Reinvestment of the Housing and Community Development Act of 1977 is a United States federal law designed to encourage commercial banks and savings associations to help meet the needs of borrowers in all segments of their communities, including low- and moderate-income neighborhoods. Congress passed the Act in 1977 to reduce discriminatory credit practices against low-income neighborhoods, a practice known as redlining.

The Act instructs the appropriate federal financial supervisory agencies to encourage regulated financial institutions to help meet the credit needs of the local communities in which they are chartered, consistent with safe and sound operation. To enforce the statute, federal regulatory agencies examine banking institutions for CRA compliance and take this information into consideration when approving applications for new bank branches or for mergers or acquisitions.

Fair Credit Reporting Act
The Fair Credit Reporting Act ("FCRA") is U.S. Federal Government legislation enacted to promote the accuracy, fairness, and privacy of consumer information contained in the files of consumer-reporting agencies. It is intended to protect consumers from the

willful and negligent inclusion of inaccurate information in consumers' credit reports. The FCRA regulates the collection, dissemination, and use of consumer information, including consumer credit information. Together with the Fair Debt Collection Practices Act ("FDCPA"), the FCRA forms the foundation of consumer-rights law in the United States. It was originally passed in 1970, and is enforced by the US Federal Trade Commission, the Consumer Financial Protection Bureau, and private litigants. The FCRA also has a positive impact on fair lending from a consumer's perspective by ensuring that they are using fair and accurately reported information.

Recent Court Decisions Related to Redlining
Redlining is defined as the practice of banks or real estate agents steering minority families away from predominantly white neighborhoods. Some recent cases show that redlining is still occurring today.

Redlining has an impact on people's lives and their ability to build wealth. The federal government has been ramping up its investigations of housing discrimination through its Financial Fraud Enforcement Task Force, a partnership of the DOJ and the Consumer Financial Protection Bureau that was started under President Obama's leadership. The task force's goal is to expose more redlining cases.

Major U.S. cities have been trying to eliminate housing practices that have negative impacts on their residents by filing suits against banks and financial services companies suspected of a variety of steering practices. Several cities have files suits against banks for "Reverse Redlining". This is a form of predatory lending where the statistics show banks offer high-interest loans to minorities more often than not. The next paragraphs explore several recent cases.

In September of 2015, the U.S. DOJ settled with Hudson City Savings Bank (NJ) for close to $33 million after an investigation found that it closed very few mortgage loans with African American and Latino borrowers between 2009 and 2013. The DOJ called it the "largest residential mortgage redlining settlement in its history". The bank serviced one of the largest housing markets in the nation, covering mortgages throughout New Jersey, New York, and even Philadelphia. But the bank went out of its way not to set up any branches in minority neighborhoods. As part of the settlement, Hudson City will have to open two full-service branches in non-white communities.

Also in September of 2015, the New York State Attorney General settled with Evans Bank for $825,000 after discovering that the bank erased black neighborhoods from maps used for determining mortgage lending.

In May of 2015, HUD settled with Associated Bank for $200 Million over redlining in Chicago and Milwaukee. The HUD complaint stated that the bank denied mortgage loans to black and Latino applicants between 2008 and 2010. As in the Hudson City case, Associated Bank will have to open new branches in predominantly black and brown communities

Miami sued 3 banks; Wells Fargo, Bank of America, and Citigroup, alleging that the banks were steering black and Latino applicants towards high-interest, "predatory" loans. Though a federal judge dismissed the suits, an Appeals Court reversed that decision, saying that banks could have foreseen the "attendant harm" that resulted from the predatory lending when they resulted in large numbers of foreclosures throughout the city.

Los Angeles sued four banks in in early 2015; J. P. Morgan Chase, Bank of America, Wells Fargo, and Citigroup. The banks were accused of both traditional redlining and also "reverse redlining". L.A. dropped the J. P. Morgan Chase suit. The suits against Bank of America and Wells Fargo are on appeal while the Citigroup case goes to trial in 2016.

FUTURE TRENDS IN FAIR LENDING

It is safe to say that fair-lending reviews will continue as long as there are laws on the books and regulators to enforce them. The CFPB has issued its guidelines on exams and they focus on the entire process in the mortgage transaction. They will scrutinize the loan officer's marketing (and understanding of what they can market), the interview process, and all the way through to the servicing of the loan. And if you think that they won't scrutinize the loss-mitigation process after the Independent Foreclosure Review of 14 national servicers in 2011 to 2013, think again.

One trend resulting from the examinations is a steep increase in penalties corresponding to a fair lending enforcement action as outlined in this chapter. Furthermore, since the inception of the CFPB there has been a steady tendency for violations related to fair lending to be referred to the DOJ. This occurs when there are allegations that a lender violated the ECOA when denying loan applications. Referrals are also made to the DOJ when there are findings of other discriminatory issues, such as pricing or credit score requirements.

Banks are exposed to several reviews from various state and federal regulators and may possibly be under penalties from both at the same time. Due to overlapping regulations, they can be exposed to being penalized by several regulators for the same violation. Theoretically, a bank could violate a regulation that is in ECOA and be investigated by the CFPB, while also violating the FHA, which would be under investigation by HUD, and violate a state regulation at the same time and be subject to a review by the state banking regulator. If you think this can't happen, you would be surprised to learn that it happened to a bank in Michigan in 2013.

U.S. Demographics

Estimates are that the United States population at the middle of the 21st century will exceed 400 million people. The U.S. Census bureau predicts as many as 450 million. This is anywhere from 75 million to 125 million more than living in the United States today.

The population is also growing older to the point that it will have a significant impact on how we view housing in this country. The portion of the population that is currently at least 65 years old—13 percent—is expected to reach about 20 percent by 2050.

Between 2000 and 2050, census data suggest, the U.S. 15-to-64 age group is expected to grow 42 percent. In contrast, because of falling birth rates abroad, the number of young and working-age people is expected to decline.

Demographic shifts and changing values will increase demand for pedestrian-friendly, mixed-use communities in both urban and suburban settings, according to John McIlwain of the Urban Land Institute. "The age of suburbanization and growing homeownership is over," McIlwain said in a recent report, "Housing in America: The Next Decade." "The coming decades will be the time of the great reurbanization as 24/7 central cities grow and suburbs around the country are redeveloped with new or revived walkable suburban town centers." This transition will be fueled by the growth of two-person households, an end to baby boomers' suburban infatuation, and public policies designed to stimulate compact development. There are four specific age groups that will affect housing:

1. *Older baby boomers* - Today, many older baby boomers are stuck in their suburban properties because of the real estate bust, which has put them underwater — owing more on their mortgage than the property is worth. But McIlwain says that older baby boomers who can sell their homes aren't necessarily following the road maps of previous generations.

2. *Younger baby boomers* - Although they are now entering their peak earning years, younger baby boomers have significant housing-market headaches in front of them. On top of the phenomenon of negative equity, many will have a tough time locating buyers for their suburban homes.

3. *Generation Y (late teens to early 30s):* The real estate bust has had a significant impact on how generation Y's 83 million Americans view homeownership. As they watch millions of Americans lose their homes to foreclosure, the allure of buying real estate has become less powerful, McIlwain said. "They will be renters by necessity and by choice rather than homeowners for years ahead," he says.

4. *Immigrants:* There are roughly 40 million foreign-born people living legally or illegally in the United States today, and this demographic is expected to grow swiftly in the coming years. McIlwain notes that immigrant populations tend to cluster together. "These clusters have moved from the central cities where they tended to gather in the past to the inner suburbs over the last two decades," he says. Housing demand from immigrants may one day flow to the larger suburban homes that are expected to face downward pricing pressure in the coming years. "The reduced prices of these homes and their larger size ... make them an attractive option for larger immigrant families, though prices will have to drop considerably for this to happen," McIlwain says.

How will these four groups affect Fair Lending? With an increased group of immigrants that invariably will reflect a higher Latino percentage of the population, the effect on fair lending will be positive. The Generation Y population, having grown up with more clarity on government's impact on housing and fairness will be competing with the "new" immigrants that will be helping populate the suburbs and the larger homes of the retiring baby boomers. Fair Lending will always be a focus of regulators; however, the reality of the market is that the lenders will adapt to the new reality of a "majority minority."

Industry Impact: The Cost of Compliance
A skilled, high-quality compliance function is expensive to build, but there is a growing realization that investment in effective risk and control functions and the infrastructures that go with it is worthwhile on many levels.

Given the continuing increase in the volume of regulatory information published, it is logical that firms are spending a considerable proportion of their time tracking and analyzing the impact of regulatory developments. No matter what the size of your compliance department, regulatory change is clearly resource-hungry, and at times will require more associates within your firm (and from outside) to shift their focus on your regulatory and fair-lending projects. Failure to track and analyze all relevant regulatory developments may put your company at a distinct disadvantage, and may mean that it runs significantly larger risks than if appropriate levels of skilled resources had been allocated.

The number of U.S. compliance teams spending more than 10 hours per week tracking and analyzing regulatory developments nearly doubled (13 percent in 2013 and 25 percent in 2014). U.S. firms are now spending significant time considering the implications of the Dodd-Frank changes. Working in an ever-changing regulatory environment has become the norm for financial-services firms in the U.S. A significant amount of skilled compliance resources will still need to be devoted to reviewing proposed regulatory changes, assessing the likely impact on the companies and, where necessary, lobbying the regulators with their input on workload impact.

The implementation of any regulatory change will always involve a range of compliance activities, not least the required updates to policies and procedures. The need to involve the frontline sales personnel in the fair-lending policies will be paramount. Even so, compliance teams are continuing to spend a lot of their time on the updating required, and they may wish to consider whether or not the business might take a more active role in this process. This might have the twofold benefit of freeing up compliance time (perhaps to consider any proposed regulatory changes in more depth) and also ensuring that there is more business involvement with, and ownership of, any resulting policies and procedures.

The mortgage industry has been overwhelmed with a flood of new rules and regulations while dealing with unpredictable origination volumes. This combination has put intense pressure on mortgage lenders to update compliance processes while producing new business volume. Violations can carry severe financial penalties or possible civil actions. Responsibility now falls squarely on the lenders' shoulders. With the scope of regulation now reaching into all aspects of mortgage operations, the days are long gone when a small to mid-sized mortgage lender can go it alone or with outdated technology. In this lending environment, that is simply too risky and leads to longer disposition cycles and lower selling prices.

Increased compliance scrutiny and pain of non-compliance has been a multi-year trend that has continued to a point of exhausting lenders, and the trend will likely continue. Lenders have made the easy corrections to their environment and now need to assess more thoughtful ways to meet the increased demands. At the same time, as lenders are feeling greater scrutiny from CFPB and other agencies at both the federal and state level, they are also experiencing increased demands on their IT infrastructure (security, cyber threats, hardware requirements, etc.) and heightened competition, with the need to produce sustainable results. So, not only must they ensure compliance throughout the origination process, they must also ensure their IT demands are met without an increase to their budgets.

These trends are getting worse, and while many lenders may have made the simple process changes, they must now take a more proactive approach to finding better resolutions if they plan to survive in the future.

Higher Origination Costs
To meet these ever-growing challenges, lenders' overhead has increased significantly to support back-office compliance, which is driving up origination expenses to the point that lenders' current practices are too expensive. That's on top of the record low production profit of $150 per loan the industry experienced in 2014, according to Mortgage Bankers Association (MBA) data. MBA chief economist Michael Fratantoni stated that "The losses are not a result of lenders aggressively pricing mortgages in order to make up for lower volume. Rather, it is due to higher expenses, especially because lenders have had to add back-office staff to deal with new compliance requirements put in place after the mortgage crisis."

These market conditions are putting intense pressure on all lenders, but especially small to mid-sized lenders trying to keep pace with their larger counterparts. With back-office costs sky rocketing, small and mid-sized lenders must find a way to contain these costs if they want to remain competitive and survive. Can they continue to compete, or are the larger lenders going to continue to throw resources and bodies at the challenges to gain more and more market share?

The answer is clear: if small and midsized lenders continue to do business as usual and are constantly reacting to changing market conditions with outdated technology, they will not survive. The good news is there is a way for these lenders to compliantly compete and be able to contain the rising costs to originate.

Automation: The Great Equalizer

Small and mid-sized lenders need to realize that the right technology and automation can be the great equalizer. That sounds great, but how can lenders benefit from automation while also containing their IT costs and infrastructure? Advanced fully-hosted mortgage Software as a Service (SaaS) allows lenders to reduce ownership and costly upgrades, simplify and accelerate system implementation, enjoy worry-free security, and benefit from a centralized data repository.

For most lenders, technology ownership is a fixed cost for a resource that rarely reaches its expected return on investment. Further, loan origination systems are notorious for slow implementation, and are subject to numerous annual upgrades that can be either expensive, or time consuming (or both!) to deploy. As a result, the right SaaS solution has become a prime candidate for outsourcing, especially for growing lenders.

Not only is it important for lenders to understand the benefits of a SaaS model, but more important, they need to realize that there are big differences in SaaS options currently available. That includes lenders who are currently using an outdated SaaS system and are struggling to maintain compliance and contain costs. Understanding these differences will allow lenders to more proactively address the deeper industry issues burdening them today and provide the framework to easily adapt to ever-changing market conditions.

Assessing a SaaS Solution
Mortgage lenders should consider the following when assessing a SaaS LOS:

- Does the vendor provide a "test drive" environment that allows access to the platform to validate that it will work for those lenders' specific needs? The key, especially for small to midsized lenders, is in an out-of-the-box solution with lending best practices already built into the solution, versus a system that requires significant configuration and support by the lender just to originate a loan. The out-of-the-box solution minimizes the time needed for implementation, and eases the burden for the lender to proactively address today's most challenging market conditions.

- Does the vendor have a transparent and collaborative culture that performs as the lenders IT partner? How is support provided? Does the lender have a designated contact? Is there an SLA in place for bugs or support tickets? What is the cost for follow-up with support tickets?

- Does the vendor have a product road map that makes sense, and does the lender have the ability to collaborate on future functionality, system design, and development priorities?

- Is the customer a big fish in a little pond, or a small fish in a big pond?

- Is the system based on the right technical infrastructure for stability and data access?

CHAPTER TWELVE: *FAIR LENDING*

- What is the vendor's track record of uptime interruptions? Has the provider had costly outages in the past?

- Does the database run on MS SQL? Does the vendor's system run on archaic flat files vs. a truly relational database? How robust is the network/ data center?

- Does the vendor support third-party vendors in a best-of-breed model or promote internal, inferior products? Does the system support the industry's best vendors with high levels of feature functionality with seamless integration? Does the LOS provider charge vendors with high "click fees" that results in the lender paying for higher charges?

- How much effort is needed to configure the system for the lenders' specific requirements? Does the system require complex coding to support lender needs or is the administration simple to apply? Are tables auto-updated for the lender when applicable? Does the lender need an extensive IT staff to support the system on an ongoing basis?

- Is the solution competitively priced? Vendor pricing varies significantly in implementation fees and transaction fees. It is critical to understand all fees on an on-going basis to truly contain costs.

In addition to meeting the IT infrastructure demands, small and mid-sized lenders must address the ever growing burden of compliance. Lenders of this size simply do not have the resources to constantly monitor, proactively address compliance changes, and interpret how these changes will impact their organization. Remember, it is not just the rising costs to comply, but also the significant ramifications for noncompliance that lenders must be able to handle. Therefore, lenders need to strategically partner with a technology provider that can handle these compliance mandates. The provider must have a compliance focus, one that proactively monitors the changing compliance landscape, follows best-practice compliance standards, and streamlines application data security.

The solution should provide lenders with the ability to ensure that compliance policies and procedures are adhered to while efficiently completing the lending process. In today's highly competitive marketplace, just having a SaaS lending solution with compliance is no longer enough. It takes the right provider to be able to deliver a cost-effective, highly compliant solution with the right IT footprint for small and mid-sized lenders to succeed. If small and mid-sized lenders are going to remain competitive and survive in these market conditions, they need a vendor who can change direction on a dime and provide them the insight, IT infrastructure, and strict compliance needed.

Small and midsized lenders can compete and succeed in today's challenging mortgage environment. It comes down to partnering with the right provider to deliver the most advanced SaaS solutions that address compliance and contain IT costs. The time to explore all your lending solution options is now.

CASE STUDIES

In 2015 alone, the Department of Justice entered consent orders against nine banks or institutions regarding their unfair pricing practices or their redlining practices. I list five case studies here of financial institutions that were charged with having policies or practices that violated fair-lending laws.

Unites States vs. Countrywide (Bank of America)

In July 2008, Bank of America closed on a deal to purchase the ailing Countrywide Home Loans' parent organization for $2.5 billion. With the purchase, Bank of America assumed liability for Countrywide's lending practices. On December 21, 2011 the Department of Justice of the United States of America settled with Countrywide Corporation, Countrywide Home Loans, and Countrywide Bank for violating fair-lending laws. Countrywide gave subprime loans to 10,000 Hispanic and African-American borrowers, while providing prime loans for white borrowers with similarly situated financial circumstances. Additionally, they charged higher fees and rates to over 200,000 minority borrowers than their similarly situated white counterparts. Subprime loans, as we all know by now, come with higher interest rates to account for the investors predicted higher risk of default. A Bank of America spokesperson said the DOJ reviewed loans made before Bank of America purchased Countrywide in July 2008.

United States vs. Wells Fargo

In July 2012, Wells Fargo Bank and the U.S. Department of Justice (DOJ) resolved the DOJ's charges that some Wells Fargo mortgages had a disparate impact on some African-American and Hispanic borrowers. The DOJ claims were based on a statistical survey of Wells Fargo Home Mortgage loans between 2004 and 2009, and the claims primarily relate to mortgages priced and sold to consumers by mortgage brokers. Wells agreed to pay $125 million to borrowers that the DOJ believes were adversely impacted by mortgages priced and sold by mortgage brokers through its Wholesale channel.

The settlement also resolved pending litigation filed in 2009 by the State of Illinois on behalf of borrowers there, and resolved an investigative complaint filed in 2010 by the Pennsylvania Human Relations Commission. The DOJ case against Wells Fargo over violation of the Fair Housing Act was the second largest fair-lending settlement in the DOJ's history at that time, after the lawsuit against Countrywide Financial. Wells Fargo separately made a business decision to leave the wholesale channel, noting that brokers were independent businesses and they had no control over the broker's pricing decisions.

Also at this time, Wells Fargo is entering into a collaborative agreement with the City of Baltimore in which the city agreed to dismiss its widely publicized lawsuit it initially filed against Wells Fargo in January 2008. Wells Fargo will provide $4.5 million for community improvement programs to the City of Baltimore, and granted the City of Baltimore $3 million in additional funds for local priority housing and foreclosure-related initiatives. Wells Fargo set a five-year home-mortgage lending goal for the Baltimore area.

United States vs. SunTrust Mortgage Inc.
In what has been a common complaint from the DOJ, they found that SunTrust Mortgage allowed too much discretion in pricing for its brokers and loan officers in determining a customer's interest rate, resulting in discriminatory prices for minorities. They were charged with violating both the Fair Housing Act and the Equal Credit Opportunity Act in charging more than 20,000 black and Hispanic customers with higher interest rates and fees between 2005 and 2009.

Prior to the settlement, SunTrust Mortgage had implemented policies that substantially reduced the discretion of its loan officers and mortgage brokers to vary a loan's interest rate and other fees from the price it set based on the borrower's objective credit-related factors. Supervisors are required to sign-off on any variations. The policies restrict compensating loan officers and mortgage brokers based on the terms or conditions of a particular loan. The settlement required SunTrust Mortgage to keep its improved policies in place for at least the next three years and continue to monitor for signs of discrimination, and provide monitoring reports to the United States. The investigation started after a referral by the Board of Governors of the Federal Reserve to the Justice Department's Civil Rights Division in December 2009 for potential patterns or practices of discrimination.

United States vs. C&F Mortgage Corporation
The Justice Department charged C&F Mortgage with violating the FHA and ECOA by raising interest rates for black and Hispanic mortgage customers. C&F did not require its loan officers to document reasons for changing a customer's interest rate from the standard rate, and increased compensation for loan officers who charged higher loan prices, creating "overages".

The DOJ and C&F settled for $140,000, and C&F began reviewing employees' compliance with nondiscrimination standards, specifically their justification for large interest-rate adjustments. The company agreed to institute new pricing policies and employee training policies.

United States vs. Prime Lending
In 2010, PrimeLending settled charges with the DOJ that stated that PrimeLending regularly set higher loan prices for African American borrowers. PrimeLending was one of the country's largest Federal Housing Authority (FHA) lenders at the time of the charges. The DOJ stated that PrimeLending's loan-officer incentive program encouraged "overages" (higher interest rates or "points") by providing higher compensation to those loan officers that utilized overages.

The mortgage company settled for $2 million, and set new loan-pricing policies and employee training requirements.

ABOUT THE AUTHOR

Stephen M. McGurl has been in the mortgage banking industry for 32 years. He spends a great deal of his free time devoted to volunteering and charitable work. As an independent consultant in the financial-services industry, Steve runs McGurl Risk Advisors, LLC. His primary focus has been providing solutions in the compliance and fair-lending space for banks, government agencies, and mortgage lenders. He has worked with numerous firms on consent orders, lawsuits and engagements touching such issues as fair lending, fraud, loss mitigation, MBS representation and warranties breaches, portfolio evaluations, and staffing capacity.

His career has afforded him the opportunity to be an executive in operations, retail, and wholesale production and account management at several to-ten lenders. Steve has owned his own mortgage brokerage and understands what is involved in building and operating a business on a daily basis. He is very active with local, state, and the national MBA as an instructor and member of numerous committees, including the HUD National Homeownership Strategy (NHS) Education and Counseling Subcommittee.

Steve graduated from the School of Mortgage Banking, received his Certified Mortgage Banker (CMB) designation in 1996, and has consulted for the education program of the Mortgage Bankers Association of America.

CHAPTER THIRTEEN

MORTGAGE SERVICING

MARIANNE LAMKIN | SENIOR VICE PRESIDENT
AMERICAN MORTGAGE CONSULTANTS

No one suspected on the morning of February 7, 2007, when New Century announced a need to restate its financials for 2006 because of *"errors in accounting"*, that the servicing industry would be changed forever. Prior to that day, New Century had been the number two subprime mortgage lender, holding a mortgage servicing portfolio of $43.3 billion (as of September 30, 2006)[1]. A short two months later New Century filed bankruptcy, and within the year a number of mortgage servicers, including New Century, would no longer exist. In fact, four of the top five largest bankruptcy filings in the United States in 2007 were subprime mortgage lenders, and the fifth was a prime mortgage lender.[2]

Thirty years ago, servicing was a relatively easy process of taking payments, managing escrow accounts, and nudging delinquent borrowers with a friendly reminder phone call. In those days, forbearances were the loss-mitigation strategy of choice, and banks used mortgages to cross-sell other products and services and manage customer relationships. As the secondary market developed, non-bank servicers entered the market, filling up niches such as subprime servicing, that the banks had ignored. The New Century failure was the beginning of the end. Since 2007 and the following crises, not only did borrowers default in massive numbers, but regulators and investors increased scrutiny on every task performed by servicers. This chapter examines the primary components that have undergone the most change.

TYPES OF SERVICERS

Banks
Mortgage servicing was traditionally performed by the banks that originated the loans, or bought them from correspondents. The top mortgage servicers are still banks, with Wells Fargo, Chase, and Bank of America leading the way as of late 2015. As the economic decline steepened in 2008, with the regulatory issues of recent years, and with Basel III capital requirements, banks have been slowly easing out of mortgage servicing. As banks struggled with the sudden surges in defaults and recognized their processes

---

1 United States Bankruptcy Court for the District Delaware, Final Report of Michael J. Missal Bankruptcy Court Examiner, February 29. 2008.
2 United States Bankruptcy Court for the District Delaware, Final Report of Michael J. Missal Bankruptcy Court Examiner, February 29. 2008.

were inadequate to effectively manage high-touch borrowers, they began selling their servicing rights to nonbank servicers who had been dealing with subprime and high-touch borrowers for years. While the top banks continue to be the largest servicers, the non-bank and specialty servicers who survived the early days of the crises grew by leaps and bounds, gobbling up MSRs as other servicers closed or banks began selling large portfolios of both private and non-performing GSE loans.

As the delinquencies surged during the crisis, all servicers struggled to manage the volume of delinquent loans, and the increasing demands to manage the newly created GSE programs to assist borrowers. Servicing larger volumes of delinquent loans created staffing shortages and a need to invest in processes and technology to manage loss mitigation efforts. Despite these pressures, as servicers failed and banks divested their inventory, nonbank servicers and specialty component servicers quickly began absorbing loan servicing offered by banks that were not prepared to deal with the newly defaulting borrowers. Specialty servicers, who were able to quickly respond and use their expertise on specific products or geographic regions, ramped up to manage the volume. Specialty servicers typically have different organizational structures than banks, and have developed the expertise to contact borrowers and focus on getting the borrower back into making payments.

Nonbank Servicers
Nonbank servicers are non-deposit taking institutions that generally focus on servicing private-label securitizations. In 2009, the top five commercial bank servicers of non-agency mortgages accounted for 72% of total private label servicing; today, these five make up less than 26% of that total. Non-bank servicers now service approximately 74% of private-label securities.[3]

Nonbank servicers have traditionally been less regulated than banks, and until the CFPB was created, were primarily subject to state-specific laws, and subject to only a handful of federal regulations, such as FDCPA and RESPA. In 2014, when the explosive growth of Ocwen, Nationstar, and Walter Investment Company caught the attention of national legislators as the fastest growing servicers, regulatory scrutiny immediately increased. How much did they grow? Between 2011 and 2014, market share for the five largest non-bank servicers grew between 30% and 350% (Ocwen, Nationstar, Walter, PHH and Quicken).[4]

Specialty Servicers
Specialty servicers grew quickly during the crises as the GSEs began pulling servicing from underperforming servicers, or simply buying the servicing rights themselves and distributing them to specialty servicers who had experience with the high-touch requirements of defaulted loans. Banks were especially happy to unload highly delinquent loans on specialty servicers in an effort to distance themselves from the headline risks

---

3   http://www.housingwire.com/articles/31409-fitch-rise-of-nonbank-servicers-threatens-private-label-rmbs
4   Urban Institute, http://www.urban.org/sites/default/files/alfresco/publication-pdfs/413198-Nonbank-Specialty-Servicers-What-s-the-Big-Deal-.PDF

incurred every time a settlement with a regulator was announced. Specialty servicers typically take on loans that are at least 60 days past due, and manage them through the loss mitigation process, turning them into performing loans, and keeping them for up to a year of performing status. See chapter 15 of this book for an extensive discussion of this topic.

Subservicers

Subservicers are servicers who perform all the functions of a servicer, but do not own the servicing rights. These entities have also grown in number and size as investors and other non-servicers acquire the servicing rights and utilize subservicers through a vendor relationship. Subservicers can be a bank, non-bank, or specialty servicer — the only difference is the ownership of servicing rights. See chapter 14 of this book for an extensive discussion of subservicing.

THE SERVICING BUSINESS MODEL (THE ECONOMICS OF SERVICING)

The basic business model for residential mortgage loan servicing generally involves receiving and processing monthly payments from borrowers and passing the proceeds to investors, notifying borrowers when payments are late, and managing defaults, foreclosures, and borrower bankruptcies. Investors pay servicers a fee to manage the loans, and typically reimburse servicers for any default-related expenses. Servicers keep any fee income from borrowers.

It can be argued that the basic business model and incentive structure for the servicing industry is all wrong. Under the current models, servicers process payments and receive a set servicing fee for every payment they collect. Servicers also retain any fees they collect from borrowers for late payments or other ancillary services. Servicers are obligated to meet the demands of multiple constituents: borrowers, investors, federal, state, and local regulators, and laws.

Recently, the Federal Housing Finance Agency (FHFA), which regulates Fannie Mae and Freddie Mac, and the U.S. Department of Housing and Urban Development (HUD) have jointly reviewed the issues around the difference between servicing a performing loan and a nonperforming loan and presented several options. The MBA Reserve Account and the Clearing House Reserve Account proposals recommended a mechanism that would give servicers accounts to draw on based on high defaults on particular portfolios or products. The third alternative proposed a fixed amount for performing loans and incentive-based compensation from the GSE's, including an option to tie excess interest-only strips to mortgage servicing rights. None of these proposals have been implemented to date.

While the GSEs and HUD debate and revisit the issues, the private-label market and small servicers have found better business models that make sense for non-performing portfolios. In at least one instance, the owner of a portfolio of non-performing loans negotiated with a servicer to pay significantly higher servicing fees tied to the status of the loan, and fixed at boarding. Non-performing loans pay a substantially higher servicing fee, and if the loan performs again, the servicing fee remains the same, and an unprofitable loan is suddenly much more profitable. In return for higher servicing fees, the investor retains all late and ancillary fees, removing incentives from the servicer to charge the borrower unnecessary fees, and providing a strong incentive to return the loan to a cash-flow basis as quickly as possible.

The Cost of Servicing
In good economic times, when loans are performing, servicing can be a profitable business. Servicing rights can be a lucrative asset, and servicers can even sell excess servicing-fee income to manage cash flows. When the economy is stressed, however, non-performing loans are costly to manage. The key to operational and servicing efficiency is the ability to aggregate loans and leverage technology; hiring hundreds of loss mitigation negotiators and managing loans on a case-by-case basis can quickly become prohibitively expensive. With uncertainty in the regulatory environment and increasing pressure from investors, accurately pricing servicing is a challenge.

Servicing profitability is driven by servicing and other ancillary fees as well as float from custodial accounts (P&I and T&I) which are held between collection and remittance to investors. Servicing fees are collected by servicers as a portion of the loan's interest rate — if the borrower doesn't pay, the servicer doesn't collect the servicing fee. GSE minimum servicing fees are typically 25 basis points for fixed-rate loans and 37.5 basis points for ARMs.[5]

Servicing costs continue to rise. Prior to the credit crisis, the typical cost to service a performing loan averaged $55 per year; today estimates are $208 or more per loan/per year. Servicing a nonperforming loan has increased from $482 to $2,357 per year.[6]

While servicing fees haven't changed in 30 years, expenses have increased substantially. Direct costs have increased with new regulation and compliance requirements, new default and collection requirements such as correspondence, and the advent of the SPOC (Single Point of Contact) requirements, as well as servicing advances and the related cost of funds, not to mention compensatory fees from the GSEs and servicing deficiencies on FHA loans. Servicing fee income for a fixed-rate Fannie Mae or Freddie Mac loan with a $250,000 origination balance would be $625.00 per year (.0025*250,000). If that loan goes into default, the servicer doesn't get any additional servicing fees, and if the loan goes to foreclosure, the cost to manage that loan can be four times the amount of the servicing fees.

Most securitizations are either scheduled/scheduled or scheduled/actual, meaning the servicer is still obligated to advance the scheduled payment of the principal and interest (or scheduled interest and actual principal). If a borrower defaults, the servicer no

---

5 Mortgage Bankers Association (MBA), "Residential Mortgage Servicing in the 21st Century" May 2011.
6 Mortgage Bankers Association (MBA) "The Changing Dynamics of the Mortgage Servicing Landscape, June 2015.

longer receives the servicing fee and not only has to finance the principal and interest advances of missed payments, but is also obligated to advance for tax payments, insurance premiums, and incur the carrying costs of default, foreclosure, and property preservation. The servicer is also obligated to expend resources to contact the borrower, determine the reason for default, and ascertain whether or not the borrower can resume payment, or will need a modification or some other workout plan. Although the investor ultimately reimburses the servicer for advance payments and for default-related vendor payments for property inspections, valuations, and attorney fees, the direct cost for labor and technology falls to the servicer.

CUSTOMER SERVICE

Servicing for performing loans is basically a customer-service and payment-processing function. Prior to the crises, Customer Service organizations did little more than answer customer questions. Now Customer Service has become the critical front end to help keep costs down and resolve borrower issues before they become full blown. As the crises developed and servicers were inundated with defaults, Customer Service was the logical front line of defense. Servicers began enhancing technology and training Customer Service to deal with escrow issues, create automated pay-off quotes, and to research and resolve basic servicing issues. Some servicers have developed a Wikipedia-like system to enable agents to conduct key-word searches to quickly and accurately answer borrower questions.

As operating and personnel costs rose exponentially, servicers looked for ways to reduce the drain of Customer Service as an expense center. Not only did servicers quickly adopt one-call resolution tactics, they began tightening metrics to answer more calls faster. Where an Average Speed of Answer (ASA) of up to 60 seconds was considered leading edge in some institutions, 30 seconds or less is now the goal in leading servicing practice, and abandonment rates of 5% or more that were the norm, are now pushed to less than 3%, with the best servicers maintaining ratios of 1% or less. With improved technology and better-trained front-end staff, leading servicers are regularly producing ASA metrics of 2% or less.

LOSS MITIGATION

A story circulated around 2011 about a borrower in New York City who had a mortgage serviced by one of the largest banks in the U.S. After her husband lost his job, she called the bank and was approved for a modification, turning her ARM loan into a fixed-rate loan at a payment she could afford. She received, signed, and returned her modification documents. A month later, the bank returned her payment with a letter saying the payment was short. After several phone calls in which she was transferred multiple times, she discovered her fixed-rate loan had been booked as an ARM with a dramatically higher payment. Even though she provided copies of the final modification documents to the bank, she was told the loan was in the servicing system as an ARM, and she needed to make the higher payment. The borrower turned to the New York Department of Financial Services, who after months of attempts to get the servicer to acknowledge that their system was wrong, finally told the borrower they could do no more for her and she should hire an attorney; however, local attorneys were unwilling to take her case, as the bank had the reputation of bureaucratic stalling tactics and siloed departments that didn't communicate with each other.

Although this story was hardly unique, it demonstrates the chaos the industry faced during the first few years of the crises. Lumbering technology was difficult to update with the new data fields that regulators and investors suddenly required, and trained staff and other corporate infrastructure was completely inadequate for the new reality.

As the crises deepened and defaults continued to climb, the GSEs and the U.S. Treasury began creating modification plans for Fannie Mae and Freddie Mac loans. Private-label loans in securitizations that were subject to Pooling and Servicing Agreements were often prohibited from being modified, particularly in instances where the borrower was technically still current. In other instances, specialty servicers had developed their own loss mitigation strategies, but either PSA or the GSEs prevented the use of those plans. Additionally, the sheer volume of defaults caused both borrowers and housing advocates to complain about response times, lost financial packages, erroneous modification documents, and failed attempts at short sales.

Banks and nonbank servicers were completely unprepared, and the industry became chaotic. Prime servicers who maintained delinquency rates of 1% or less, suddenly found themselves with soaring delinquencies up to 11% by 2010, and borrowers who no longer paid with a gentle reminder. Subprime delinquency rates closed in on 40%-50% in some portfolios, and even the high-touch tactics of the subprime world were no longer effective.

Borrowers were losing their jobs, and stopped paying their loans and answering their phones. Servicers finally had to admit that many of their prime borrowers were now subprime borrowers, and they needed completely different strategies to manage those borrowers. Servicers had to get creative, and they had to get borrowers to pick up the phone.

Servicers had to completely revamp their collections and loss-mitigations processes. Prior to the crises, most loan-workout options were centered on repayment and forbearance plans. Modifications were the workout plan of last resort. When delinquencies began to soar, collections and loss mitigation departments were woefully understaffed and technology was inadequate. As servicers tried to hire, train, and deploy new employees, processes began to break down, and borrower complaints to the regulators increased.

Servicers were quickly trying to set up processes and, through trial and error, refining procedures almost daily. Departments and processes had to be established to take verbal financials from borrowers, receive and inventory paper copies or imaged financial statements and applications for HAMP and other modification programs, and update systems to reflect the most recent requirements of GSE guidelines as modification and other loss mitigation programs were developed. Although servicers rapidly implemented technology to manage these new processes, the various systems often either weren't compatible or there simply wasn't time to design the interfaces.

Many servicers did not have adequate call-center technology, and as dialers reached borrowers, there were often no agents available to take the calls. Incoming calls from borrowers were routed to the first available agent, who likely had never spoken with that borrower before. Loss-mitigation agents were often so busy that most calls from collections or customer service could not be transferred to an available agent. Considering that in 2012, even after borrowers were fairly well educated in the options available, servicers generally reported that it often took more than 25 attempts to get a borrower on the phone to discuss payment options; the possibility of not making the connection could lose the borrower forever.

Borrowers frequently complained that it was impossible to speak with either a live agent or even the same agent who was already familiar with their loan. Although many small servicers had used the single point of contact concept for years, larger servicers who managed staffing levels in relation to call volumes simply routed calls to the first available agent, who relied on system notes from prior agents. Servicers are now required to have separate teams of SPOCs (single point of contact staff) to make the initial introductory call to borrowers to explain options, provide continuity, and keep borrowers informed of the status of their workout.

All of these difficulties, along with regulatory requirements, resulted in several innovative strategies. Once borrower contact was made, if the borrower indicated that the time was inconvenient, many servicers began scheduling appointments with the borrower. Once the modification is complete, some servicers have established special "Mod follow up" teams to call borrowers for up to six months after a modification has been finalized, to remind them of payment amounts and due dates to reduce recidivism. Other servicers with large private-label securitizations established separate certified credit-counseling departments to help borrowers manage their finances in the hopes of refinancing the mortgage within 12 months.

HOW COULD ESCROW BE CONTROVERSIAL?

Collecting tax payments and insurance premiums and making the payments to the related tax authority or insurance carrier is another process that has become more complex. The business of tracking tax payments due has almost always been outsourced to vendors who have established relationships with tax authorities, as has insurance tracking.

Many prime borrowers elect to pay their own taxes and insurance and manage their cash flow. Subprime borrowers have always been encouraged, but not required to create escrow accounts. As loans went into default, borrowers not only stopped their principal and interest payments, but also allowed taxes to become delinquent and hazard insurance to lapse, creating more risk to servicers and investors. GSEs and other investors began to make escrow accounts compulsory for borrowers who received modifications. Servicers are required to analyze borrower's escrow accounts annually to determine if there will be enough cash in the account to make the required tax and insurance payments. When a borrower has not maintained hazard-insurance coverage, or lost coverage, the servicer force places an insurance policy to protect the investor in the event of loss or damage and passes the cost along to the borrower. Force-placed insurance (now called Lender-Placed) only protects the unpaid principal balance, not borrower's belongings. Lender-placed insurance is usually a last-resort placement, is more expensive than borrower-secured insurance, and servicers invest in significant resources to ensure borrowers renew their hazard insurance yearly.

In past years, servicers looked for revenue outside servicing fees, and many set up affiliate companies to take on tasks previously delegated to vendors. One common affiliate was an insurance company to receive insurance commissions paid by the insurance carrier. As regulators began scrutinizing servicing practices, insurance affiliates and the cost of lender-placed premiums became very controversial. Most servicers have divested their insurance affiliates and no longer collect commissions from the carrier.

IT'S ALL ABOUT TECHNOLOGY

The servicing industry has generally lagged behind banking and other industries when it comes to technology. Upgrading technology is critical to addressing the challenges faced by servicers. Some servicers have been able to mitigate increased costs of servicing with technology, but legacy platforms have generally left servicers with expensive and time-consuming changes needed to adapt to the rapidly changing regulatory requirements and changes in efficiency and process improvements.

Smaller, more flexible organizations have been better positioned to react to technology challenges than larger organizations that are reliant on third-party servicing platforms, or those who had not created their own data warehouses or front-end user interfaces. The large servicing platforms are not easily redesigned to capture new data or create new calculations, and with the difference in code ownership, getting all clients on the same version takes time.

Leading servicers are deploying technology to validate data and compliance at every possible point. Transaction monitoring and rules-based data-integrity systems are providing in-line controls which can identify issues earlier in the process and reduce the costs of dealing with borrower complaints and regulatory issues downstream. Although servicers are automating and continually upgrading their internal loan-audit programs to catch data discrepancies related to loan transfers, a fully automated system isn't here yet. Since loan documents are generally stored as pdf documents, and data is usually provided in excel or other similar format, there's nothing to compare electronically, and that often results in large staff dedicated to *"stare and compare"* exercises to validate data, and still leaves room for human error. With the CFPB cracking down on loans in the process of loss mitigation during transfers, servicers are spending a lot of money to try to fix bad data.

Technology: What's Next?

Servicing platforms haven't changed much since the 1980's when it comes to front-end users: many servicers are still using *"green screens"* and employees are required to memorize screen names or complicated pathways to retrieve loan information. Most servicers have invested in IT resources to build their own data warehouses over the last 10 years, and many are looking to technology to reduce costs and gain efficiencies. In fact, some servicers have made their data warehouses the *"system of record,"* and the servicing system is simply the vehicle to accommodate day-to-day operations. Technology will continue to be the key driver of servicing operations in the foreseeable future.

Servicers are looking to other industries for creative technology and customer-friendly solutions that will reduce human contact and staffing costs. The most promising are advances in self-service technologies. Self-service platforms allow borrowers to retrieve information and complete transactions either over the phone with IVRs, or over their computers or mobile devices. Banks have been using self-service technology since the 1990's, although there were a few mortgage companies that were early adopters such as E-Loan and Deep Green Bank.

Mortgage servicers have begun to embrace self-service as a way to provide easy customer service and reduce operating costs. Customers can make on-line payments, review transaction histories, set up automatic payments, retrieve escrow analysis and other documents, and download payoff quotes with this technology. Servicers are adopting web-chat functionality as well, and a 2013 study by McKinsey & Co quoted in the August 2015 *Mortgage Banking* magazine revealed that providing digital chats with customer service representatives *"is 56% of the cost of running a support system through a call center"*. With the addition of self-service technology, however, servicers will have to include training on the use of its applications for customer-service representatives. Self-service options are one of the least expensive and most customer-pleasing technologies, and as millennials come of age, their comfort with technology and desire for instant gratification will drive down costs even further.

SERVICING COMPLIANCE

Early in the crises, regulators felt that mortgage servicers were under-regulated.[7] As regulated entities, banks were better positioned to manage all the new regulations that have been implemented since 2007. Servicing in general has always been less regulated than originations, and most servicers did not have the staff or the infrastructure in place to manage all the new compliance requirements. Although banks have been developing

---

[7] Mortgage Bankers Association (MBA), "Residential Mortgage Servicing in the 21st Century" May 2011.

their compliance-management systems for more than 20 years, for many nonbank servicers, compliance systems were little more than an excel spreadsheet to keep up with allowable fees and state requirements, a few internal auditors, and a staff of attorneys that focused more on litigation and other corporate matters than overseeing servicing processes.

Mortgage servicing compliance has always been a complex web of state and federal laws, and investor servicing requirements. In addition to federal regulations, each of the 50 states has their own laws and regulations, particularly around foreclosure and bankruptcy, and each securitization's Pooling and Servicing Agreement has specific servicing requirements, as do each of the GSEs and other government agencies (FHA, VA, USDA/RD, and PIH).[8]

With the passage of Dodd-Frank Wall Street Reform and Consumer Protection Act, compliance was suddenly front-and-center at mortgage servicers. The Act, which established the Consumer Financial Protection Bureau (CFPB) as a new regulatory entity, granted this new entity direct supervisory authority over all banks with more than $10 billion in assets and all non-bank institutions engaged in the mortgage markets. Other attempts to rationalize and standardize federal regulations and GSE servicing resulted in Helping Families Save Their Homes Act of 2009, the Attorney General Settlement between five of the largest bank servicers and a coalition of 49 state attorney generals which became known as the National Mortgage Settlement, and the GSE Servicer Alignment Initiative. The National Mortgage Settlement has 304 mortgage servicing standards and 29 performance metrics to which servicers must adhere.

While banks generally had one or two regulatory agencies, depending on their charter, and had developed long-standing relationships with the regulators, non-bank servicers had only been subject to state regulatory exams, investor audits, and rating agency overviews. Stringent oversite was a complicated adjustment.

In addition to the federal regulatory and investor compliance changes that have been implemented over the past few years, states continue to pass their own laws. Recently, California implemented a Homeowner's Bill of Rights, and shortly thereafter, Washington and Illinois passed their own versions with state-specific requirements.

Local municipalities can also create headaches for servicers. Property code violations can create obstacles to liquidating properties and transferring titles. Complaints to county and city offices from neighbors in a subdivision with abandoned or unmaintained properties often leads to code-violation fees that can be very costly to servicers. If code violations go unnoticed, liens may be attached to the property, which may prevent the transfer of title. Property preservation and maintenance can be expensive. Servicers have to maintain a balance between repairs that will keep neighborhoods safe and the neighbors at bay, and reimbursable expenses from investors. Any errors on the servicer's part, such as unnoticed code violations, are generally not reimbursable to the servicer.

---

8 Federal Housing Authority, Veteran's Administration, U.S. Department of Agriculture, Rural Development, Public and Indian Housing.

Another new regulatory requirement that was new to nonbank servicers is the *compliance management system,* which includes vendor management. Servicers, who previously allowed business units to manage vendor relationships, are now required to complete risk assessments on all vendors, and compliance staff are taking a much more active role in conducting vendor oversight. Outsourcing is a business strategy that creates dependencies on service providers, some of whom are vital to the servicer's operations. Although the requirements are not new, servicers have had to develop formal compliance policies and procedures, and complete formal risk assessments on each vendor for senior management.

The cost of non-compliance is harsh; the CFPB and other agencies are requiring higher and higher settlement fines, and in 2013 Ocwen was required to provide $2 billion in principal reductions for servicing errors, and another $125 million in cash to borrowers who had already lost their homes to foreclosure[9], GreenTree was required to pay $48 million in borrower restitution for servicing errors and another $14 million in fines,[10] and SunTrust Mortgage was required to provide $540 million in borrower relief.[11] Specialty servicers are not immune, Residential Credit Solutions was fined $1.5 million for failing to honor modifications for loans transferred from other servicers.

Servicing Compliance: What's Next?
The level of complexity in federal, state, and local regulations has driven the cost of servicing up to record levels which will ultimately be passed on to consumers in the form of higher interest rates and fees. As employment levels trend back to pre-crises levels, and the industry begins to recover, federal, state and local regulatory and compliance requirements need to be rationalized into a standard system that not only protects consumers' and investors' rights, but provides servicers with a compliance model that is affordable to both small and large servicers. Technology will have to keep up as well. The bulk of servicers utilize one of the three major servicing systems, FiServ, LSAMS, and Black Knight. The cost to develop and maintain a proprietary servicing system is not only operationally and technologically challenging, but adds a new level of compliance and headline risk only the largest servicers can afford.

Regulatory enforcement is a balancing act; too much enforcement could cause servicers to be so distracted by the regulators that it becomes difficult to remediate the processes and technology for compliance. This has been especially true of Ocwen. In March 2015, Ocwen held over $410 billion in servicing rights, and if regulatory actions had caused Ocwen to shut down, it would have been nearly impossible to find other servicers who

---

9   http://www.consumerfinance.gov/newsroom/cfpb-state-authorities-order-ocwen-to-provide-2-billion-in-relief-to-homeowners-for-servicing-wrongs/

10 http://www.consumerfinance.gov/newsroom/cfpb-and-federal-trade-commission-take-action-against-green-tree-servicing-for-mistreating-borrowers-trying-to-save-their-homes/

11 http://www.consumerfinance.gov/newsroom/cfpb-federal-partners-and-state-attorneys-general-file-order-requiring-suntrust-to-provide-540-million-in-relief-to-homeowners-for-servicing-wrongs/

could absorb the nearly 2.2 million loans. Additionally, Ocwen has been the largest subprime servicer and many of its borrowers are minorities in blighted urban areas.[12] Regulators have expressed concern that there is a need for specialty servicers such as Ocwen, which are willing to take challenging portfolios.

As servicers try to manage the increasing level of federal and state government intervention in the mortgage industry, it is likely that there is still more to come. Fannie Mae, Freddie Mac, and the FHA continue to be pressured by political interests to expand borrower eligibility, while simultaneously the CFPB is implementing affordability requirements.

CONCLUSION

If we have learned nothing else from the trials and tribulations of the years since 2007, it is clear that the servicers who succeed will be those who are nimble and capable of innovating and leveraging technology. Staying on the cutting edge of technology and deploying solutions rapidly is critical in a fast-changing environment. Government and investor regulations will not get any easier — in fact, they will probably only get tighter, requiring servicer to be creative in order to manage increasing costs effectively.

The business model of servicing is not likely to change anytime soon. Complicated regulatory schemes to provide servicers some relief in the cost of managing non-performing loans seem unlikely. While small and captive servicers are changing the nature of incentives and servicing fees, the rest of the industry still has to find optimal solutions, and given the number and sizes of the organizations involved, change may be off in the distance.

On a brighter note, as delinquencies and foreclosures decline, the industry can move out of crises mode and focus on borrower experience, process improvements, and technology enhancements.

The industry has made a great deal of progress and banks are re-entering the servicing markets, even buying MSRs from non-bank servicers such as Ocwen. Banks are still shying away from non-performing loans, but are opportunistically buying servicing rights to newly originated, performing GSE loans. While growth will be constrained by Basel III capital requirements, banks seem to be adapting to the new regulatory environment.

---

12 Berry, K.,"Disconnect", Structured Finance News, March 2015.

ABOUT THE AUTHOR

Marianne Lamkin has more than 20 years of professional and consulting experience in Mortgage Origination and Servicing operations, Investor Reporting, Treasury Operations, Regulatory Compliance, Risk Management and Investor Reporting. Ms. Lamkin currently leads the mortgage servicing consulting practice at AMC, and manages teams performing regulatory compliance reviews, originations and servicing operations reviews, CMBS and RMBS related advance verification, due diligences, and document custodian compliance reviews.

Prior to her tenure at AMC, Ms. Lamkin was an Associate Partner at Capco, and a Senior Manager at Bearingpoint, Inc. Ms. Lamkin is a Commissioned Bank Examiner with the Federal Reserve and spent 7 years with the Federal Reserve Bank of Philadelphia in Safety and Soundness.

CHAPTER FOURTEEN

CHOOSING AND WORKING WITH A SUBSERVICER

DAVID J. MILLER, JR. | EXECUTIVE VICE PRESIDENT, BUSINESS DEVELOPMENT DIRECTOR

CENLAR FSB

Subservicing is the outsourcing of traditional administrative servicing activities to a third party for a fee. The subservicing industry has grown from a small, relatively select group of users to a widely accepted form of servicing for a broad cross-section of financial services participants. Historically, banks and credit unions have been the holders of mortgage servicing rights (MSR), with a few mortgage bankers retaining servicing rights when they sold their loans to Fannie Mae, Freddie Mac, and Ginnie Mae. During the last several years, we have seen dramatic shifts in this business as more mortgage bankers retained the MSR, and with the entry and growth of non-traditional servicing buyers (REITs, Private Equity) interested in ownership of the MSR. As a result, subservicing has become an accepted form of managing loan-servicing activity, and has evolved into a significant driver for participation in the market.

The most common, traditional subservicing arrangement is where a company contracts with a subservicer to service their portfolio for them. The portfolio can either be serviced in a generic name, or on a private-label basis with the servicing branded to provide a high-quality, consistent customer experience.

Subservicers are tasked with everything from developing reports, to handling escrow, to delivering branch-payment systems, to providing outstanding customer service. Specifically, the loan-servicing activities performed by subservicers include:

- New Loan Set-up
- Data Integrity Review
- Customer Care/Service
- Cash Processing and Loan Payoff
- Default Administration
    - Collections
    - Loss Mitigation
    - Foreclosure
    - Bankruptcy
    - Claims Processing
    - REO
- Investor Reporting/Corporate Accounting
- Escrow Administration
- Adjustable Rate Management
    - Property Releases
        ~ Easements

~ Loan Modifications
 ~ Partial Release
 ~ Assumptions
 ~ Satisfactions
- Process Improvement
- Transfer Operations – inbound/outbound
- Year End Reporting
- Compliance

The subservicer typically also provides access to loan data, integration with other operating systems, delivery of industry-standard and customized reports, and support of management-reporting needs. Perhaps most important, the subservicer will provide 24 x 7 customer support, and be able to measure and deliver the results through call statistics, turnaround times, performance measures, and high-quality contacts with the customer. While most subservicing arrangements today include all or most of these loan-servicing functions, in some cases just a few of the loan-servicing functions can be outsourced.

In sum, while you have entrusted the daily operational activity and the responsibility of servicing performance to a third party, YOU continue to own the servicing rights and the customer relationship, while retaining the rewards and benefits associated with the servicing asset. An important point to remember is that despite the fact that you have outsourced the servicing asset, YOU are still obligated to the investors (Fannie Mae, Freddie Mac, Ginnie Mae, private, etc.) for the performance of the servicing activities. In order to administer your responsibility, you will need to develop a strong oversight program to assure that the servicing is being performed in accordance with all applicable requirements, as well as in accordance with your business strategy.

TYPES OF SUBSERVICERS

There are several types of subservicers, so it is necessary to be sure that you select the right type of partner with the appropriate credentials. Does the company that you are considering do this as their primary source of business, or is it a sideline or subsidiary company that they have set up to utilize capacity that will compete with their other business interests? Just as important, are they in your marketplace competing for deposits, loans, or other services?

As you begin to think about subservicing, one of the benefits available to you is the ability to service on a private-label or branded basis. Be sure to think about your business objectives and how you want to face your customers. Private-label solutions vary, but in essence your brand will be used to service your customers. You will need to decide where and how deeply you want this branded service to be delivered. A thorough private-label solution begins with a process to attach your logo to all outbound customer-facing correspondence and communication. This should include letters, coupon books, monthly billing statements, notices, year-end statements, credit bureau reporting and all customer points of contact. Your subservicer can also create dedicated, branded contact channels for your customers that include both voice and data. A dedicated toll-free number can be established for your customers to utilize. A custom script can be developed to greet your customers with your branded information, answering calls using your company name.

A similar customer experience can be developed connecting your web technology with the subservicer's to provide a seamless experience for the customer. Subservicers are now providing access via the web to customers to allow them to look at loan balances, payment amounts, escrow information and history transactions. These websites can be customized to provide a private-label experience to customers with hyperlinks built to your site so that the customer can move seamlessly between the sites to obtain the desired information.

Performing and Specialty Subservicers

There are two broad types of subservicers that you will need to understand to assure that you align your business with their programs. The terms generally used today are *performing subservicers* and *specialty* or *non-performing loan subservicers*. A performing subservicer is one that will handle portfolios that are mostly current. These subservicers should have a full-scale default team with all of the necessary resources and experience to handle your delinquent loans, but they generally focus their operations on performing portfolios. A non-performing loan subservicer is a company that specializes in servicing delinquent loans and has built their servicing operations around default mitigation. They are often compensated based on the amount of money that they can recover on the servicer's behalf.

A rule of thumb as you consider options for your portfolio is that around an 8% - 10% delinquent rate would typically be the high end for a performing servicer. Of course, there are benefits to both types of subservicer, but because the cost to service delinquent loans is significantly higher than the cost to service a current loan, your cost would be commensurate with the services provided by these companies.

BENEFITS OF USING A SUBSERVICING PARTNER

There are numerous reasons that you might want to consider subservicing as an alternative to an in-house servicing operation. But let's start with perhaps the most challenging consideration today: *compliance*.

Compliance

In today's environment, the compliance and regulatory landscape has become increasingly complex, with updates and changes being issued seemingly every day. Moreover, the costs for non-compliance have risen dramatically, with higher penalties and compensatory fines being imposed by the different regulatory authorities and mortgage agencies. How can you keep up with the alphabet soup of requirements and compliance issues without a small army of specialists in your operation to review a change, determine its operational and technical impact, build a solution, and then test to assure that you will be in compliance by the due date? It's certainly a daunting task. A relationship with a subservicing partner with broad expertise can therefore help you achieve these objectives, assuring that your loans are serviced in compliance with all State and Federal regulatory parties, GSE, investor, and all insuring, entity guidelines and requirements, while delivering a process that is built on servicing best practices.

Federal Regulatory Agency and Regulation Landscape

AML	FDICIA	OCC
Basel III	FRB	RESPA
BSA	Ginnie Mae	SCRA
CFPB	GSEs	State Regs
Dodd-Frank	HOA	TCPA
ECOA	HOPA	TILA
EFTA (ACH)	HUD	UDAAP
Fair Trade	NCUA	VA
FCRA	NMLS/SAFE	
FDCPA	OFAC	

Cost Effectiveness and Scalability

As you think about your strategic goals and objectives and begin to build out your five-year plan, you likely find yourself thinking about how to manage and control costs while retaining flexibility in your operations. Subservicing allows you to lock down your servicing costs while still having the flexibility to better manage portfolio volume changes to take advantage of market opportunities. Typically, working with an established and major subservicing company will be more cost effective than building a new in-house servicing operation or using an existing servicing platform with less volume. The costs for the required servicing technology, trained staff, different support systems, and compliance monitoring all make it extremely difficult to be cost competitive without servicing at least 150,000 loans. If you are a buyer of loans or MSRs, subservicing obviates the need to expend the capital to build the infrastructure and resources to take advantage of opportunities. Using a subservicer enables you to adjust your volumes more easily in response to changing market conditions and secondary market pricing opportunities, without having to support the fixed costs for an in-house servicing operation. Taken all together, subservicing can be a cost-effective alternative given the resource constraints that we all face.

Subservicing also allows you to offer new products to your customers and expand your services. We all know that technology isn't cheap, and the economy of scale that a subservicer can bring to your business allows for a much broader approach to your business plan. Specifically, by working with an experienced subservicer with a strong staff and technology, your firm can offer a wider range of fixed-rate and adjustable-rate loan programs, provide various types of conventional and government loans and access specialized housing agency and other financing programs without having to develop and support the required servicing for these different products internally.

Best execution – isn't that what it's all about? Many originators today who are servicing themselves find that they are tied into a specific delivery method because of either a systems limitation or limited investor-reporting capabilities. A good subservicer will support all of your selling strategies, as well as supporting your business if you do private securitizations. But, in order to do that, they will need to be rated by the appropriate agencies and have the right controls in place to administer the reporting requirements of the transactions.

Some additional benefits to using a subservicer:

- Allows you to expand your product mix without having to learn all the details associated with a particular product or investor that are required of a day to day servicing operation

- Allows you to expand and shrink your portfolio without worrying about the staffing needs of your own organization

CHOOSING A SUBSERVICER

Many years ago when I started in this business, a senior executive at a prospective banking company said to me, "economics are important, but only after I have assured myself that you are the right fit for our business. Cheap is cheap and I know that you need to make money. Why would I want to cut the service to the most valuable asset that we have built in our business?"

So here is a list of some of the things that you should be asking for as you consider a subservicer.

- *Company strategy and focus* – is subservicing their primary source of business, or is it one of many products that they offer? Will you be competing for resources, decisions, and enhancements against their in-house operations? How will servicing protocols be administered? A simple example: whose delinquent loans will they call first, yours or theirs?

- *Management strength and experience* – look at the experience and depth of the management team. Ask questions about background, accomplishments, and experience.

- *Management commitment and industry activity* – how important are you to their business? Are you going to be an important client and how do they demonstrate that? Will their executive management take your calls? Are they committed to the business and to the industry? Ask about their involvement with the Mortgage Bankers Association (MBA), the American Bankers Association (ABA), NCUA and Credit Union and other industry affinity groups. Do they have leadership positions in these groups?

- *How are they staying abreast of industry, technology, regulatory, and compliance changes?* Make sure that you dig deep into these areas. These are areas that, if not managed properly, will quickly get you into trouble. Make sure that you understand how they will support you with state, CFPB, OCC, NCUA, GSE, and investor audits.

- *Discuss and review their GSE and Ginnie Mae relationships.* How do they manage this very critical part of their business? And are there any major issues outstanding that could impact your business?

- *Evaluate their Risk Management Program.* Understand how they manage risk for both you and their overall business. Is it a formalized process, and are the components documented and available to you for review?

- *Make sure that they are continuing to grow and expand their core service process and that you are the beneficiary of those changes.* Ask about key initiatives and enhancements that were recently delivered and what they have scheduled for delivery.

- *Capacity* – ask about their growth strategy, their technology and space capacity, and how they balance and manage both to assure the best service to you.

- *Security and Privacy Policy* – make sure that your data is safe and that your subservicer has a sound plan to safeguard not only your data but your customers. Headline risk is damaging to their business and, more important, to yours!

- *Review financials* – ask for the financials. Make sure that they have the financial capacity to do the kind of business that you are contemplating. Do they have the capacity to withstand failures in their business?

- *Approvals* – do they have the appropriate state and GSE approvals? If they are an unregulated institution, ask them to provide you with copies of their state approvals.

- *Check references* – ask for a list of references and then check them!

- *Conduct a site visit* – there is almost nothing more important than getting in front of your proposed partner. Go look at their operations. Meet their management team. Look at the way that they do business. Are they a partner that you believe would properly manage your portfolio and your customers? Can they help you to build value in your portfolio?

- *Product development* – what is their attitude and approach to developing new products and services? You want assurance that a lack of commitment to this process doesn't stagnate your business or leave you behind your competitors.

- *How do they define quality service?* Will they treat your customers with an approach toward service to maintain an experience that will create a lifelong customer?

- *Are they flexible enough to integrate your business model and strategy into theirs?*

BUILDING THE OVERSIGHT PROGRAM

As the Master Servicer, you are fully accountable to Fannie Mae, Freddie Mac, and Ginnie Mae for the subservicer's actions, servicing and process fails, and more specifically, for compensatory penalties. You also ultimately remain accountable to the regulators for servicing performance. The ownership risk — that is, the representations, warrants and indemnifications — also remain with you.

In a traditional subservicing arrangement, the subservicer will take responsibility for their servicing failures, but you, as the Master Servicer, will continue to retain the credit risk for the portfolio. The subservicer will indemnify you for their fails, so be sure that the subservicer has the financial capacity to accept those obligations.

You will need to build a strong oversight program staffed by experienced servicing personnel to satisfy the requirements of Fannie Mae, Freddie Mac, Ginnie Mae and CFPB. A key requirement will be to build and document an oversight program that is comprehensive and assures that you are taking the appropriate care to manage all aspects of the relationship and servicing activities. Each of the aforementioned entities have published oversight guidance on their websites which should be incorporated into your program. Some of the key elements that should be included are as follows:

- Build policies and procedures for your oversight program.
- Obtain access to your subservicer's policies and procedures.
- Conduct audit and quality-control reviews to assure compliance.
- Establish your Master Servicer management team.
- Engage and communicate regularly with your subservicer. Schedule no less frequent than monthly meetings to review performance, goals, and objectives.
- Stay actively involved in all regulatory and compliance requirements; make sure that you understand the impact on your servicer and that they are servicing in accordance with these requirements.
- Assess the quality of the subservicer's risk management systems to identify acts or practices that materially increase the risk of violations of Federal consumer law.
- Review cash controls and reconciliations.
- Review your customer service expectations with your subservicer and establish a process to assure that you are both aligned on service delivery.
- Conduct annual financial reviews.
- Obtain access to the servicing system so that you can monitor loan level performance.

MANAGING THE SUBERVICING RELATIONSHIP

As with all relationships, building a strong foundation is the key to maintaining a successful partnership. That starts with open dialogue and communication on a regular basis. You should be willing to share information about your business strategy that the subservicer can use to build a stronger program for you and your customers. The subservicer should regularly provide updates on the programs, technology, and service improvements that they are developing.

The subservicer will assign a relationship manager to oversee the account. It's important to understand that you are probably not their only client, so build a solid and regular communication process with them to discuss performance, goals, and objectives. Clearly communicate your expectations to your subservicing partner and make sure that they understand your expectations on the turnaround times needed as well as the urgency of your request, specifically when the matter is of a more critical nature. Explain the rationale behind your request and solicit ideas on how to best achieve results. Be open to multiple approaches. If you work together as a team, you will find that the relationship manager can become your best friend and advocate.

Also, be sure to clearly communicate your organization's culture and the service expectations and business processes that are most important to you. In doing so, your subservicer will be better prepared to deliver on and meet your expectations.

Seek transparency as if this were your in-house service operation. Establish data and reporting analytics that will provide the appropriate information to validate the servicing process. Apply best-practice techniques in all areas of servicing as you perform your oversight functions. Seek to prove positive results rather than negatives or failures.

You should establish performance measures that will capture cycle times and accuracy and that will also expose adverse trends. Develop a testing process and schedule periodic reviews to assure that your subservicer is performing to your expectations.

Value the relationship that you build with your subservicer. Be demanding but reasonable and they will work extremely hard for you. Remember – trust but verify!

ABOUT THE AUTHOR

David J. Miller, Jr., Executive Vice President and Business Development Director for Cenlar, and a member of the bank's Executive Committee, has over 25 years of experience in mortgage servicing administration, project management, accounting, operations, systems management, loan administration and strategic planning. Dave has managed portfolio conversions and deconversions and has extensive experience with servicing systems. He served as chairman of the Loan Servicing Committee for the New Jersey League of Community Bankers and is a member of the Mortgage Bankers Association Loan Administration Committee.

Dave earned a bachelor of science in business administration from Temple University.

CHAPTER FIFTEEN

RESIDENTIAL MORTGAGE SPECIAL SERVICING

BILL COPPEDGE | SENIOR MANAGING DIRECTOR

FAY FINANCIAL, LLC

When Jess Lederman approached me to ask for a chapter on special servicing, I checked around to what had been written about this industry which used to be, in my humble opinion, one of the less exciting aspects of the mortgage business. As the keeper of a dedicated mortgage blog since 1998, I would like to think I am reasonably abreast of news in the mortgage industry. Since the housing crisis of 2008, there has been much published discussing many of the problems associated with special servicing. However, there is no single source that describes the core elements of special servicing in any real depth or that describes how those elements have changed in reaction to the crisis. Not only did the crisis bring about the downfall of some of the largest originators and special servicers, but it also created opportunities for new business models that could address the shifting needs of the industry. Given that lack of information on special servicing and the dynamic nature of the industry, I was delighted to write this chapter, and it is a privilege I greatly appreciate.

For over 30 years I was a mortgage-backed bond salesman and most of the accounts I covered were large mortgage origination companies that had minimal exposure to special servicing and loss mitigation. Most of the people reading this book can probably make the same statement about their knowledge of special servicing. While there were many twists and turns in the mortgage space over the years, nothing has changed the industry more than the housing crisis of 2008, and special servicing perhaps changed the most. The investors and operating companies that were most levered to the risk of default were either destroyed or forced to permanently change their business model. Since then, special servicing has become an entirely different animal, which I learned firsthand when I joined Fay Servicing's business-development team in 2010. I am excited to share details of this interesting world in which I have been directly involved for the last five years, but tied to for my entire career.

We will start this chapter from the ground up and, when it is appropriate or useful, I will use my firm, Fay Servicing, as an example. The chapter will cover the following areas:

1. Key Special-Servicing Definitions
2. Rise of Third-Party Special Servicing
3. Three Functions of Special Servicing
4. Compliance and Regulation
5. Items to Consider in the Selection of a Special Servicer
6. Conclusions

CHAPTER FIFTEEN: *RESIDENTIAL MORTGAGE SPECIAL SERVICING*

KEY SPECIAL SERVICING DEFINITIONS

If you are familiar with these definitions, please jump ahead to 'Rise of Third-Party Special Servicing' on page 6.

- **Mortgage:** A debt instrument secured by the collateral of specified real estate property, that the borrower is obliged to pay back. Mortgages are also known as "liens against property" or "claims on property." If the borrower stops paying the mortgage, the lender can foreclose.
  http://www.investopedia.com/terms/m/mortgage.asp

- **Property Lien:** A notice attached to a property claiming the property owner owes the creditor money. A lien is typically a public record and is generally filed with a county records office.
  http://www.nolo.com/legal-encyclopedia/what-property-lien.html

- **Deed:** A legal instrument that transfers a property right in real estate. Deeds contain a description of the real estate involved, the names of the respective parties, and the signature of the person transferring the real estate.
  http://realestate.findlaw.com/buying-a-home/what-are-property-deeds.html#sthash.Aw0hnhJX.dpuf

- **Title:** A formal document, such as a deed, that serves as evidence of ownership. Conveyance of the document may be required in order to transfer ownership in the property to another person. For real property, land registration and recording provide public notice of ownership information. In United States law, evidence of title is established through title reports written up by title insurance companies, which show the history of title (property abstract and chain of title) as determined by the recorded public record deeds.
  https://en.wikipedia.org/wiki/Title_(property)

- **Mortgage Servicer:** A company that manages all aspects of a mortgage loan once it has been originated. The duties of a mortgage servicer typically include (but are not limited to) the accepting and accounting of mortgage payments; calculating variable interest rates on adjustable rate loans; payment of taxes and insurance from borrower escrow accounts; negotiating workouts (including liquidation) and modifications of mortgage upon default; conducting or supervising the foreclosure process when necessary; and disposition of Real Estate Owned (REO) Properties.
  https://en.wikipedia.org/wiki/Loan_servicing

- **Special Mortgage Servicing:** A specialization within the mortgage-loan-servicing function that begins when a borrower is delinquent, or is deemed likely to be in imminent default. A special servicer can service either loans it owns, or on a third-party basis. If it is not possible to bring a defaulted loan current through reinstatement, the special servicer begins the process of loss mitigation.

- **Loss Mitigation:** A process of negotiating mortgage terms for the borrower that will prevent foreclosure. Forms of loss mitigation include loan modification, short-sale negotiation, short-refinance negotiation, deed in lieu of foreclosure, cash-for-keys negotiation, a partial-claim loan, repayment plan, forbearance, or other loan work-out strategies. All of the options serve the same purpose: to mitigate the loss the owner of the loan is in danger of realizing.

There are three categories of terms within default management: Home Retention, Non-Retention, and Latter Default Stages.

Home Retention
- **Loan Modification:** A written agreement between the borrower and lender outlining new terms of the borrower's mortgage. The modification is permanent and both parties are bound by the new terms. The new terms of a borrower's mortgage include but are not limited to: lowering the interest rate, extending the term (either actual loan term or amortization term), capitalization of arrears, and reduction of principal balance.

- **Forbearance:** An agreement in which the borrower will make no monthly payment or a reduced monthly payment, typically for a period of three to six months. Sometimes the lender will require the borrower to be put on a repayment plan when the forbearance has been finished to bring the loan current, while other times the lender will modify the loan at the reduced payment amount at the conclusion of the forbearance period.
https://en.wikipedia.org/wiki/Loss_mitigation

- **Short Refinance:** A resolution in which the lender reduces the principal balance of a borrower's mortgage in order to permit the borrower to refinance with a new lender. The reduction in principal is designed to meet the loan-to-value guidelines of the new lender (which makes refinancing possible). FHA launched a special 1023 program for short refinances. At the time of this writing, the FHA 10213 program is scheduled to sunset at the end of 2016.

Non-Retention
- **Short Sale:** A disposition option in which the lender accepts a payoff that is less than the total debt due (principal plus delinquency arrears plus advances), in order to permit the borrower to sell the home for its actual market value. This applies to borrowers that owe more on their mortgage than their property is worth. Without such a principal reduction the borrower would not be able to sell the home. A short sale may contain a deficiency judgment.

- **Deed in Lieu of Foreclosure ("DIL"):** A disposition option in which a borrower voluntarily deeds collateral property back to the lender in exchange for a release from all obligations under the mortgage. If it is not possible to sell the home through a short sale, DIL is another option. Lenders might also prefer a DIL over a short sale so they can feel they can make impactful repairs and then ultimately sell the house for a higher price. A DIL may not be accepted by the lender if the borrower can financially handle his mortgage payment.

- **Cash-for-Keys Negotiation:** A disposition option in which the lender will pay the borrower or tenant to vacate the home in a timely fashion without damaging the property either prior to or after foreclosure. The lender does this to avoid incurring the additional expenses associated with evicting such occupants. Cash-for-keys compensation is often included as part of the DIL process.

- **Deficiency Judgment:** A court order making the borrower personally liable for unpaid debt. They are often associated with Foreclosures, Short Sales, and DILs, when a home's selling price is not enough to cover the loan balance. It is the lender's option to pursue this unpaid balance or not when permitted by the state.
http://banking.about.com/od/loans/a/deficiencyjudg.htm

Latter Default Stages
- **Pre-Forclosure:** A legal status of a property which is in the early stages of being repossessed. Reaching pre-foreclosure status begins when the lender files a notice of default on the property (typically at least after 61 days of delinquency) that informs the borrower that the lender will proceed with pursuing legal action if the debt is not addressed. At this point, the borrower has the opportunity to become current, pay off the outstanding debt, or sell the property before it is foreclosed upon.
http://www.investopedia.com/terms/p/pre-foreclosure.asp

- **Bankruptcy:** A legal status of a person or other entity that is claiming that it cannot repay the debts it owes creditors. In most jurisdictions, bankruptcy is imposed by a court order, often initiated by the borrower.
https://en.wikipedia.org/wiki/Bankruptcy
For many borrowers, bankruptcy is a stop along the path to foreclosure. Chapter 7 and Chapter 13 are the two types of bankruptcy that most commonly occur in residential mortgage servicing.

- **Chapter 7 Bankruptcy** is a liquidation of assets that completely wipes out general unsecured debts, such as credit cards and medical bills. To qualify for Chapter 7 bankruptcy, the borrower must have little or no disposable income. If the income is above a certain level, the borrower is required to file a Chapter 13 bankruptcy.
http://www.experian.com/blogs/ask-experian/2012/02/01/difference-between-chapter-7-and-13-bankruptcy/

- Most Chapter 7 bankruptcy filers can keep their homes as long as they are current on their mortgage payments. Some lose their home if they have significant equity that can be used by the trustee to pay unsecured creditors.
http://www.nolo.com/legal-encyclopedia/home-chapter-7-bankruptcy-32498.html

- **Chapter 13 Bankruptcy** is an Adjustment of Debt plan under which the court may approve a repayment plan. Under Chapter 13 bankruptcy, the consumer must make partial payments under a repayment plan to multiple creditors periodically over a period of several years. Once the repayment plan is complete, the bankruptcy is discharged. http://www.experian.com/blogs/ask-experian/2012/02/01/difference-between-chapter-7-and-13-bankruptcy/

- When you file for Chapter 13 bankruptcy, you do not lose any property to the bankruptcy trustee (including your home), nor does the bankruptcy filing affect your mortgage. However, although you won't lose your home through the Chapter 13 bankruptcy process, you can still lose your home through foreclosure. This means that you must continue to make your mortgage payments during Chapter 13 bankruptcy if you want to keep your home. If you are facing foreclosure, Chapter 13 can help. It allows you to make up mortgage arrears through your plan (something you cannot do in Chapter 7 bankruptcy).
http://www.alllaw.com/articles/nolo/bankruptcy/chapter-13-affects-mortgages-foreclosure.html

- When you file either a Chapter 13 or Chapter 7 bankruptcy, the court automatically issues an order called an "automatic stay". The automatic stay directs your creditors to cease their collection activities immediately. If the home is scheduled for a foreclosure sale, the sale will be legally postponed while the bankruptcy is pending — typically for three to four months.
http://www.nolo.com/legal-encyclopedia/bankruptcy-help-with-foreclosure-29631.html

- **Foreclosure:** A legal process in which a lender attempts to recover the balance of a loan from a borrower who has stopped making payments to the lender through repossession of the property. The foreclosure process begins when a "notice of default" has been filed against the borrower in the county court of the property's location. That means that the borrower stopped making mortgage payments and the lender has advised that unless the payments are brought up to date, the property will be repossessed and auctioned to the highest bidder. The most common reason for a foreclosure is payment default. Not all homes that fall into foreclosure proceed to auction, because the owner has the opportunity to bring payments current within a specified period.
http://www.everythingre.com/overview-of-distressed-sales-foreclosures-short-sale-reo.html

- **REO:** An abbreviation for "real-estate owned" property. REO refers to the actual property that has been foreclosed on and taken back by the mortgage lender or trustee. REOs and foreclosures are not the same thing. An REO is produced as a result of an unsuccessful sale at a foreclosure auction when the property fails to meet the reserve price minimum, or, alternatively, once a DIL has been executed. The mortgage lender repossesses the property to sell separately.
http://www.everythingre.com/reo_vs_foreclosure

CHAPTER FIFTEEN: *RESIDENTIAL MORTGAGE SPECIAL SERVICING*

Government Regulators and Agency Related Programs Affecting Special Mortgage Servicing

- **Federal Housing Administration (FHA):** A U.S. government agency created as part of the National Housing Act of 1934 that insures loans made by banks and other private lenders for home building. The majority of loans in Ginnie Mae securities have FHA insurance. (VA loans do not.) In 1965 the Federal Housing Administration became part of the Department of Housing and Urban Development (HUD).
https://en.wikipedia.org/wiki/Federal_Housing_Administration

- **United States Department of Housing and Urban Development (HUD):** A Cabinet department founded in 1965 with a mission to develop and execute policies on housing.
https://en.wikipedia.org/wiki/United_States_Department_of_Housing_and_Urban_Development

- **Federal Housing Finance Agency (FHFA):** A conservator of Fannie Mae (FNMA) and Freddie Mac (FHLMC) created in July 2008. FHFA is also regulator of Fannie Mae, Freddie Mac, and the 12 Federal Home Loan Banks (FHLBs).
https://en.wikipedia.org/wiki/Federal_Housing_Finance_Agency

- **Government-Sponsored Enterprise (GSE):** A financial services corporation created by the United States Congress. The two most well-known GSEs are the Federal National Mortgage Association, or "Fannie Mae", and the Federal Home Loan Mortgage Corporation, or "Freddie Mac".
https://en.wikipedia.org/wiki/Government-sponsored_enterprise

- **Home Affordable Modification Program (HAMP):** A federal program of the United States, set up to help eligible home owners with loan modifications on their home mortgage debt. HAMP assists homeowners who are in danger of foreclosure.
https://en.wikipedia.org/wiki/Home_Affordable_Modification_Program

- **Home Affordable Refinance Program (HARP):** A federal program of the United States set up by the Federal Housing Finance Agency in March 2009 to help underwater and near-underwater homeowners refinance their mortgages. HARP benefits homeowners whose mortgage payments are current, but who cannot refinance due to dropping home prices.
https://en.wikipedia.org/wiki/Home_Affordable_Refinance_Program

- **Home Affordable Foreclosure Alternatives Program (HAFA):** A federal program of the United States that provides homeowners the opportunity to exit their homes and be relieved of their remaining mortgage debt through a short sale or a deed-in-lieu of foreclosure. HAFA also provides homeowners with $10,000 in relocation assistance. Before HAFA approval, the borrower is evaluated for possible HAMP modification.
https://www.makinghomeaffordable.gov/steps/pages/step-2-program-hafa.aspx

- **Consumer Financial Protection Bureau (CFPB):** An independent agency of the U.S. government responsible for consumer protection in the financial sector. Its regulatory jurisdiction includes banks, credit unions, securities firms, payday lenders, mortgage originators, mortgage-servicing operations, foreclosure relief services, debt collectors, other financial companies operating in the United States. The CFPB's creation was authorized by the Dodd–Frank Wall Street Reform and Consumer Protection Act, passed in 2010.
  https://en.wikipedia.org/wiki/Consumer_Financial_Protection_Bureau

- **Office of the Comptroller of the Currency (OCC):** A regulator that charters, regulates, and supervises all national banks and federal savings associations as well as federal branches and agencies of foreign banks. The OCC is an independent bureau of the U.S. Department of the Treasury.
  http://occ.gov/about/what-we-do/mission/index-about.html

RISE OF THIRD-PARTY SPECIAL SERVICING

This section describes the evolution of Third-Party Special Servicing over three time periods:

I. Pre-2007 – Housing prices accelerate, as 2000-2007 underwriting guidelines deteriorated
II. 2007-2008 – Housing Crisis, delinquencies rapidly rise, home price decline begins
III. 2009-2015 – Housing prices stabilize, building of loss mitigation capacity where none existed, increased regulation, emergence of servicing bifurcation

I. Third-Party Special Servicing Pre-2007

A 26-year overall decline in interest rates was a large factor in spurring house price appreciation. Interest rates peaked in 1981, with U.S. T-bills yielding over 20%, and the 30-year U.S. Treasury Bond yielded 14%. Fed Chairman Paul Volcker's vow to stem inflation set into motion an environment for interest rates to drop that continues to exist as I write these words in late 2015. Paralleling this rate drop period, national housing prices mostly rose until their peak in 2007, ahead of the housing crisis of 2007-2008. Prior to 2007, housing prices increased and delinquencies remained low or even decreased. The need for loss mitigation at mortgage originators and servicers slowly decreased. Why maintain a large loss-mitigation staff when housing prices would rise forever, minimizing the possibility of losses? At a number of originators, loss-mitigation staff were either transferred to the regular servicing function, or laid off. This de-staffing continued until the housing crisis began. Most of the largest mortgage originators, especially the largest banks, performed servicing and loss mitigation internally. But the degradation of underwriting guidelines from 2000-2007 created an environment in which it was much more likely that a large number of defaults would accompany a severe housing price correction.

II. Third-Party Special Servicing 2007-2008

Prior to the housing crisis, most mortgage servicer operations were built for 1% delinquencies, yet, by the end of 2008, they were seeing delinquencies of 9.2%. https://en.wikipedia.org/wiki/Subprime_mortgage_crisis

With lean staff default expertise, mortgage servicers were forced to scramble and rebuild their loss-mitigation departments. Operational metamorphosis and regulation were coming. This environment led to massive whole-loan and mortgage servicing rights (MSR) sales spurred by the related and broader 2008 financial crisis. Most of these asset sales were from banks to non-banks. Banks needed liquidity; with few natural buyers in the market with meaningful capacity, these distressed assets were predominantly purchased by private equity funds, hedge funds, and non-bank servicers. The shift in ownership of MSRs and whole loans to non-banks set into motion changes in the structure of the special-servicing industry that exist today.

III. Third-Party Special Servicing Post-Crisis, 2009-2015

Great effort has been spent rebuilding special-servicing capacity since the housing crisis. Re-staffing, workflow redesign, and an increase in compliance and regulation have been the primary drivers shaping the industry's approach to loss mitigation. Besides banks initially growing their loss-mitigation headcount, large private buyers of distressed loans bought or built their own servicing platforms. At this time, a number of privately owned third-party special servicers began to appear. Overall, the industry is now better equipped to handle the challenges of residential mortgage loss mitigation than in 2007.

After the housing crisis, a new trend developed; owners of non-performing loans began to either sell or have them sub-serviced on a third-party basis. Performing loans are generally serviced in-house, or sub-serviced by high-volume/low-cost servicers that focus on cleaner loans (see chapter on subservicing in this volume). Non-performing loans are increasingly being transferred to third-party special servicers for loss mitigation, usually once a loan becomes 45-60 days delinquent. This process of separating performing and non-performing loans is known as *servicing bifurcation*. Bifurcation has become most common at large banks.

Historically, bank originators' primary strengths have been the underwriting, originating, and servicing of clean, performing loans. Additionally, the primary business for non-bank originators has been the origination of similar clean, low-delinquency loans. However, in the aftermath of the housing meltdown, we now see higher costs due to the complexities of loss mitigation, increased compliance, and regulation. These factors have reinforced the trend toward servicing bifurcation, and troubled assets continue to find their way to specialists.

For example, one large bank originator/servicer (top 20 in the U.S. as measured by total assets) recently publicly announced that 10% of its employees are devoted to regulation fulfillment, compliance, and internal/external audits. Even with this high level of bandwidth dedicated to these functions, the bank is still bifurcating their servicing by outsourcing loss-mitigation functions to special servicers once loans go 45 days delinquent.

There are three considerations for Special Servicing Bifurcation if special servicing is not your primary business:

- Operational costs of building and maintaining a fully compliant special servicing group
- Cost of penalties and reputation risk
- Performance

Operational Costs
Operational Costs fall into three areas: people (both management and operations), process re-engineering, and technology (both ongoing and new investment). Increasing costs of running an internal special-servicing operation raise an overall barrier of entry to a loan-servicing operation.

Before the mortgage meltdown, when delinquency rates were 2% (http://eyeonhousing.org/2014/11/mortgage-delinquency-rates-fall-2/), the largest servicers were generally able to keep their costs to service a performing loan to below $50 per year. Compliance now takes a central role in origination and servicing, and will continue to be a primary focus. Servicing costs, especially for loss mitigation, have sharply risen. In 2015, publically traded companies saw annual costs for servicing performing loans vary from $60-$160, and the annual cost of servicing non-performing loans vary from $600-$2500. Post-crisis compliance headcounts at publically traded companies have risen by as much as 500%.

The Mortgage Bankers Association (MBA) provides servicing costs for prime loans. In 2014, the MBA published that direct servicing costs per loan per year for ALL loans (both performing and non-performing) were $173 per loan. Default costs were $73 of the $173 total, or 42.6%. Compliance costs for non-performing loans were $423 /loan/year in 2008, *rising to $1,809 /loan/year in 2014.*

A white paper jointly written by Price Waterhouse Coopers and the MBA in 2015 states that non-performing loans cost $482-$2,315 per year to service depending on resolution outcome.

Penalties and Reputational Risk Cost
As we have seen in the years following the housing crisis, the costs of fines and penalties as well as the reputational damage associated with poor distressed-servicing performance can cripple an organization in various ways. The robo-signing scandal is an excellent example, as it caused a $25 billion settlement with five banks in 2012, and a $9.3 billion settlement in 2013 with 49 state attorneys general and federal regulators. In a judicial

foreclosure state, the lender must demonstrate that the homeowner has defaulted on a mortgage and that the lender owns the mortgage. These facts are proven by submitting documents and a written statement signed under oath (called an affidavit) by a person (usually a bank employee) who has reviewed the documents and who is supposed to have some personal basis for believing the facts to be true. In 2010, it was revealed that several large banks routinely used affidavits signed by employees who did not personally review the documents and had no basis for believing that the homeowner was in default or that the bank owned the loan. Employees testified that they signed many thousands of these affidavits a month — hence the name "robo-signers." http://www.nolo.com/legal-encyclopedia/false-affidavits-foreclosures-what-robo-34185.html

Since that time, the magnitude and breadth of penalties has continued to grow. An August 2015 Wall Street Journal article highlights several large settlements post-crisis. Many of the largest banks agreed to settlements in the hundreds of millions to several billions of dollars. http://blogs.wsj.com/cfo/2015/08/17/biggest-banks-crisis-era-settlements-petering-out-report/

While difficult to assign a dollar cost to reputational risk, maintaining and strengthening brand value is critical to originators, servicers, and mortgage investors. Any impairments to that brand or reputation could cause significant loss of business, and in many cases it has actually driven companies out of business.

Performance

There are many different ways to measure performance of a special servicer, but two that I will focus on are timelines and resolution outcomes.

- Timelines – How long does it take the servicer to reach each resolution outcome? Would a third-party special servicer shorten those timelines, and if so by how much?

- Resolution Outcomes – Given various levels of delinquency at boarding, what kinds of results is the servicer achieving? Generally, the better the servicer is at avoiding foreclosure, the better the economics will be for the owner of the loan. We at Fay Servicing use "Delinquency at Board" to measure resolution outcomes, and that term refers to the number of days a loan is past due when boarded onto a servicing platform.

The following chart is based on actual Fay Servicing data. It shows that the percentage of favorable non-foreclosure outcomes declines as the level of delinquency at boarding increases. The earlier the delinquency stage when loss mitigation begins (generally), the better the outcome. In earlier stages of delinquency, there is a higher likelihood to re-engage the borrower, and the property is less likely to experience deterioration. Comparison of resolution-outcomes relative to delinquency is a good first step in consideration for utilizing a third-party special servicer.

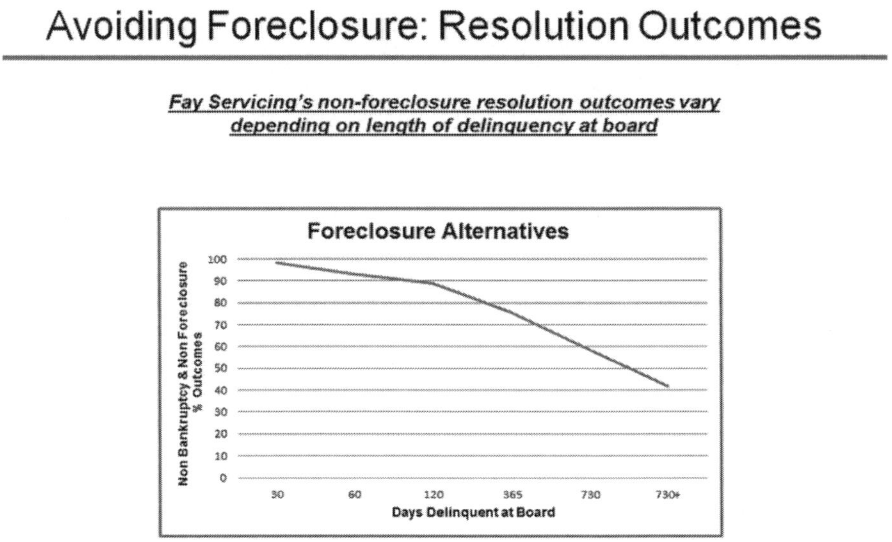

Avoiding Foreclosure: Resolution Outcomes

Fay Servicing's non-foreclosure resolution outcomes vary depending on length of delinquency at board

Foreclosure Alternatives

(Chart: Non Bankruptcy & Non Foreclosure % Outcomes vs. Days Delinquent at Board — 30, 60, 120, 365, 730, 730+)

THREE CORE FUNCTIONS OF SPECIAL SERVICING

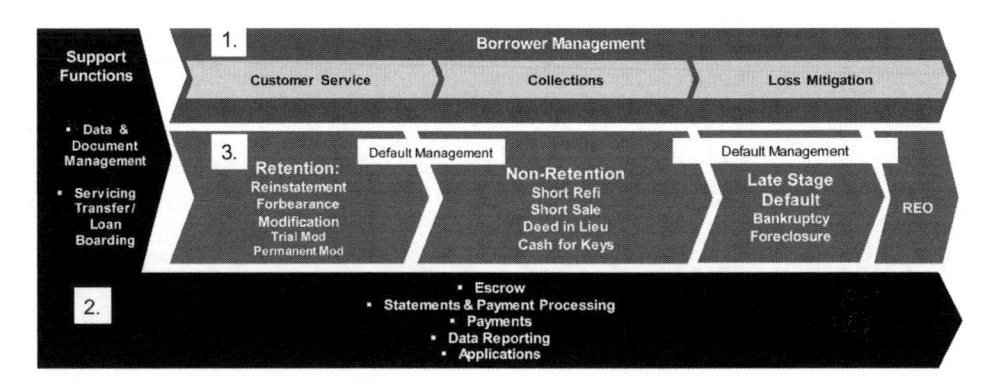

Three Functional Areas of Special Servicing Lifecycle

Every functional area contributes to building and maintaining a strong borrower relationship

Support Functions
- Data & Document Management
- Servicing Transfer / Loan Boarding

1. Borrower Management
- Customer Service
- Collections
- Loss Mitigation

Default Management
- Retention: Reinstatement, Forbearance, Modification, Trial Mod, Permanent Mod
- Non-Retention: Short Refi, Short Sale, Deed in Lieu, Cash for Keys

Default Management
- Late Stage Default, Bankruptcy, Foreclosure
- REO

2.
- Escrow
- Statements & Payment Processing
- Payments
- Data Reporting
- Applications

Many processes happen simultaneously to a loan undergoing special servicing. Every special servicer differs in the way functions and processes are handled. Fay Servicing divides the process into three broad functions.

Function #1 – Borrower Management:
- Customer Service
- Collections
- Loss Mitigation

Function #2 – Support Functions:
- Data and Document Management
- Servicing Transfer
- Loan Boarding
- Escrow
- Statements & Payment Processing
- Reporting
- Applications

Function #3 – Default Management:
- Retention
- Non-Retention
- Late Stage Default
- REO

We will be referring to this chart often in the discussion below.

Function #1 – Borrower Management: Customer Service, Collections, and Loss Mitigation

Borrower management encompasses customer service, collections, and the loss-mitigation process. However, borrower management is not executed the same way at all special servicers, and this can lead to varying results in loss mitigation from one servicer to another. This makes borrower management an important consideration in the selection of a special servicer.

The Rise and Evolution of Single Point of Contact ("SPOC")

- **Pre-2007 Crisis:** Immediately after the mortgage crisis, mortgage servicers were under-staffed and using a loss-mitigation model designed for pre-crisis times.

- **Post 2007-2008 Housing Crisis Troubles Arise Using Old Platforms:** With a large increase in delinquent loans, the legacy approach to handling the borrower was to use the existing pre-crisis loss mitigation structure passing the borrower down the resolution stage chain. This meant the borrower would have to talk to five to eight different areas (reinstatement, modification, short sale, etc.), and explain their situation over and over. From the borrower's perspective, most servicers had little to no communication between each resolution stage and among the different departments.

- **CFPB Creates SPOC:** In 2013, the CFPB and State Supervisors issued a Coordination Framework document describing the requirements for Single Points of Contact.
  http://files.consumerfinance.gov/f/201305_cfpb_state-supervisory-coordination-framework.pdf Section IV.C.1. through 3.

- **Interpretations of SPOC:** SPOC implementation can differ greatly among special-servicing companies. Many servicers have the SPOC function as what is essentially a receptionist who speaks with the borrower, primarily serving as a coordinator of communication between various departments as the borrower moves through various loss mitigation stages. Yet other servicers use the SPOC to own the relationship with the borrower and directly manage him through the appropriate loss-mitigation path. Whatever version of SPOC a servicer employs, they are all an improvement for the borrower, given the simplified and improved access to the servicer, relative to pre-SPOC models.

- **Fay True SPOC:** Since its founding in 2008, Fay Servicing has practiced what we call a True SPOC model. Account Managers (AMs), who conduct Borrower Management, are closely aligned with each of the two other functional areas of the mortgage-servicing lifecycle. By True SPOC we mean that we have combined the responsibilities of customer service, collections, and loss mitigation into one role. That role is carried out by our AMs who will build the relationship with the borrower, managing him through the entire mortgage-servicing lifecycle. Fay Servicing AMs average eight years of mortgage-industry experience before joining our firm. 62% of incoming calls at Fay Servicing are directly dialed to the AM.

Personal Budget Analysis
At Fay Servicing, we give borrowers an option to work with our staff using an underwriting tool called the Personal Budget Analysis (PBA) to help guide the Borrower Management process. With over 85 questions that can be asked of the borrower, the PBA helps accomplish two valuable objectives. First, the servicer and the borrower gain an accurate understanding of the borrower's financial picture. Second, the PBA process begins to establish a personal relationship between the borrower and AM, ultimately enhancing borrower engagement.

The PBA tool helps to ascertain true affordability by showing if the borrower has enough residual income for a modification to make sense. Traditional metrics of affordability became less relevant after the 2008 housing meltdown. Residual income looks at the borrower's ability to pay for food, clothing, transportation, medical expenses, and other day-to-day living expenses after paying home-related expenses. Fay Servicing views residual income as a crucial measure of affordability in determining the chances of a delinquency. The Veteran's Administration seems to take a similar view. For years, VA loans have required a measure of residual income within the underwriting process, and its loans saw much lower delinquencies through the crisis than any other lending programs, which do not measure residual income. The Urban Institute has written a paper about VA loan performance and discusses residual income in more depth. http://www.urban.org/sites/default/files/alfresco/publication-pdfs/413182-VA-Loans-Outperform-FHA-Loans-Why-And-What-Can-We-Learn-.PDF

The time spent at the beginning of a relationship doing a PBA has more than shown its worth. Every loan, every property, and every borrower is a little different, and information captured within the PBA often helps tailor solutions that to match the borrower's unique problems.

Residual income as a measure can point out important differences between borrowers that otherwise might look financially identical. The use of a PBA can provide useful information in conjunction with following a consistent Loss Mitigation waterfall (see graphic below).

At Fay Servicing, AMs are front and center. Both Support departments and Default departments, such as foreclosure and bankruptcy, are in continuous contact with the AM, who provides continuity as the borrower's primary contact.

Account Management: Loss Mitigation

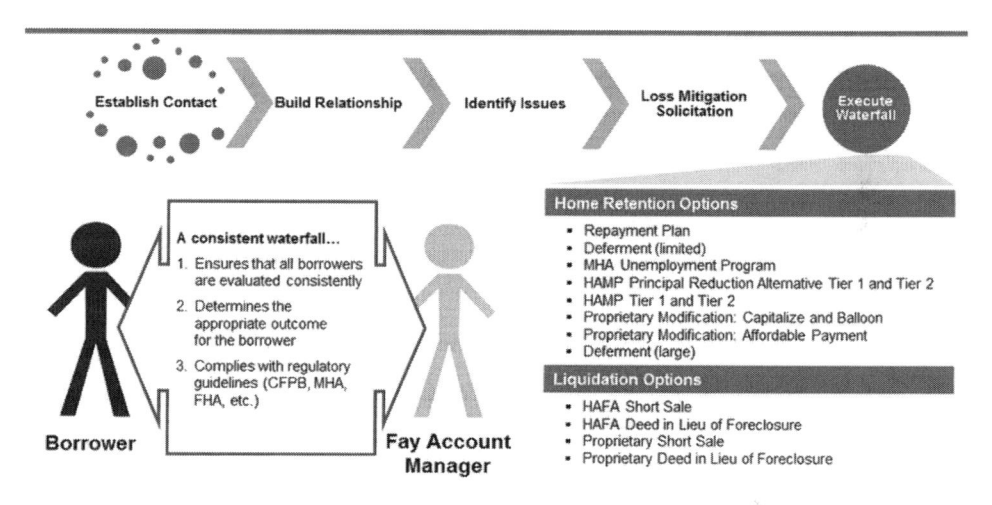

Establish Contact → Build Relationship → Identify Issues → Loss Mitigation Solicitation → Execute Waterfall

A consistent waterfall...
1. Ensures that all borrowers are evaluated consistently
2. Determines the appropriate outcome for the borrower
3. Complies with regulatory guidelines (CFPB, MHA, FHA, etc.)

Borrower ↔ Fay Account Manager

Home Retention Options
- Repayment Plan
- Deferment (limited)
- MHA Unemployment Program
- HAMP Principal Reduction Alternative Tier 1 and Tier 2
- HAMP Tier 1 and Tier 2
- Proprietary Modification: Capitalize and Balloon
- Proprietary Modification: Affordable Payment
- Deferment (large)

Liquidation Options
- HAFA Short Sale
- HAFA Deed in Lieu of Foreclosure
- Proprietary Short Sale
- Proprietary Deed in Lieu of Foreclosure

Function #2 – Support Functions: Data and Document Management, Servicing Transfer, Loan Boarding, Escrow, Statements & Payment Processing, Reporting, and Applications

Support management is at the core of special servicing. Every other procedure relies on accurate information about the loan and the ability to see what happens to the loan as it moves through the loss-mitigation process. Remember the old computer axiom, "Garbage In, Garbage Out." Clean and accurate data rules the day. As you will see from manager comments later in this chapter, extraordinary care must be taken on the front end of this process to ensure we have accurate information boarded to avoid unnecessary delays at each step and procedure. Time delays cost real money (tax and insurance payments, home deterioration, etc.) and have a large impact on overall performance and loss recovery.

Data and Document Management, Servicing Transfer, and Loan Boarding
There has been a great change in how this area is handled over the last few years. Immediately after the mortgage meltdown, owners were overwhelmed, and selling non-performing loans was an avenue to get rid of those loans as quickly as possible. In many cases, lax attention had been paid to the documents in a loan file, and specifically their completeness and accuracy. Many non-performing loans traded multiple times with multiple servicing transfers. Warehouse banks that had lent to the large subprime originators ended up 'inheriting' many problem loans with incomplete loan files. What

a mess! The time required to obtain proper loan documentation created a huge unknown in the expectation of resolution timelines and recovery performance. The special servicer receiving loans in the servicing transfer had no advance knowledge of missing documents or accuracy of data before transfer, and yet had primary responsibility for validating all data.

There is hope, because we have come quite a long way since the beginning of the mortgage crisis. A recent transfer with a large seller of non-performing loans (who was also the servicer of those loans), provides a great example of the progress the industry has made. This seller showed exemplary willingness to work with us and ensure that the information transferred was as complete as possible. Multiple conference calls were held discussing loans at each stage of the servicing lifecycle. Meetings were held for Escrow (see definition below), understanding special loans such as Payment Option Arms and Hybrid Arms, Short Sale, Deed in Lieu, Bankruptcy, Foreclosure, and REO. Both parties found and resolved a number of misinterpretations of the same data and definitions. The conference-call process was well worth the effort and increased the likelihood of fewer problems later for the seller of the non-performing loans, and also increased likelihood of quicker timelines for us as servicer to resolve the outcome of the loans.

- **Escrow Payment:** Common term referring to the portion of a mortgage payment that is designated to pay for property taxes and hazard insurance. It is an amount "over and above" the principal and interest portion of a mortgage payment.
  https://en.wikipedia.org/wiki/Escrow

    Escrow is much more complex than collecting or disbursing property tax and hazard insurance premiums. At Fay Servicing, approximately 100 of the 280+ data fields we request in a servicing transfer are related to escrow items.

However, the industry still needs a common definition and understanding of each data element, in addition to a list of required data fields, so that as much of the servicing-transfer process can be as uniform as possible to minimize data discrepancy. For example, Fay Servicing asks for and provides 283 loan data fields in a servicing transfer. Another servicer might only be able to provide 170 data fields, with some of those fields being different than the ones that we requested. Yet another servicer during a transfer might request 320 data fields, and we still provide the same 283 data fields.

Document management is also a critical part of the servicing transfer process. These documents will be referred to many times during the servicing lifecycle and must be available to multiple servicing departments. Blurred and crooked copies and scans plus missing documents must be corrected, can delay timeline execution, and could impair loan value. Delinquent loan packages with missing documents tend to trade at lower values.

Data, Reporting and Applications

Continuous access to accurate data and documents, with all functions seeing and sharing this data, is the central nervous system of Special Servicing. Each function of the servicing lifecycle needs to know what is going on not only in its area, but also in others. At Fay, our Account Managers need to see this same information to help them perform their customer service, collections, and loss mitigation functions. Further, both internal and external auditors and regulators need access to this vital information, as well as the clients that own the loans.

Insights from Fay Servicing Managers for Function #2 – Support Functions

- Some loans have had seven or eight prior transfers and documents in the loan files are incomplete or missing. How do you get an Assignment of Mortgage ("AOM") from Ameriquest, who went out of business in 2006, in this type of situation? There are many other possible document nightmares.
- How do you capture data from faded and crooked document scans?
- What if documents are fake? What is the solution?
- The most notable change in the past two years has been regulatory scrutiny of process and procedures – CFPB, States. Reg AB, SOC Audits.
- Non-Performing Loan ("NPL") escrow is different than prime escrow. More attention to detail, research, oversight, exceptions, and processing is required.
- NPL Escrow advances are out of pocket for investors. Investors must agree to pay them. Each investor has different priorities regarding items they are willing to pay.
- Inaccurate and incomplete data received at loan boarding causes major problems in accounting for adjustable-rate mortgages and bankruptcies.
- Bankruptcies put foreclosures on automatic stay, yet payments must still be made.
- Automated payments have increased greatly in the past three years; this is great for servicer efficiencies and minimizing borrower effort. But when a borrower with recent delinquency calls to pay at Fay Servicing, the borrower is given the opportunity to first talk with their Account Manager. This is well worth the cost as it helps in understanding any issues that may have changed with the borrower's situation, and it also helps us build stronger relationships.
- Inaccurate and incomplete data can impair loan resale value.
- Origination requires standardization of documentation. Servicing does not. Why?

Function #3 – Default Management

Definitions were given at the beginning of this chapter for stages of Default Management:

- Retention (Reinstatement, Forbearance, and Modification)
- Non-Retention Resolutions (Short Sale, Deed in Lieu, and Cash for Keys, and Short Refi)
- Latter Default (Bankruptcy and Foreclosure)
- REO

The interaction of the servicer relationship with the borrower at each resolution stage has evolved by necessity, over the years.

Default Management before 2007 and through the Housing Crisis
Before 2007, as home prices rose, bill collection was largely a process with little regard for the borrower. Given that most mortgages tended to have positive equity, the

borrower could sell his home if he could no longer afford the mortgage payment. The world was a binary place: collectors simply told borrowers to pay or sell the home, and borrowers would do so.

Then came the Housing Crisis in 2008. By the end of 2008, 18% of U.S. homeowners experienced negative equity in their homes. http://bit.ly/1SjGBDt. Selling the home was, for many delinquent borrowers, no longer an option, and things were getting worse. By 2010, 23% of U.S. homeowners had negative equity in their homes. As the housing crisis spread an evolution took place in the loss-mitigation process. Managers in Payment Resolutions, Non-Retention Resolutions, and REO had to expand their skill sets in order to maximize cash flows for their investors. Rather than relying on full repayment or REO sales as servicing did pre-2008, Payment and Non-Retention Resolutions became more flexible, evolving into more borrower-friendly resolutions. Loan resolution at earlier stages of delinquency aligned the best interests of both investor and borrower.

Default Management in 2015
The introduction of SPOC requirements in 2013 has grown in 2015 to encourage a more collaborative relationship with the borrower. Unless the borrower has abandoned the house or refuses to communicate, borrower buy-in greatly increases the best resolution outcome for both borrower and investor. The loss-mitigation process is increasingly focused on giving the SPOC tools for support and borrower engagement.

Default Management beyond 2015
Post crisis, underwriting guidelines have been more restrictive, with fewer borrowers qualifying for mortgage loans. Repurchase demands from FHA and the GSEs have made lenders more reluctant to lend.

Efforts have been made to broaden homeownership by making lending less restrictive. Both easing of underwriting guidelines and efforts to provide clarity of repurchase demands are attempts to encourage a lending increase to millennials, lower-income borrowers, and other groups who have been denied entry into homeownership.

In order to broaden homeownership, both FHA and the GSEs have loan programs accepting 3% to 3.5% down payments. Fannie Mae stopped requiring pay stubs. Credit bureaus are using "trended credit data" to broaden numbers of people that can qualify for a mortgage. Extended families living together can pool income to broaden income qualification.

Home-price appreciation and low unemployment are required to keep default rates low. If severe home-price depreciation occurs, many of these newer loans will be among loans to experience large increases in default rates and will need special servicing.

Predictions: The definition of SPOC will continue to evolve toward more collaboration with the borrower. Home-price stabilization or appreciation is necessary to keep default rates low.

CHAPTER FIFTEEN: *RESIDENTIAL MORTGAGE SPECIAL SERVICING*

REO "Value-Add" Market Creates a New Profit Opportunity for Investors:
- As a special servicer, we have seen first-hand how much value is lost at REO sale, as many REO managers have sold properties "as is."
- With proper management, it is possible to capture the 'fix and flip' profits rather than see these profits captured by REO investors.
- A rehab-intensive approach strives to capture the 'fix & flip' value creation for our clients as if it were our own investment.
- Unlike traditional REO firms, we view selling "as is" as a last choice and we prefer to retail properties post-rehab.

Glenn Brooks, SVP, Fay Servicing and head of the REO division, has the following thoughts on adding value to REO utilizing rehab:

"At the beginning of the mortgage crisis, large amounts of REO came to market, overwhelming industry capacity. A focus was placed on liquidation speeds and not on maximizing asset values for clients. REO departments were forced to manage volumes, hit timelines, minimize holding costs, and maximize liquidity. Why focus on rehab when housing prices were rapidly falling? This created fantastic opportunities for REO investors.

Despite REO inventories coming down, as-is sales direct to investors remain high compared to pre-crisis levels. REO managers that can apply a rehab focus and retain some of those 'fix and flip' profits for their clients are better positioned than others who maintain their focus on speed. Rehabs are not a cookie cutter business. The asset manager should know its markets well and have a sense for the broad range of enhancements that can positively impact the sale, which can vary by neighborhood. Some areas can add value with granite countertops and stainless steel appliances. Older areas might see a value rise by turning a small extra bedroom into a master bath and walk-in closet. Many neighborhoods can increase the buyer pool substantially by bring a property up to FHA standards. The REO manager must understand all these dynamics, in order to maximize post-rehab REO value to be realized by the investor."

Insights from Fay Servicing managers for Function #3 – Default Management
- Post 2009, increasing numbers of people over time wanted loan modifications as the HAMP program became more widely known. House-price appreciation has encouraged more short sales. Continuous changes to HAMP have helped more borrowers to modify.
- HAFA now encourages short sales with a $3,000 to $10,000 payment directly to the homeowner.
- Some sub-servicers have exited the business because they improperly priced their product and suffered penalties by not strictly following loss-mitigation timelines from FHA and the GSEs.
- Accurate data maximizes timeline efficiency of each resolution stage.

COMPLIANCE AND REGULATION

The level of scrutiny on the servicing industry after the great recession has never been greater. In response, legal and compliance functions within a servicer have grown significantly and the cost of compliance is high.

The Consumer Financial Protection Bureau (CFPB) servicing rules became effective on January 10, 2014. These new national standards were changes to Regulation Z, Truth in Lending Act, and Regulation X, Real Estate Settlement Procedures Act. The final rules implemented provisions of the Dodd-Frank Act regarding mortgage loan servicing. In addition to other federal regulatory agencies (depending upon the type of institution regulated) and state regulators, the CFPB has regulatory oversight over most financial-services institutions. For non-bank institutions, the CFPB is its only federal regulator.

The CFPB expects servicers to have a Compliance Management System (CMS) to monitor and maintain protocols for identifying noncompliance and reporting. A robust and effective CMS requires commitment from top leadership, involvement of the board of directors, management of risk, and is comprised of three lines of defense. The first line of defense, quality assurance, performed within the business operation and checking work quality largely before it leaves the department; the second line of defense, quality control, separated from the business and within the compliance group; and the third line of defense, internal audit, helping to manage and control risk through the organization, reporting directly to the board of directors.

Being responsive and transparent with consumers and building open and transparent relationships with regulators is key.

ITEMS TO CONSIDER IN THE SELECTION OF A SPECIAL SERVICER

As you have seen, there are many processes simultaneously happening during the delinquent-asset resolution process. Proper due diligence of a special servicer entails investigating each piece of the process. Here are a few items that we think are important, but under-appreciated in the selection of a third-party special servicer.

- What types of loans are third-party special serviced? FHA, agency, re-performing whole loans, and non-performing whole loans all have different loss mitigation investor criteria and each have different performance benchmarks. What experience can they point to? It is critical to understand which products each servicer is best at servicing and why. Different kinds of loans can and should leverage different servicing strengths, leading to different performance metrics. What are the servicing costs relative to loan performance? The lowest dollar expenditure for servicing does not necessarily yield the optimum performance outcome. Therefore it is important to think about these items together with a cost-benefit framework. It does not take many instances of foreclosure avoidance to justify paying higher servicing fees. Another theme that has gained traction since the crisis (which we expect will continue) is the notion of *paying for performance.* We believe that a servicer and client should attempt to align interests at every opportunity. Servicers willing to put their compensation at risk based on their performance tend to make decisions easier for potential clients for obvious reasons.

- What are the performance goals of the loan portfolio? A private equity fund might view a loan portfolio as an investment with relatively high yield and IRR targets. A bank, on the other hand, might want to manage loan portfolios to minimize capital requirements. It is important to understand what your goals are for your portfolio so that you can choose the servicer that will be the best fit for your strategy.

- Is the servicer profitable? Choosing a special servicer is a major commitment. Make sure the special servicer has financial stability and can afford to maintain a state-of-the-art compliance regime. Anything less than maintaining strong compliance increases investor risk.

- How does the special servicer handle borrower management and SPOC? Spend time with individual account managers that speak directly with borrowers. Do these SPOCs seem capable of doing what the servicer's management claims they can? Spending time with those who are closest to your borrowers can often give you the most valuable information with which to make your servicer selection decision.

- Does a special servicer's operation seem qualified and nimble enough to achieve your goals? Is the special servicer's approach at all customizable or is there limited flexibility in the types of programs and campaigns that you can employ to meet your specific needs?

- How smooth is the boarding-transfer process? Ask to see a track record, demonstration, and procedure manual.

- Get references from each special servicer, and go into great detail with each contact about their experiences.

CONCLUSIONS

- Accurate loan boarding and data transfer is of vital importance. It has a tremendous impact on borrower management, loss mitigation, and liquidation aspects of special servicing from start to finish, and ultimately will have a direct bearing on key performance metrics.

- A SPOC program, properly designed and administered, can be a special servicer's greatest advantage in maximizing performance, borrower satisfaction, and client satisfaction.

- The evolution of better data transfer has been spurred by the presence of regulators. This benefits the borrowers and our industry as a whole.

- More standardization is occurring with in-flight modifications, benefitting both borrowers and investors.

- The time spent by an Account Manager building a relationship with the borrower pays dividends. Having a relationship increases the likelihood the AM will know if there is a change in the borrower's financial circumstance and ability to pay. And if remaining in the house is not possible, a borrower is more likely to a leave a house voluntarily and undamaged if they believe their servicer has done everything they possibly could to both understand and fix the problem.

- Selection of the proper special servicer allows a lender to return to their core competency of originating and servicing high quality performing loans. A properly selected special servicer can improve portfolio performance, limit reputation risk, and minimize the increasing costs associated with running a fully compliant default servicing operation.

- A servicer who claims to be great at everything is, in all likelihood, probably not good at anything.

Thanks to the following Fay Servicing managers for their valuable insight: Mike Wocjik, Matt Schuster, Greg Reed, Wanda Montgomery, Glenn Brooks, Shlomo Sahadeo, Lucy Przybyla, Tim Ridolphi, Victor Fuentes, Tucker McDermott, Joe Biczak, Loren Morris, Andy Laing, and Ed Fay.

ABOUT THE AUTHOR

Bill Coppedge is a Senior Managing Director of Business Development at Fay Financial, a residential mortgage Special Servicer. Bill has been actively involved in the mortgage finance industry for 39 years, 31 of which were spent at large investment banks (Kidder Peabody, PaineWebber, Oppenheimer, Bank of America) in institutional mortgage sales covering large mortgage originators and REITS in the areas of RMBS (agency and non-agency), pipeline hedging, servicing hedging, and residential whole loan transactions. Bill also worked at a large regional bank in the purchase and sale of whole loan consumer assets, maintaining contact with over 150 commercial banks, regional dealers, private equity and hedge funds, servicers, and money managers in the performing and non-performing space. For the past five years, he has had the opportunity to learn the finer points of default management at Fay Financial. Bill is also the editor of FayMortgageNews.com, a mortgage blog read by senior management in all areas of mortgage acquisition, distribution, and securitization.

INDEX

audits, *See* quality-control audits
automation, *See* mortgage automation

compliance, *See* regulation
Consumer Financial Protection Bureau (CFPB), 118, 161-164, 175, 188

data security, 123
Dodd-Frank Wall Street Reform and Consumer Protection Act, 160-164, 166-167, 175
    criticism of, 146
    damage to mortgage technology infrastructure from, 82-84
    mortgage operations affected by, 115

eClosings and eMortgages
    cost savings and efficiencies with, 133-135
    definition of, 125
    eDocuments, 128
    electronic vaulting, 131
    eNotarization, 131-132
    eNote ownership, 129-131
    eRecording, 133
    eSignatures, 127-128
    implementation and adoption of, 136-138
    industry standard for, 126-127
    legal framework for, 125-126
    security of, 135-136
    tamper-evident seals, 129
    warehouse lending and, 138

fair lending
    case studies of, 194-196
    Dodd-Frank and, 175-176
    helping lenders and consumer, 177-179
    history of, 176-177
    laws supporting, 181-184
    risk mitigation, 180-181
    trends in, 188-194
    types of lending discrimination, 184-188
fraud, *See* mortgage fraud

HMDA, See *Home Mortgage Disclosure Act*
Home Mortgage Disclosure Act (HMDA), 122, 158

loan origination process
    building of, 7-9

    data use in, 4-7
    historical perspective on, 1-2
    opportunities and challenges in, 10-12
    process-oriented approach, 2-4
loan origination system, 6-7
loan processing, 8, 9, 10, 11
    future of, 123

mortgage automation
    compliance and, 192-194
    Ellie Mae, 111-113
    Future of, 121-124
    history of, 107-111
    human spackle syndrome, 117-119
    mortgage meltdown and, 113-114
    trends in, post-meltdown, 114-117
    TRID and, 120-121
    warehouse lines and, 138
mortgage cooperatives
    examples of, 66-68
    need for, 65
    regulatory compliance and, 68-69
    services provided by, 70
    servicing and, 69
mortgage fraud
    2000-2006, 26-28
    automation and analytics to combat, 40-42
    causes and common elements in, 28-33
    emerging threats, 42-43
    prevention and detection of, 37-40
    types of, 33-37
mortgage insurance companies
    claims, 60-61
    cost of mortgage insurance from, 59-60
    overview of, 57
    regulation of, 58
    working with, 58-59, 62-63
mortgage servicing
    See also special servicing, subservicing
    compliance, 205-208
    customer service, 201
    economics of, 199-201
    escrow, 203-204
    loss mitigation, 201-203
    technology, 204-205
    types of servicers, 197-199

INDEX

mortgage technology
    See also mortgage automation
    accomplishments, 76-80
    common securitization platform and, 91-94
    diffusion of, 89-91
    Dodd-Frank damage to, 82-84
    future of, 94-105
    government versus private-sector investment in, 81-82
    history of, 74-76
    industry conundrum, 85-89
    model-based management, 80-81
    reverse mortgage origination, See reverse mortgage origination technology
    underinvestment in, 84-85

quality-control audits
    case studied, 54-56
    foundations of, 45
    grading, 50-51
    present and future of, 51-54
    reporting, 47-50
    sample size, 46-47
Qualified Mortgage (QM), 167

Real Estate Settlement Procedures Act (RESPA), 157-158
regulation
    ATR/QM/QRM, 166-167
    CFPB and loan data requirements, 169-170, 172-174
    CFPB and UDAP, 170-171
    Dodd-Frank, 161-164, 165-166
    history of, prior to 1900, 147-150
    history of, in the 20th century, 150-160
    history of, in the 21st century, 160-174
    servicing compliance with, 205-208
    TRID, 168-169
    unfair, deceptive, and abusive acts or practices, 171-172
RESPA, *See* Real Estate Settlement Procedures Act
reverse mortgage origination technology
    compliance and loan quality, 142
    document preparation, 142
    fulfillment services integration, 142
    future of, 144-145
    reporting and analytics, 143
    sales, 143-144
    shared loan access and, 141
    success-based pricing, 144
    wholesale partner support, 141

servicing, *See* mortgage servicing
special servicing
    compliance and legal issues in, 236
    definitions, 219-224
    operational costs, 226
    penalties and reputational risk, 226-227
    performance of, 227
    rise of, 224-228
    selection of special servicer, 236-237
    three core functions of, 228-235
subservicing
    benefits of using, 212-214
    managing relations with subservicer, 216-217
    oversight of, 216
    overview of, 210-211
    selection of, 214-215
    types of, 211-212

technology, *See* mortgage technology
TILA, *See* Truth in Lending Act
TILA-RESPA Integrated Disclosure Rule (TRID), 120-121, 168-169
Truth in Lending Act, 156-157

underwriting
    four C's of, 14-15
    investment properties, 15-18
    jumbo loans, 18-21
    self-employed borrowers, 21-25

warehouse lending, 138

Made in the USA
Middletown, DE
18 March 2016